Embracing Writing

Ways to Teach Reluctant Writers in *Any* College Course

Gary R. Hafer

Foreword by Maryellen Weimer

JB JOSSEY-BASS™
A Wiley Brand

Cover design by Adrian Morgan
Cover image : © Red Sky | Getty
Consulting editor : Maryellen Weimer

Published by Jossey-Bass
A Wiley Brand
One Montgomery Street, Suite 1200, San Francisco, CA 94104-4594—
www.josseybass.com/highereducation

Jossey-Bass books and products are available through most bookstores. To contact Jossey-Bass directly call our Customer Care Department within the U.S. at 800-956-7739, outside the U.S. at 317-572-3986, or fax 317-572-4002.

Wiley publishes in a variety of print and electronic formats and by print-on-demand. Some material included with standard print versions of this book may not be included in e-books or in print-on-demand. If this book refers to media such as a CD or DVD that is not included in the version you purchased, you may download this material at http://booksupport.wiley.com. For more information about Wiley products, visit www.wiley.com.

Library of Congress Cataloging-in-Publication Data
Library of Congress Cataloging-in-Publication Data has been applied for and is on file with the Library of Congress.
ISBN 978-1-118-58291-6 (cloth);
ISBN 978-1-118-58378-4 (ebk.);
ISBN 978-1-118-58369-2 (ebk.)

Printed in the United States of America
FIRST EDITION
HB Printing 10 9 8 7 6 5 4 3 2 1

Contents

To my wife, Marjorie,
from whom I've learned much,
and still love much.

Foreword

How do I know when a book is really good? It changes what I do. A good book makes me think. It makes me want to share its content with colleagues. It makes me want to read more on the subject. But after reading a really good book I'm doing some things differently, and that's what happened with this book.

Like many faculty I've always thought that freewriting was kind of a waste of my time. How can you start writing when you don't yet have the ideas? What's the point of taking the mess and muddle in your mind and putting it on paper? How can this writing free-for-all contribute anything toward the polished prose of academic scholarship? And writing it by hand when I can key text three times as fast? How sensible is that?

I wasn't even sure it was a good use of student time. So many of them don't write well, and I'm suppose to encourage the writing equivalent of "Just Do It." All those errors in spelling, grammar, punctuation, and sentence structure they get to make freely and without consequence. And that's supposed to improve their writing?

Gary's book is big on freewriting. His arguments are well constructed and persuasive, but I still wasn't convinced—or at least I didn't think I was. Then one day in Staples I found myself buying three bright, spiral notebooks for 99 cents each. I slid mechanical pencils into their spines and put one in my purse, one in the car, and one next to my favorite chair. Without much conscious consideration, I started writing in them—here and there, now and then—mostly on current projects, a blog post, a book chapter, ideas for a presentation, feedback on a colleague's paper. The writing was as awful as I expected, although I was surprised by how quickly the ideas came when I didn't think I had any. I was also taken aback by how easy it was to clean up the muddle once I had it down. Even when I didn't look at the freewriting in the notebook, writing the real first draft was a breeze. Normally I experience first drafts as hard-fought battles against strong headwinds. Before too long I was back in Staples buying more notebooks.

Embracing Writing is a book that offers fresh versions of various ideas. Freewriting isn't a new idea, but how Gary recommends you use it in class and in your own writing is. He doesn't preach or hype about how well it and the other strategies he recommends work. He doesn't tell you to try them. But when you do, you discover that he's right, and you learn new things about approaches you thought you understood. I so appreciate books that get beyond rehashing the ideas of others, books that build new structures out of familiar ideas, and books that challenge conventional thinking about the way things are or the way we think they have to be.

The Writing Across Curriculum (or WAC) movement is a relevant example here, too. Its proponents have managed to convince most faculty that students need to be writing in every course—not just in their English and composition courses. It didn't take a lot to persuade most of us; we see how students write. But to many teachers adding writing assignments seems like one more thing "good" teachers are supposed to do. The WAC movement has helped, generating a plethora of writing activities and assignments that teachers can use. But to get students to take them seriously, most of them have to be graded. Teachers new to teaching writing have discovered that grading written work is a time-consuming struggle with disappointing results. It's hard to see much improvement in student writing, or there's no change in how fervently they disdain the activity. It feels like WAC and the rest of us are doing some wheel spinning.

Gary's observations about all this are provocative. He thinks the teachers now trying to improve student writing are often not all that in love with writing themselves. They have chosen fields where they can advance knowledge in labs, by solving problems or with other kinds of hands-on work. However, writing is used to advance knowledge in every field. Faculty who don't like to write still have to. Professional advancement often depends on it: publish or perish. Could they too be reluctant writers? Do they have trouble getting their papers started? Do they wait until the last minute before they begin writing, sometimes missing deadlines? Do they struggle with rewrites, find criticism painful, and handle it poorly? Could the solutions that Gary has discovered work well with reluctant writers in the classroom also work for their reluctant writer teachers?

Embracing Writing is about teaching students who don't like to write and don't do it well—that's the book's main focus. It proposes a variety of interesting ways teachers can improve student writing and their attitudes about it—ways that involve the role of writing in the classroom, approaches to rewriting (not revising, because Gary makes important distinctions between the two), ways of providing feedback, and a whole different orientation to grading. This isn't the way writing is usually taught, in composition courses or any other courses for that matter. But it's an approach that makes sense and one that offers options to teachers who are regularly or occasionally frustrated by their attempts to teach writing. They are options they may not have considered or perhaps should reconsider.

And this returns us to the intriguing subtext that runs through the book. Could these approaches help teachers who don't like to write or help any writer struggling with a writing task? For example, Gary recommends that students write in every class (beyond their customary note taking), and he encourages faculty to write along with students as he does in every class. His classes begin with everybody writing—maybe they're working on a thesis statement, maybe they're rewriting a sentence or paragraph, maybe they're jotting notes on the assigned reading, maybe they're answering a question or writing questions. And there is the teacher writing along with students—crossing things out, writing sentence fragments, occasionally misspelling. Whatever happens the rest of the period builds on or grows out of this first writing. Often class ends with writing as well. This shared writing experience makes the class literally and figuratively a community of writers who work together to support each other's writing endeavors. Being in that kind of community changes attitudes, gets students writing more, and ultimately improves their writing.

The content of this book rings with authenticity. It is a well-written story of one teacher's twenty-year journey to a new and quite remarkable way of teaching, a way that does encourage reluctant writers to embrace writing. There are memorable stories, like the book Gary wrote in fifth grade and conversations with students where he makes points that help them and us see familiar attitudes and writing practices from different perspectives. It is a book you'll enjoy reading and that will make you think, and it could very well change how you teach and write.

And yes, I did start this foreword with a freewrite—in the Detroit airport while waiting (none too patiently) for a delayed flight. Freewriting, as Gary proposes one practice it, is open to digression. Among the first-pass expression of possible ideas are tirades against winter travel and airline incompetence. The tirades took care of the tension; the first pass at ideas whacked out the underbrush and gave the better ideas room to grow. Thank you, Gary.

Maryellen Weimer

Preface

I welcome you to *Embracing Writing: Ways to Teach Reluctant Writers in Any College Course*, my response to a growing dilemma that many teaching faculty face as they exercise writing for learning in their college courses.

On one hand, I find that the faculty with whom I talk recognize writing as essential to their scholarly and professional responsibilities. They are the first to acknowledge that disciplinary knowledge is closely tied to rhetorical knowledge; that is, they appreciate that they must be able to write prolifically and competently about their discipline in ways that speak clearly to their colleagues and other audiences, such as their students. They know it isn't enough to dump information in the laps of their readers: They must also *commune* with them in interesting and profound ways. Making a professional finding takes on added significance when such scholarly work culminates in a journal article or a book, bringing its own reward in tenure, promotion, and professional recognition. In short, faculty value not only that they must speak with authority in their discipline but also that they must possess the requisite skills so that their writing accomplishes something. In other words, their writing must invoke readers *to effect* some change in them: agreements, disagreements, confrontations, denials, connections. Integrating writing and disciplinary knowledge are notions that faculty implicitly acknowledge.

On the other hand, that understanding—as genuine and as real to the discipline as it may be—can seem unreachable when professors try to integrate writing into their courses. In fact, college courses may be the *worst* place to learn how to do that kind of writing. At those sites, students interpret first efforts as finished products that deserve a grade, no matter how persistently their professors emphasize process. As faculty can testify, writers go through countless drafts, revisions, dumps, and rewrites—let alone feedback of varying helpfulness from colleagues and editors—that all work toward crafting their final products. This context is removed from most student encounters with writing. In its place is what students believe really matters: the transaction that brings about good high-stakes writing, they being unreceptive to final writing as a pastiche assembled from messy processes. Who can blame them for being reluctant to move into the full writing process when the grade is synonymous with the polished final version? Given the exigencies of the modern classroom, it's hard for faculty to create the incentive—let alone supply the time, circumstances, and feedback necessary—for a rich and integrated writing environment in their courses.

That teaching professors feel daunted as they face these intricate problems is understandable. Most teach content courses, not skills-based courses like writing. They don't have the time or the resources to design writing to carry that content. As one professor on a writing-across-the-curriculum committee confessed, "I'll tell you right now: I haven't the foggiest idea of how to teach writing. I know it's important, but I don't feel confident in teaching it."

It is that dissonance I wish to span with *Embracing Writing*. Won't you join me in making writing a more meaningful bridge for learning in your classes?

Purpose

I wrote *Embracing Writing* not only to give teaching faculty the tools to make their students more effective learners and better writers but also to make those tools accessible and manageable to faculty. No matter their successes in using writing in the class-room or at their own writing desk, all instructors can become more compelling when they use writing for learning. To appropriate these tools, readers must recognize several things. First, they need to recognize the significant resources inside the actual writing process that, when embraced, will resolve problems students have with writing. I understand how circular this pronounce-ment sounds, but writing is powerful enough to solve its own problems when integrated fully into courses. Second, as much as learning is involved in this enterprise, there is an even greater amount of *un*learning required. The negative outcomes of much school-sponsored writing—summarized in what I call the *Writing Problem*—jeopardize students' future success unless they are countered, and countered demonstratively, by an approach rather than just a series of unrelated techniques. Third, faculty who want to honor writing in their courses need to be shown ways to circumvent teaching writing as a second subject. This point may seem counterintuitive until faculty come to know the important (though neglected) epistemic qualities—those qualities that direct writing as learning—within writing itself that facilitate teaching course content to students. Last, faculty themselves can and should practice this approach to writing both in their responses to student writing and in their scholarship.

This book presents writing as the entry point to demonstrate that writers—professors and students—can teach and learn course content effectively and with an insight that gives shape to their learning. Both faculty and students know writing is not only some-thing they must do but also something they must do well. This book gives faculty a method to effect that learning and to produce more self-conscious writers.

Writing Practices

Instead of beginning with sets of rules and regulations that appoint hit-or-miss outcomes, this book starts with typical writing practices. In themselves, these practices are empowering, teaching creative options that open pathways to more powerful writing. For example, this book positions low-stakes writing opportunities for students to give them scaffolded practice with the kinds of writing they will need to produce when the stakes grow higher. It also allows for better teacher intervention while students are shaping their writing rather than professors delaying feedback until the process is completed and the final grade assigned.

Taken individually, these writing practices are not new, since writers instinctively pursue writing as craft. At the same time, writers secure a process that faculty typically ignore or are discouraged from integrating into their courses because they fear the workload involved. This book's approach gathers writerly practices together with what good faculty are already doing expertly: teaching course content.

Shared Understandings

What is available when both you and students write are better opportunities for writing together, ones that you can embrace because this book's approach centers on four understandings.

First, students and faculty must share a similar attitude toward writing. That is, they must be convinced that writing is a uniquely effective way of learning. I remain convinced that the kinds of writing activities I advocate in this book bring about better writing because students are encouraged to take great risks to bring about greater learning. For example, the *checksheets* in this book emphasize effort in writing, summarizing tasks for students to explore so they can distribute the cognitive workload over several drafts.

A second understanding calls attention to how writing works by encouraging faculty to participate together with their students in its processes and products. For instance, the kind of low-stakes responses I encourage them to make opens up writing as a way to help students and themselves with writing dilemmas.

This book collects writerly habits for cultivation, encouraging faculty to build a routine for writing in their professional life and in classroom routine. The chapter on daily writing, for example, profiles one way to energize the writing of teachers and their students.

Finally, this book investigates a number of writerly practices for the college curriculum by developing a repertoire of strategies that help students gain mastery over their writing. These practices have the added benefit of uniting faculty's professional life with their pedagogy.

Workload

I am particularly aware of many faculty members' reticence about teaching writing, compounded by the prospect of ever-increasing teaching workloads. At teaching workshops I've attended and in others I've led, the most frequently requested workshops all centered on writing in disciplines outside the English department: how to require, grade, and survive it. Within those same workshops are the zealous participants who need to make their sponsorship of classroom writing practical and easily implementable.

I address many of these concerns because they were mine when I began teaching writing twenty-five years ago. For instance, in the first chapter I show what writing activities faculty should privilege in apportioning their time and which ones they should demote. I'm giving fair warning now that I am a huge fan of conferencing and copious feedback. But I'm an even bigger fan of integrating those activities into a course without increasing workload. Such integration makes writing as a tool for learning manageable and enjoyable.

Audience

My primary audience is higher education faculty in *any* discipline where reluctant writers are among their students, including those

- committed to developing students' writing skills but who may hesitate because of the increased workload.

- who are trying to use writing in their courses but do not possess specialized training.

- who do not embrace writing and recognize a similar attitude in their students.

- who rate their own writing skills as weaker than they should be.

- who are unsure of ways to teach content through writing.

- who have been using writing in their courses, perhaps even for years, and would like an integrated and more manageable approach.

- already teaching writing-intensive courses as part of a program, such as writing across the curriculum.

In addition, this book reaches across divisions that historically mark those with tenure and those without, who teach part-time, who teach composition, and who teach beginning students in first-year seminars. They are all writers whom I speak to and support in this book.

Another audience includes writing program administrators who are responding to the growing trend among colleges and universities to assign first-year writing courses to new hires, regardless to what academic department they owe allegiance. For example, a new faculty member in anthropology may be required to teach a first-year writing course within her field. I count this community among my audience.

Perhaps more than ever before, faculty are responsible for advanced disciplinary courses or capstone courses that include high expectations for written work. They feel pressured to design writing assignments even though they may lack the knowledge and experience to place these assignments within a larger writing pedagogy. Welcome aboard!

I recognize that my descriptions may be unusual, but then again, so is this book: an approach that capitalizes on writing as an instructional tool that also benefits faculty's own writing. My intent is to make writing much more embraceable!

The Story of an Approach

My student days prepared me for the opening years of my professional life as a professor and reluctant writer. I took on any writing project with trepidation whenever I had to use writing in my teaching or as the capstone to my scholarly projects. I knew I was not alone. Some of my fellows described the feeling as *inertia*, a shrinking from the commitment that writing commands. For them and for me, writing became an infinitely complex process, and teaching with writing, an intolerable complication. Both impeded my own writing process. I just *couldn't* write: my encounter with the writing problem.

Yet I now use writing in all my teaching, and I write every day, with and apart from my students. What happened? That is the story of this book.

Brief Overview of Contents

In Chapter 1, I tell how a simultaneous crisis in my teaching and in my writing found aid only after I worked my way back into the life of a writer. In Chapter 2, I focus on writing a syllabus that invokes a student audience since it is the first encounter students have with a professor's writing. In Chapter 3, I take faculty through the first day of class with a series of discrete, brief activities that in Chapter 4 become the basis for the writerly habits in the course. Those activities, when strung together, become the basis for the longer assignments I discuss in Chapter 5, making rewriting, as opposed to revising, possible, the subject of Chapter 6.

Different modes of feedback comprise Chapters 7 and 8, particularly how to make such effective for students and manageable for professors. Chapter 9 addresses the last things in a course that privilege writing: final portfolios and conferences. Finally, Chapter 10 focuses on how to grade the writing processes and products of the course. The spirit of this book doesn't end with its final chapter, however. The approach I share can still be written as professors practice a method rather than a series of unrelated canned techniques.

When I look back now, the approach I advocate looks obvious. Yet my experience and those of my colleagues convince me that the *obvious* in teaching is not nearly so obvious after all but is the core of inductive teaching, which unites writing with course content. In these pages, I'm happy to share the not-so-obvious, not as an unrealistic wrap-up with every loose end tied tight but as a continuing thread that revisits where it started: with an embrace.

Embracing Writing: Ways to Teach Reluctant Writers in Any College Course shows learning and writing are longitudinal, lifelong processes, made feasible—and enjoyable!—by integrating them with the content faculty already teach.

Acknowledgments

I am thankful for the invaluable assistance of two wonderful writers. Maryellen Weimer, who initially encouraged me with this project, gave me a nuanced reading to a very early draft. I could not have completed the book without her. Equally encouraging and insightful was my wife, Marjorie Maddox Hafer, a writer whose giftedness in writing and every other subject I can think of overshadows my own.

I belong to a community of great writers at Lycoming College, and I want to acknowledge Sascha Feinstein in particular for the practical advice he offered to me as a fellow writer. David Rife provided me early feedback that helped shape important sections later in the process. I am always amazed at the writing abilities of my colleagues.

Of course, I am indebted over many decades to my many teachers and students who taught me so much about the patience necessary for good writing and learning, but especially for this advice: practice what you preach.

Any shortcomings in this book, however, are exclusively my own.

About the Author

Gary R. Hafer is the John P. Graham Teaching Professor at Lycoming College in Williamsport, Pennsylvania, where he teaches writing to students from all disciplines. His short studies on writing instruction have appeared in *College English*, *Journal of Developmental Education*, *Teaching Professor*, and *Computers and Composition*. Hafer is also production design editor for *Brilliant Corners*, a journal of jazz and literature. He lives in Williamsport with his wife and two children, Anna Lee and Will.

1

Write from the Beginning

A s professors, we love learning. It is something we enjoy doing, and we do it well. When we share our learning with colleagues, we explore anew much of what we have investigated, through writing, in professional journals, and conference papers. Slowly, over a long period of time, we acquired writing skills valued in our disciplines, not by listing precepts to be slavishly followed but by example: practicing our own craft as writers, building from examples to those precepts. We have observed how other writers we admire in our profession do their writing, and if we were lucky we may even have seen how these writers went about fashioning their writing—how they invent ideas, where they write, which technologies they use, and the like. In such situations, we learn much because it is always instructive to see how mentors produce writing rather than to speculate on their composing process when we have only final forms: essays, articles, books.

But do our students share in those same learning experiences? Are they euphoric with their writing in the disciplines, seizing writing as a way to discover, to ask deeper questions, to study through problems, to find out what they don't know? In my thirty years' experience as a writing teacher, and as much of the professional literature demonstrates, only a few students come to a general education class eager to write.

Nevertheless, how can we improve on their experiences? We may justly feel ambivalent adding value to their encounters with disciplinary writing: What kind of commitment will such a workload require of us? Does it mean more grading? What kind of assignment design will it demand? How can a writing assignment be designed so it is enjoyable for students and us? At the same time, as lovers of learning we cannot help but be concerned with the weak writing we see pass our desks every day and the great gulf that spans our experiences with powerful writing and theirs.

On the other hand, can those experiences be much different from ours, especially their school experiences? My colleagues regularly observe that it is so easy to become buried in the busyness our professional life demands that inventing new and invigorating writing assignments is too burdensome. And the burden didn't just appear. When we entered the teaching profession we were thrust into writing committee reports, institutional assessments, and scholarly papers. Not long thereafter, we were probably asked to teach a course in our discipline that requires a good deal of writing. The pressure builds. The enormity of those competing tasks at hand can quickly diminish our joy in writing. If we step farther back, we can even see ourselves joined with our students in their experiences with writing. We can even feel like students in these circumstances when—if you're anything like me—your history with school-sponsored writing as a student has been mixed.

But perhaps you lack confidence about your own writing skills. You may feel like a decent writer, but teaching writing in your discipline seems daunting and even frightening. You may value writing in the classroom but ask, as one of my colleagues does, "Who am I to teach writing? I just don't feel qualified. And even if I did, I don't have time to teach a second subject."

If the difficulties seem insurmountable, the benefits of using writing in a content course seem miniscule. What can you expect if you bring a fuller-bodied writing into your classroom and into your professional life? Specifically, what can you anticipate, as a professor in a content course, from reading this book and participating in the approach I advocate both for your own and your students' writing? Very little, unless you covet a passion and energy for writing itself.

If you have that exuberance already, let me invite you into ways that can sustain or even increase that love for your own and your students' writing. If you lost that passion in the busyness of your professional life, let me help you recapture that first love. If you have never known that deep passion for writing—or know it only as an acquaintance—let's move together through this book to secure that closeness to writing in the same way you have for learning. In short, wherever you are in your journey with writing in your profession and in your pedagogy, this book is written for you.

How can I be so sure? Because like you, I share in the *Writing Problem.*

What Is the Writing Problem?

Even though I savor the times I reserve for writing and often find composing joyful, I haven't always enjoyed the pathways to writing that my elementary school teachers taught me to tread. Straightjacket outlines. "Correct" prose. "Think carefully before writing." Those high-stakes goals always eluded my grasp. Even now, I still have to untangle long arguments, work hard to synthesize a committee report so that the document sounds like it ascended into one voice, or pause over starting a single e-mail. But now these occasions are less frequent and more readily repairable. Part of that is because of greater experience. But experience doesn't explain everything. I like to walk to the college and have been for a good deal of my tenure there, but I don't think I'm a better walker to school than I was ten years ago. Something else entered into my stride.

With that greater experience—that is, the longer I teach and the more I write—I identify more closely with the struggles of many of my colleagues who do not find writing enthralling. Moreover, I have found another community that writes and grapples with the same writing difficulties: my students. Though we may vary in magnitude—whether we agonize or are blocked or hesitate—we unite in the same dissonance: the need to produce effective writing yet the failure to attain it by willpower alone.

This puzzlement is what I call the Writing Problem, and it has four components.

1. Through schooling, students conclude that good writing equals an absence of error, an inference they base on feedback from their previous experiences with school-sponsored writing.

In *Vernacular Eloquence*, Peter Elbow observes that most students learn to read from hearing their parents or guardians—or someone who loves them—read to them regularly. They learn to write, however, within the sterile environment of school and from someone outside their family (Elbow, 2012). I would add that during those early encounters with writing in school students learn—and they learn it well—that their school-sponsored writing is incomplete without teachers marking up their papers. In such environments, students initiate writing only when they deem it is worth doing, when it is available as a receptacle for correction—marginal notes, special symbols, and terminal comments. Good writing, in such a view, occurs when something is absent: teacher corrections. But such absences are rare. One conscientious colleague I know carries mountains of student papers home every weekend to "correct." As she reports, "I see so much bad writing. I feel guilty if I don't mark everything I see."

I discovered that uneasy status of school writing firsthand in fifth grade when I sponsored my own writing project, for which I reluctantly recruited my English teacher into my audience. Since my parents were not avid readers, she was the only adult reader I knew. My novel, *The Great Alaska Mystery*—the product of a full year of drafting on a Royal manual typewriter with persistently stuck keys and overinked o's—was enthusiastically received by Mrs. Ruttenburg. After I tentatively offered my unsolicited book to her, she asked her colleague in the art department to construct a hard cover and bind the pages of my manuscript to make a "proper book." Every week or so I would ask Mrs. Ruttenburg if I could be excused to travel down the long hallway to the elusive art room to check on the status of the book binding. I could hear my heart beating heavily as I struggled to produce my question to The Artist. And then finally, after weeks of silence, there it was, mystically appearing on Mrs. Ruttenburg's desk: a beautiful hand-bound volume, black stitching on the spine. The art teacher had drawn a green outline of Alaska with magic marker, along with parallel interior lines.

"Very art-like," I thought, overjoyed. "A proper book."

And it was beautiful. When I opened it, however, I immediately saw the splash of color: the teacher's red pen branded its pages. The burning marks pointed to punctuation mistakes marked for dialogue, rules I didn't even know that suddenly appeared and were quickly applied. The sweetness and bitterness I experienced was hard for a fifth grader to process. It's still hard.

I struggle to this day with what the teacher actually taught me about my writing: perhaps that it's not worthy of a book but let's make it into a book anyway? My embarrassment at having made so many errors overshadowed my joy at having my loose pages bound as a book. The teacher told me later that my yearlong effort had inspired many in the classroom to write their own books.

"Jonathan started one today," she beamed.

The other students never finished, however. And we never returned to the subject of writing in that classroom again. My writing produced no lasting, edible fruit. However, the red stains remained.

Is it any surprise, then, that our students come to us with a developed avoidance strategy concerning writing? Even some of the brightest students, such as the entering class from Stanford University, arrive as "pretty confident writers" but find that confidence "considerably shaken" after their first year when college exposes them to a broad range of assignments and genres (Haven, 2009).

Students communicate effectively every day in acts they don't think twice about initiating—sketching, painting, doodling, talking, blogging, messaging—without teachers assigning subjects or composing prompts, in and out of school. Unlike their school-sponsored writing, these acts are prolific, are part of their lives, and do not require a teacher-audience. This writing accomplishes something for them: it has legs and brings about some change, no matter how great. Students participate in all sorts of self-sponsored writing, even though they and their teachers may not acknowledge it as real writing.

What if we could harness that inventiveness for school-sponsored writing?

2. As a rule, school-sponsored writing equals high-stakes writing.

Teaching writing, especially in a content course, is difficult. Seldom are there pay rewards. There are workload incentives to avoid writing too, such as its heavy grading demands. Then there is the issue of training. I've heard some faculty declare quite openly, even among writing-across-the-curriculum (WAC) committee members, that they have no business teaching writing. They confess that they serve on writing committees and teach WAC courses because they feel administrative and departmental pressures to do so. They meet their professional obligations, but they can avoid the compartmentalized writing course when they can. Who can blame them?

Writing in school settings seems to invite resistance. Very early in my career, I remember discussing our students' collective hatred of writing with a colleague. I lamented how students confessed their horror stories of school-sponsored writing. Yet, one had really shocked me that day: A freshman reported that one of his teachers never returned his major research paper because, the teacher admitted at the end of the year, he had written "unkind messages on it" and crumbled the student's paper in anger. How could I possibly reach this student now with how writing could be joyful? I told my colleague I was frustrated to teach those courses where writing was the cornerstone, a foundation students worked eagerly all semester to dislodge, no matter if the whole building would topple.

In that struggle, I told him, I was exhausted: "Why can't I just teach a few English courses?" I laughed.

He laughed too, but for another reason. "I hate writing too," he blurted out. "I do it, yes, because I have to as a scholar, but I certainly don't like it very much." And this confession came from a literature professor!

I think he overstated his case. I know many, many colleagues throughout our profession who enjoy writing. But my friend's comment made me think of all the ways I avoid a particular kind of writing: where the stakes are high, the cost is great, and achieving success is rare. When I first started teaching, I concocted excuses for why I didn't write. For example, I reasoned I couldn't write in my office because it was too noisy; the library, on the other hand, was too quiet. How could I possibly work on a long project when I had no extended block of uncommitted time or on small ones since my days were fragmented? Of course, if I would get a topic, I promised myself, I would be in a position to write; however, I didn't have an immediate subject, so any writing done now would be premature, even wasteful. After all, my first job to my students was as a teaching professor and the second as a writer who writes. This scaffolding served me many years.

I persisted in that view too because I knew I was not alone: I was in the company of a population who do not write readily and enthusiastically and by choice in school: our students.

Many faculty wrestle with writing in the same ways their students do. Yes, they write—as our students write—but are equally compelled to write for high stakes. For faculty, high-stakes writing means promotion, scholarship, and other professional gains—if they succeed. For students, essay examinations and research papers mean better grades and even better jobs—if they succeed.

Even for faculty who do write regularly and do it well, they still face, at times, internal resistance, a critic that voices doubts throughout their writing. It can stop them from finding meaning or starting from a blank sheet. It can occur anytime, too, unpredictably, and even when faculty writers want desperately to generate it.

As a result, both students and faculty have plentiful incentives to avoid it, procrastinate over it, and sometimes grow into a stance where they hate writing.

3. *The pressures inherent in high-stakes writing alone persuade faculty and students that low-stakes writing is not worthwhile.*

Students are incentivized to see only writing that's graded as worthwhile and, even then, only writing that supposedly records what is already mentally planned. Academic culture encourages professors to think that only work that has passed the grading of referees and editors in a disciplinary field is worthwhile. Thus, student and faculty writing communities face the same attitudes that high-stakes-only work affords—anxieties, impatience, fear, and even hatred of writing. In many ways, we are knotted together as one community in the Writing Problem.

In school environments, it is common to hear both faculty and students talk similarly about writing. Next time, listen for the parallels in the way both describe missed deadlines, whether it be student papers or scholarly journal submissions. How do they explain their unedited final drafts, whether research papers or dense faculty committee reports? Or perhaps you will hear both discuss the declension of their "underwritten" essays, whether it is students who pull all-nighters or faculty who compose just-in-time journal articles. Maybe you have caught yourself sounding like your students when freely discussing your own writing with trusted colleagues. I know I have.

At the same time, I hear very little discussion about low-stakes writing within school settings. In serving many years on a WAC committee, I notice faculty have difficulty designing assignments in writing-intensive courses that are informal, or low stakes. Even then, there is the difficulty of how they fit into a high-stakes writing regiment where grading is the centerpiece. At the same time, I also have students wanting to show me the low-stakes writing they produce on their own—their fan fiction and blogs—but they lack their instructor's permission or the skills to bring that kind of writing into coursework. They are experimenting with low-stakes writing on their own.

How much better our pedagogy would be if we could transition students—and our own writing—from low-stakes to high-stakes writing.

4. For both faculty and students, writing often occupies an uneasy second-subject position in the content classroom.

Today, there are many associated communities trying to mimic WAC successes, such as initiatives for diversity and information and computational competencies. Yet the proliferation of these other skills and competencies prods WAC to move beyond labeling courses as *writing intensive* into more integrative roles, as some have argued (White, 1990).

I recall one faculty member in the sciences who confessed he "had to teach writing because the writing in his classes is so bad" but who nevertheless questioned how specific techniques could fit into a comprehensive whole. New and junior faculty typically have to teach the assigned WAC course. In some universities, new hires must teach freshman writing courses within the discipline of their fields. It is easy, though unfortunate, to conclude that teaching writing means teaching a second subject, one that competes with the primary focus. One chemistry professor once complained to me in a faculty writing seminar that he had so much material to cover that he didn't have time to teach writing. I find similarly busy professors in all disciplines conflicted over their responsibilities to teach what they refer to as two subjects.

Within writing-across-the-curriculum and writing-in-the-disciplines programs at various liberal arts and general education colleges, writing morphs into an appendix to regular catalog courses. It can become distracting to have committees and commissions to promote writing, like designating W-courses, which in turn becomes a code for additional workload for both faculty and students. That those same courses are often taught without a writing emphasis reinforces a stereotype: that writing is a supplemental, secondary subject, complete with an extra chapter of assignments. It is common to hear students complain that the PSYCH 350 offering this semester is a W-course that requires an "extra" research paper.

What we need, instead, is an approach to teaching course content through writing, a manner that both honors the fullness of writing and makes it likable. That conclusion I faced in my own bumpy ride back to writing.

My Journey Back to Writing

I have a long life history with the Writing Problem. When I look back on my experiences with school literacy, I never recall seeing my teachers write. I thought keeping writing private was connected to the job of the professional, something writers were expected to do. Only amateurs like my fellow students should expose their unfinished works to the teacher and others in peer groups. To me, it was an unfathomable mystery of how writers produced writing, let alone good writing, since I had never seen it performed live.

Even in college, I wondered if instructors started out as badly as I did and, through rewriting, persevered to the good. Certainly when I heard writing talked about in the classroom, I never saw my teachers performing it for us. The closest I came was an instructor who demonstrated freewriting on the board, but it wasn't real writing, in my mind, and he never repeated the exercise again and never expected us to imitate it.

When I began teaching, I didn't change perspectives since I saw that most of my professors assigned to teach writing in their content courses or who felt professionally obliged to include writing never-theless expended much effort to avoid it. I felt their pressures too, those that began with despising the assigning, reading, and grading required for writing courses. Then there was the time commitment! In effect, I came to see that I was teaching my students what I could not achieve. I had become, in essence, a nonwriting writing teacher. Over time, I felt quite comfortable dispensing pious advice that none, including myself, could follow.

I came to this conclusion when I finished a graduate degree in rhetoric and began teaching freshman writing courses full time. When I taught those same courses as a graduate instructor, I was writing research and reaction papers for graduate classes, so I was doing writing. At my first job, however, I didn't have even those extrinsic assignments. I reasoned I could wait on writing new journal articles and the like since I had a backlog of pieces gathered from those school-sponsored assignments, ones I could easily send out for publication later. Besides, I reasoned, I was now at a teaching institution where scholarship was nice but not required. My writing abruptly ceased.

When I spoke before those initial college classes, I didn't rec-ognize my voice; I sounded like a teacher and not like a writer or even a teacher of writers. I came to studying a skill that I myself had ceased to practice. In my pedagogy, I found myself substituting other things, like heuristics and composing diagrams and theories of writing, but whatever space they occupied in the classroom, they always came at the expense of my daily practice and outside of a community I was supposed to be creating with my student writers.

I began identifying with my wife's book bag, its slogan lament-ing writer's block and procrastination: "I sat down today to write, but my coffee was cold so I went to warm it up, and when I got to the kitchen ... " and it goes on like that, within one meander-ing, branching sentence, until it ends with "but after 45 minutes I insisted I had to get back to writing, so I hung up, grabbed my mug, and went to my desk, but my coffee was cold so ... " My wife remarked, "Isn't it so true? I bought the bag at a writing conference."

To gain perspective on that dilemma, I looked back. I remembered seeing myself as a writer—just a person who writes—hunched in a rowdy elementary school grade classroom. I remembered writing about every school subject that interested me, and the writing drove that interest in history, geography, and science. It was hard to determine what came first: interest in the content or the writing. My writing became so regular that the study hall proctor, the vice principal of the school, asked me just as regularly, "Do you have a story for me today?" It was the only occasion from early school-sponsored writing where I felt the teacher had read my work.

Years later, I saw the same kind of punishment as an undergraduate when teachers assigned research papers to any student who earned less than an A on the midterm. Students earning A's were rewarded with a reprieve from writing. Writing became the punishment for feeble performance, writing that probably was never read and certainly never welcomed. Incidents like these convinced me that if any force could squelch the powerful urge to write, school-sponsored writing was the best candidate.

What This Book Will Do For You

I offer this book to you, the teaching professor, as an approach to working through the Writing Problem in your courses and in your own writing. This method empowers you as colleagues, no matter your inclination to teach writing, to use the epistemic power of writing to serve your courses. You can accomplish this role for writing because this book seizes the potent forces already established in your own courses and in your own writing, building a structure that complements rather than compromises what you already find working. In short, this book gives you a method that equips you to use writing in the classroom and on your writing desk.

Allow me to nudge you, gently, in ways that gather the kindling to ignite that passion for writing.

That nudge is my way of writing this book for you, a wide range of teaching professors who value writing and want to carry the content of their course *without* carrying burdensome workloads such concerns often demand. In other words, I want this book to serve as a resource for using the power of writing to enable a deeper reflective experience in students by opening them to use writing for their learning in your course. Giving writing a centerpiece in your course accrues another benefit: it adds to your writing craft. As such, this book is not an English professor's book. Instead, it offers choices to combine your passion for your discipline, the students enrolled in your courses, and your own writing.

In short, I want this book to work for you. To me, this means that a series of isolated canned techniques won't suffice. We all need catalysts to help us think more constructively about writing for learning in our courses and in our scholarly work. I seek to give you an approach that guides and recommends without prescriptions. Sometimes in this book I launch into what I've learned through my own trial and error; other times I give examples of how you might carry out a recommendation. Please realize that no matter what arrangement I choose I don't have it all figured out; I am always learning new things from my writerly colleagues—professors and students. My advice is, "Here's what I do; here's what you can do."

As a result, I never ask or expect you, as the content specialist, to teach writing as a second subject. So many professors tell me they prefer specialists like the English department to teach writing. I'm sympathetic to their viewpoint. Similarly, I don't tell you how to teach your own discipline in the classroom; your training and expertise is something I take for granted here. Consequently, the toolbox I open in this book is for you to rummage through, the content specialist.

Instead of teaching writing, I am asking for a different kind of commitment. For our purposes, I want you to think of writing not as a subject or discipline right now but as a powerful way to encourage writing in your students and in your professional life. This working perspective on writing, after all, is everybody's affair. It can enrich your teaching as it feeds your own writing. Those twin benefits can make writing truly enjoyable.

Thus, the overruling principle in this book is more of a reminder than an argument. You already believe this premise: Teaching helps students achieve continuous improvements, and in that way teaching can be just like writing. The Writing Problem is shared by all of us, including our students, no matter the degree. To lessen its severity, we need partnerships—learning to writing, professor to student, writer to writer. We are forever learning to teach, and we are forever learning to write. The powerful urge to learn is never discouraging in teaching; neither should it be with our own or our students' writing.

Structure of the Book

I organized this book as the walkthrough for a content course that privileges writing as a way of learning. The book doubles as a preparation for your own writing. The space writing occupies in this approach does not replace but rather facilitates your pedagogy and your professional writing life.

Chapter 2, "Plan with the Syllabus," grows out of the low-stakes exercise I ask you to start at the end of the present chapter and builds a conversation about writing practice in your pedagogy. Since the syllabus is the first exposure students have to your writing, it gives them insight into what you write as well as how you write.

Chapter 3, "Open That First Class with Writing," shows you how to acquire writing from students on the very first day and to make that low-stakes practice a satisfying exercise.

Chapter 4, "Write Daily: Practice Before Polish," pulls students away from extrinsic motivators like grades and demotivators like past writing experiences. Instead, this chapter emphasizes how to practice, something students don't know how to do. It is also something from which all writers can benefit.

Chapter 5, "Make Long Assignments Manageable for Everyone," argues that you can segment lengthy assignments so students can work on discrete, specific tasks comfortably. This process can work for your own writing.

Chapter 6, "Prepare for Rewriting," distinguishes between rewriting and the more involved revising. You and your students can initiate rewriting at any time, without lengthy training and explanations, familiarizing students with choosing the better among their generated options.

Chapter 7, "Offer Feedback for Classwork," explains how to give student writers the kind of formative feedback that does not overextend your workload.

Chapter 8, "Give Feedback During Short Conferences," shows how to make writing conferences manageable or how, in very large classes ways, to do the next best thing.

Chapter 9, "The Finals: Portfolio and Conference," develops the final, summative assessment as a culmination to all the low-stakes practice students perform earlier in the course.

Chapter 10, "Offer But Two Cheers for Grading Writing," explains how to use Peter Elbow's conclusions about contract grading to define student performance so that you can concentrate on weightier matters like the writing itself. In such an approach, you delay grading so that students focus on their writing craft. It also frees you to assess your writing quickly, forming your low-stakes practice.

The appendix stimulates writing in the classroom with some exercises that work in conjunction with your content course.

A Way Forward

Some time ago, a student told me that I think all problems can be resolved by writing. I had to think about that for a moment. "Yes, that pretty much sums it up," I said. "If writing is the problem, then writing must be the solution."

Just now, my son Will spied over my shoulder at this section while I was composing it in our kitchen. "It sounds really professional," he said.

I frowned. "Really?" I said. "I don't want it to sound that way. I want it to sound like how my readers talk because I relate so closely to what they're experiencing."

"That's good," my fourteen-year-old replied. "But they want to know how you do it; they don't want just someone to relate. Look, if they're going to pick up this book, they want to start working right away. They want to know how to carry it out."

Okay. So let the writing son teach the writing father. Let's take notice again of how we just got started. Let's not allow another moment to go by without bringing writing not only to how we research but also to how we teach in our discipline. This time let me be your writing fellow, your colleague, as we return now—you and me—as students of writing.

An Exercise to Get Us Started

Marilyn Roberts identifies the syllabus as a "document in process instead of a finished text to be 'put to bed'" (2013, 109). If we also can think of our pedagogy as a continuing process of making classroom observations, we can also see syllabus writing as a great exercise for low-stakes practice that gets us thinking about using writing in the classroom.

But where can you start? One way I've found productive, and I think you will too, is to think about what you want to accomplish. But first, consider making a *brain dump*. What I'm recommending is time to get the messy and disconnected thoughts you have for the syllabus all in one space so you see what you're thinking. In this context, writing captures and creates thinking all in one place.

Here's something I do, and you can do it, too: I just openly freewrite about the present syllabus I have for a course I've taught, am teaching, or am planning to teach. Freewriting is the spontaneous, active transfer of your brain to your pen, writing not as fast as you can but as nonstop as you can. When you freewrite, you push ever onward without hesitating or going back or crossing out or editing in any way. There's no recursive movement backward, only forward—figuratively and mentally. You want contact not with your internal critic but with your subconscious mind, which has been doing its own unrecorded writing. In freewriting, you push to the next word, the next line, the next page. Peter Elbow (1998) formalized this technique first in *Writing Without Teachers*, but it has many practitioners.

You can start with generating a focused freewrite of your syllabus. Start with a list or an instructive line like, "One thing I want to change about my syllabus is ... ," which you complete and go on from there. Don't worry about grammar or spelling or striking out text right now; don't concern yourself with staying on topic. If you can't think of what to write, transcribe, "I can't think of what to write." You'll soon tire of that mantra and circle back to writing about your syllabus. Just keep the writing moving—no retracing. We want not a seesaw but a bullet train through problems, difficulties, triumphs; whatever occupies your hand about your syllabus will engage your mind. Limit yourself to ten minutes.

Then let it settle, incubating until we address it in Chapter 2.

The Freewriting Habit and Quality

Without exception, every aspect of the Writing Problem for both faculty and students can have the same writerly solution, even if that solution, at first glance, looks counterintuitive or simplistic. This principle guides the book, starting with the sample exercise from the last section. It seems obvious but it's worth stating: we need to start somewhere.

We know it's often difficult for students to get started with writing a paper. The solution is to start writing anywhere, whether it's the germ of an idea or a search for meaning. We can call those first words a beginning. In a classroom situation, you can ask students to write prolifically and without stopping or other constraints for ten minutes—freewriting, for example—after first announcing a major assignment in class. Thus, as simplistic as it sounds the answer for nonwriting is writing. Later in this book, I provide sample focused freewriting examples that you can adapt to your classroom and which can envelope your present high-stakes assignments.

When I presented this example in a writing seminar, one professor vehemently objected. "How does freewriting help them?" he asked, exasperated. "They are already bad writers. Freewriting is nothing more than more bad writing."

However, we know that these so-called bad writers do not freewrite. Rather, they begin by fitting leaden prose into the structured, high-stakes genres assigned in class that do not tolerate bad writing. These bad writers need that freewriting beginning; they first need a place to dump their bad writing, a sanctioned space to overcome inertia to achieve something more (so-called good writing). If students can learn to freewrite habitually, they find the bad prose they produce becomes repetitive and boring; exhausted, they collapse, often unconsciously, into bursts of occasional and unplanned good writing. We occasionally witness this phenomenon when some students grind out a long paper at the last minute and a small insight appears, bookended by the bad writing. Unfortunately, student writers seldom see such and rewrite to shape that insight into a better paper.

There are also other considerations associated with bad writing. Those bad writers did not develop overnight; they entered into a process that led to ineffective writing. Some had very little writing instruction in school; others had very little experience with school-sponsored writing, and what they did have was largely negative. Many are just indifferent to writing and see it as something they *have* to do. No matter their past experiences, however, students can become better, even competent, writers, but it involves teaching some new habits. One of those, freewriting, enables us to start the journey.

It is precisely because so many of us start out as bad writers—professors and students—that we need to rehearse our language in a private forum to open up our thinking in prose. We need other habits, too, like becoming good rewriters. It takes time and practice to accomplish a good end product. Consequently, anyone's judgments about *good* and *bad* at this initial point—including the writer's!—are premature.(That so many students exhibit bad writing behooves us as professors to lengthen their writing process so that the writing can have time to develop.) Acknowledging some of our own quick writing as bad, we can appreciate why we need to lengthen the writing process so we can generate a better product. In fact, when we characterize any academic writing as bad, we can just as accurately call it premature or unfinished.

In other words, students need a better process that extends their practice from the initial private domain—the bad—before going public with a better product. It is the professor who can best guide that practice. It starts with little structure and mushrooms to greater structure. Out of that greater structure, content can flourish. Consequently, there is never a shortage of content or structure—only time. Moreover, the relationship between content and structure is tight: distinguishable but inseparable. If we judge writing prematurely or divide the grade between structure and content—that is, before writers ripen their content and structure—we cut the vine before it blossoms.

Writers begin with a structure, the schema they import from their reading histories, their reading in a discipline, the way you have shaped the course. But they often cannot delve deeply into that structure yet. Freewriting is the bridge from their initial *unstructure* to the final structured product that we want them to achieve.

So yes, bad writers do need freewriting to transition content into a given structure. That means many rehearsals in an extended writing process so they have time to wed content to structure, something readers demand.

What About You?

Now look at your own writing habits. Have you tried freewriting? Have you worked the pen to open up your mind to new ideas that writing can introduce? Have you put aside thoughts of bad writing so that you can push, later, toward the good?

The way to lessen the Writing Problem is to start writing, and the easiest and most prolific way is to start today with freewriting. Find a comfortable pen, devote a new notebook exclusively to writing (called a daybook), and take ten minutes to write continuously, without stopping. Follow this delightful invitation before attempting any structured writing project and just before any class starts. Try that freewriting out by longhand, too—choose *analog*—so your optimal technology is the minimal: a nucleus of pens. The coordination of eye, brain, and hand presents an earthy physicality that births writing. As you freewrite, you build a fluency and experience with language, experimentation without evaluation. Freewriting also encourages rewriting when you read it to yourself and then to others, a rewriting that you engineer before others even hear.

In summary, when you next begin a writing project, by either assigning it to students or executing your own, start by writing about it. Freewriting is one useful strategy to get started. As helpful as thinking about the project or talking about it with a colleague might be, recognize that these activities are not writing. The best writing you can do is when you start early, allowing the writing to invent your ideas and to inform your conversations with a colleague. When this way becomes a habit, you will not only produce more writing and with greater facility but will also ease it into structured, formal writing. Suddenly ideas will bud. A structure will emerge in your mind much more easily when the content is carried in your writing. The messy, "bad" writing in your own notebook gives birth, given time and permission, to the more structured enterprises that follow.

Then encourage students to follow your lead by inviting them to write without stopping for a few minutes at the start of any writing enterprise, whether class meeting or project. It becomes both of you then to write from the beginning.

2

Plan with the Syllabus

A typical syllabus is very easy to write. Anyone reviewing syllabi across disciplines and schools will see all the familiar headings: listings of assignments, office hours, learner outcomes, and statements of mutual accountability. The pedagogical literature also observes what professors should include in a syllabus (Baecker, 1998; Eberly, Newton, and Wiggins, 2001; Habanek, 2005), including its announced purposes (Albers, 2003; McKeachie, 1986; Singham, 2007).

The typical syllabus and the literature are mum, however, regarding how professors can compose a readable one that invokes its audience of students. That task is also the most difficult to achieve in writing a syllabus. Since it is the first sample of your writing that students see, it is also students' first experience with how you will deal with the Writing Problem in your class. Of course, they won't use that term, but students really want to know how you receive student writing in the course and what your writing looks like because they believe you are immune to the Writing Problem. I believe a comprehensive, detailed syllabus that students enjoy reading is the first step for any course that uses writing for learning. In other words, I'm asking you to consider writing the *un*typical syllabus.

That syllabus is a most effective way in opening a written dialogue with your students. It serves as a natural way to deliver your writing to them on the first day. As such, it must be detailed and comprehensive but also accessible and even enjoyable for them to read, which means it must also be enjoyable for you to write.

Sounds impossible, doesn't it? Fortunately, we can write a solution to this dilemma by harnessing the power of writing to solve its own problems. Capitalizing on the freewriting exercise from the previous chapter, we can use this same process now for two purposes: to find a writing voice that dialogues with our students and to discover the kinds of things we want our student writers to know in our course. By taking the time and effort to write a comprehensive syllabus, we show our fellow writers we value writing from our very first day with them.

Have you started with the open freewriting exercise from the previous chapter? May I nudge you, gently, to take a glance back there and begin with that exercise before moving on in the book?

Start Writing at the Beginning of Thinking

One evening very early in my teaching career I told my wife about a new teaching assignment I was excited about. She looked equally excited for me, as she always does in such situations, but after a few minutes I saw her face grow concerned. "That's wonderful," she said, "but how will you teach it?"

I couldn't answer her. It required some thought, so I set about finding those thoughts by exploring her question, the question every syllabus poses, through writing. Just as you did in the last chapter, I started freewriting.

Do you have a daybook, an everyday notebook dedicated solely for writing? I had mine handy, inserted the date, and copied her question to the top of a new page. Starting with the phrase, "What I really want to do in this course … ," I made a new entry by completing the sentence. Soon I was on to the next and the next, following the pen as it seemed to generate my thinking. Blissfully oblivious to spelling, grammar, and syntax, I continued to write without stopping, unconcerned how pretty it looked on the page or how good the writing was. Whenever I felt tempted to stop, I wrote it away by reasoning on paper that I don't have time to stare at a blank page or to worry about what constitutes good writing. I was devoting my writing energies at that moment on unstructured thinking: pushing forward, one word upon another, one idea stacked haphazardly on the former. I felt my writing take over when I became a witness to its rocking between clusters of ideas, exploding from the pen to full lines where I wrote nothing more significant than "I don't know what to write about." I stopped a short ten minutes later and looked briefly over what I had just written. Without a joining thread among them, I saw my thinking as a pastiche of ideas—oils mixed with water—consisting of how students could use field research, compose a portfolio with their chosen artifacts, and benefit from workshops. In short, I was freewriting about goals and grading and objectives and homework assignments.

After dinner, I freewrote again for another ten minutes. I was still generating material, finishing a partially completed sentence from last session to gain momentum. Ten minutes passed. To incubate those ideas, I cleaned up the kitchen. I next drove to the office later that evening, used a stand-up desk, and wrote for twenty more minutes, filling pages of my notebook.

The blank page produces inertia; the writing of the page, thinking.

At the end of that day, I had a whole lot of stuff in my notebook, but when I reviewed it, two things emerged. First, I wrote about students as writers. And second, even more surprisingly, I wrote as if I believed they could see themselves as writers too.

Those two insights gave me a voice for the syllabus and the class: In the classroom, I am one among my fellow writers. Suddenly, I felt free to share my own successes and failures in writing and to incorporate them into the structure of the course. I could account for missteps like false drafts that pushed me unproductively. I could now show them written feedback from editors, especially ones that explicate why my article was rejected. Most importantly, I could explain what was going on in my writing life at the time, to place it in context so that my students can see how writing is made.

By drawing from the real, commonplace experience of writers, I endeavored to welcome writers into my classroom.

If you already have syllabi you've used in the past, don't discard them! Instead, look back at the freewriting you incubated from Chapter 1. Any insights emerge? Anything different from what you expected to write? Do you see any connections?

If not—or even if you did—try extending your freewrite. This time, start by freewriting in a comfortable voice, centering on things you want students to care about in your course. The more deeply you plunge into your freewriting, the more you will find a natural dialogic language that will transform that syllabus into a genre that invites student writers to write to you. It's one thing to know that your present syllabus is the best in the biology department, but a syllabus requires thinking beyond colleagues to reach your student writers, your primary audience. How marvelous when students see themselves represented in your syllabus as you share your passion, say, for numbers or biology.

Can you begin to see the benefit of depicting yourself and your students as writers?

You obviously care about words and language, but how do your students see your commitment? It is through visible action that you take on the role of a writer. Notice the definition that John Braine gives: "A writer is a person who counts words" (1975, 19). As writers, you know you already care about words and own the words you use. Yet students must see evidence of how you *do words*. Braine mentions *writing* and *counting*, actions that are visible and, given nurture, can accomplish something—move, persuade, stimulate, and encourage an audience. Using language self-consciously, to be pedagogical, must be observable. I have a retired laborer friend who never completed high school but who is conscious of his language in his actions. He likes to ask me questions about usage when he writes in the margins of his drafts: "Should I have used *I* instead of *me*?" and "Is *this* the right word here?" as he points to a passage in his letter. He loves crosswords and learns words that he works to put into the context of his daily life. He counts his words. He cares about words, the way they fit into puzzles and his own writing. I see him do writing. He is a writer.

Paradoxically, carefulness in language can begin with the abundant flow of words in freewriting. After that burst of spontaneous writing, your later drafting is free to settle on just the best words, which become the basis for the syllabus. As Eberly et al. observe, the syllabus is "rarely considered as part of curriculum redesign" (2001, 56), but it should be for both (re)structuring a course and finding a voice. That can make the syllabus a fluid document to reach ever-new students with your own writing.

In planning any course—a first-timer and a reliable repeater—you can testify to the epistemic power of writing by writing as children do: simply by writing nonstop, without hesitating. It is the single greatest anomaly that lifts both of us from our quandaries by working our language muscles before the big game of structured discourse.

The Focused Freewriting in the Middle

In the last chapter, I asked you to freewrite for ten minutes, to write without structure so that the freewriting might coax insight and an ensuing structure for your syllabus. (Again the writing paradox: the unstructured leads to the structured.) Have you found some hints toward structure? If not, maybe you need another ten-minute span for writing.

Another way you might try is to take a week to freewrite about your syllabus in another place. For example, take a daybook, that journal devoted exclusively to writing, to places where you expect to wait for something else to occur: the dentist's waiting room, the coffee shop, the minutes before class begins. After a week, look back and highlight centers of gravity that you keep returning to or circling around. Here are some of mine:

1. An Introduction to the Course
2. Nature of Writing in This Course

3. Required Texts

4. Statement on Grading

5. Assignment Design

6. Portfolio and Examinations

7. Plagiarism

8. Policies for Submitting Work

9. Attendance

10. Outcomes

The next step in this kind of syllabus project is to take those areas and perform a focused freewriting on each center of gravity: five minutes on each. You could perform freewriting on each in the waiting spaces of two full weekdays. Even when you get off-topic, you can still circle back in the writing to return, the journey appearing as a spiraling staircase that collapses into its subject. At such times, you want ideas, the energy to push forward so that a complex task like a structured syllabus is distributed into discrete chunks of time that you can manage.

In the span of two days, you can write a lot, without much effort and without consuming whole days. First, you may even find additional subjects when you find yourself off-topic. You can then expand the task if you like, such as freewriting about your or your students' experiences with the Writing Problem.

Here's another alternative. If you are freewriting about a course you're teaching again, try a quick freewrite in your own daybook after finals are in and the course is still fresh in your mind. It's tremendously liberating to freewrite at the end of one course, long before you restart the next; your mind is ready to dump pedagogical problems into one word followed by the next and so forth. There's a permanence to that recording, too, that you can reference later if you wish. As you trust the process, you find gentle release and relief from the heavy memories you've been carrying.

Yet another alternative is to start by listing your Big Ten areas or taking mine to get you started. Then make some focused freewriting on those ten areas—just five minutes each—for about one hour's worth all together just for the purpose of exploration. Or break the ten freewrites into separate days. I like to go early to a coffee shop, find my usual corner, and just focus-freewrite for an hour.

In such a relaxed scenario for writing—freewriting is both writing and relaxing—I eschew the responsibility of bringing writing fully into the classroom in one gulp. Otherwise, I face leaden prose or blank pages or tons of abstract thinking, writing that doesn't *do* anything. Instead, elect for freewriting, the energy drink that you sip.

The Structured Rewriting at the End

After a few hours, days, or weeks—but only after the initial freewriting—you will now feel free enough to communicate to your audience. If you don't, try freewriting some more. You want the raw material to come out without imposition—to give content its due.

Now is time for the refining fire. Take the raw material of the freewrite and stoke it, through rewriting, so it begins to take on the structure of a syllabus. You can accomplish this by breaking the ten areas into chunks, brief assignments that you rewrite until you achieve a good faith effort that satisfies for the present. This time, I suggest switching modes to drafting, where you fashion salient ideas from your freewriting into sentences and paragraphs. Or you can craft sentences that have only dim resemblance to the freewriting that preceded it. The purpose for your freewriting was to release your language; that done, the task becomes to shape language and refine it through drafting.

I also recommend changing technologies for the drafting: go digital this time. I like to break the ten areas into separate folders or subfiles in a software program like Literature and Latte's *Scrivener*

(Blount, 2009), which allows me to keep all ten in one file but benevolently restricts me to see only one center of gravity at a time. You can certainly do this activity in any program, but try to find one that limits your exposure to the whole structure until all the chunks—the ten areas—are in *good faith effort* territory. (More on this concept later.)

While you are drafting, become aware of the primary audience for your syllabus: your students. Since you are communicating with these fellow writers you can find your voice as you converse in writing. Whenever I get to drafting, I spend some time finding that conversational voice because I want my voice to match my intention in appealing to writers first and to students second. Voice allows us to make that connection. It will also give your writers a benchmark in writing back to you.

I excerpt particular sections here that can apply to any college course, along with a few comments so you can see continuity in voice among sections. You can find a complete syllabus for an introductory course in the Appendix.

Remember you are drafting to achieve *good enough* status. Return the next day or week to bring those sentences and paragraphs to *better* status. Your subconscious is working on that writing while you are doing other things. That incubation between on-again–off-again writing can work until deadline. When I'm constructing a syllabus, I look for the last day I can get the college print shop to produce it or Web services to publish it online and move my deadline back one week or, in the summer, one month. That calendar allots time to edit, to proofread, and to let a colleague or trusted friend read over it and give advice.

The Welcome

On the first day of class when you distribute the syllabus, consider creating an initial writing exercise as a way to spark discussion. To establish a clear and concise point of view, think about using the first person (*I*/*we*) and address the audience directly using the second (*you*). Obviously, you want to make your voice approachable to students.

In the sample sections, I excerpt from an introductory course. I aim to show examples of how I've done it and how you can do it, too. These are not templates but samples that you can adapt to your own classroom and subject. I believe strongly in the inductive method when discussing writing because it is one that your students can latch onto from the very first day in seeing how you do writing. So I offer my examples here, not so much for imitation but to give you a sense of how you can make voice a powerful feature to connect with your students:

> Welcome to the course. I hope that through our opening exercise you see that writing is the most important thing we can do in this class.
>
> To keep writing in that central role, I teach by syllabus, a guide to the standards, responsibilities, policies, and purposes of any course, especially one that uses writing to deliver content. I also have composed this syllabus as an open conversation between us as we pursue the craft of writing together. I reserve the right to modify the provisions outlined in this syllabus if a need arises, but in such cases, I will always strive to be fair.
>
> The syllabus also keeps us on task. I will hold you to its terms, and I expect you to hold me to them just as rigorously. As writers—as people who write—we need to be mutually accountable to one another. Therefore, view this syllabus as one approach to sharing our joint responsibilities as writers.
>
> Along with these responsibilities are specific learning goals I expect us to reach. In this syllabus, I also introduce nine other areas, such as how I prefer assessing over grading, class policies, and perspectives on writing about

subject matter that makes us better writers. These areas all reflect my experiences as a writer and as a teacher of writers.

In every course I teach, I enlist student writers to engage course subject matter through their writing. This course is no exception. That means that, as a writer, you must work to strengthen all aspects of your writing process—inventing, drafting, rewriting, copyediting—which will help you and your peers to become better writers and rewriters. Since writing is a process—a long and complicated one—I will give you plenty of both practice and guidance.

I recognize that there are many ways to teach a course through writing. My perspective on learning approaches course content through writing about it. As a writer, I am always exploring new ways that benefit my learning of content, with writing as the driving force. I want to share these with you so we can learn together.

Here is an opening that applies these principles to an advanced education course in which all students have taken the introductory course with the same instructor:

I designed this course for students who must meet teacher certification requirements, but I want it to do more than just satisfy a category. I want to show how educational issues shape the society in which we will live as well as in your new career as an educator. I'm also interested in cultural and linguistic diversity—you may remember these distinctions from the introductory course. These two components help form a good education for any student.

As an educator, you will be expected to speak and write well and to be able to research a topic using scholarly sources. I will help you develop these skills as we explore the major units of the course.

In both cases, students see that the course assigns an important role to writing but one they may not be accustomed to: a way to learn course content.

Nature of How Writing Functions in This Course

It's essential for you to establish how you view writing, no matter how briefly. A principle grounded in a practice ("to write a handout or share it") and dialogue ("Let's just write five minutes on that question") can help students understand.

> Because it is difficult (impossible?) for me to talk precisely about writing until you write for this class, there will be some uncertainty in our daily operation. I want the freedom, when I notice a particular writing problem or question persists, to write a handout and share it during workshop without worrying about keeping pace with the syllabus. I also want to be able to stop a puzzled or overwhelmed class to say, "Let's just write for five minutes on that question." Similarly, you may ask for additional help in class regarding any specific writing topic with which we are struggling.

Grading

Student writers expect grading to occupy a central place in a syllabus. One way to meet that expectation yet reject the stereotypes common to school-sponsored writing is to identify yourself as a student of writing. If you can successfully adopt this relational role in your syllabus, you can sidestep much resistance and thus open the path to course content. By addressing students' concerns first as students, you can show that you have listened to student concerns, particularly with writing, in the past.

The Contract for B is covered in more detail in Chapter 10, where I discuss how to incorporate writing assessments into a traditional course. The contract recognizes the instrumentality of effort required for writing and how greater effort means more rehearsals, drafts, and rewriting than what students normally do, all of which you want because those actions contribute to better performance. I include this introductory section here to show that the conversational style you establish in the opening can continue as you share common ground with your readers and their concerns:

> No subject in the classroom provokes more mistrust, distrust, resentment, hostility, anxiety, bitterness, resignation, envy, and rancor between students and their professors than grading. At best, students perceive traditional grading as a subjective judgment of their learning and their person. At worst, they discern it as a weapon used against them.
>
> My best answer (so far) is to introduce better measures of fairness into the grading process, but those are not enough. I want to ease student writers into thinking constructively about their writing more often and that means grading less often. Together, we must forget grading up to the point where learning to be a better writer takes over. You see, I choose far less grading in favor of far more assessing; I choose one grade at one time rather than many grades all the time.
>
> That reduction doesn't mean I won't evaluate, respond, comment, judge, and even like your writing. I will reserve plenty of time for feedback. I use what writing professor Peter Elbow calls a *home studio* approach, commonly called *assessment*. Imagine you are enrolled in a painting or cooking class; perhaps you could be a scout looking to complete a merit badge or a new driver looking to pass a competency test. These contexts are ones I covet for my writing classes, ones where assessment—not grading—is the rule.
>
> I first thought along these lines after a student showed me a news article in which some school districts

proposed homework-free weekends but found that students used these time-outs to catch up on overdue homework. In short, they worked harder than ever. What if I could host grade-free weeks in which we worked harder than ever but instead of catching up to a grade we strove for writing excellence, something we should be doing as writers anyway? Peter Elbow and Jane Danielewicz arrive at the same notion:

> We would have classes or workshops or lessons, but there would be no official grading. Of course I'd give you evaluative feedback … , pointing out where you've done well and where I could suggest an improvement. But I wouldn't put grades on your individual paintings or omelets or give you an official grade for the course.

Imitating those same evaluative conditions, I sponsor workshops, conferences, and handouts in this course. My job is to create a learning environment: as professor, I also am your mentor and fellow writer. I will give you a rich supply of feedback on your writing; I will even write with you in class. In these roles, I will not assign letter grades for fourteen weeks—big assignments and small—but I will provide plenty of feedback for rewriting (or revising, if you want it). In fact, after the first day until midterm, I refuse to talk about grades entirely and will do so only then by request during a conference.

That said, if you complete the tasks assigned to this course—work really, really hard—I can assure you of a final grade of B. I call this understanding the Contract for B.

Assignment Design

Here is a great place to show how course writing assignments fit particular purposes for writing in your course and then aligning them to assessments. For unstructured, low-stakes writing, you are free to assess according to the appropriate degree of *finishness*: just enough feedback without overwhelming its recipient. Transitional writing is midstakes, a mixed category that gives students more feedback to guide and to stimulate their thinking toward rewriting and revising (I distinguish between the two in Chapter 6) as they rehearse for high stakes. In summary, high stakes is graded, final, summative, and light in feedback. It is critical for educators to have high expectations and demanding courses, but it is just as important to recognize that students seldom reach those expectations on a first attempt, making feedback essential before the final grade.

These categories, however, are meaningless unless instructors infuse writing with a purpose, an aim to ground students in writing that accomplishes something outside of itself. A purpose goes beyond organizing principles or formatting to the core of writing itself. Traditional purposes are to persuade, to evaluate, to show causes or effects, to propose. Have students notice that writing is poised to do something to someone. A story can help. The owner of my favorite coffee shop recently showed me a solicitation letter he received that was grammatically correct and professionally typed but that "said nothing." As he explained it, the letter "was a perfect opening for a cover letter because it introduced the charitable organization in three tight paragraphs but never explained exactly what they wanted and when and how." Everyday examples of writing that fails to do something purposeful to an audience fill our days. Let students hear one story from you about how you value writing that has a purpose to do something.

To situate writing within the classroom, metaphors can work wonders in humanizing what can be pretty dry stuff that students easily forget. I use a baseball metaphor to describe writing because it grows from my own interests but primarily because it's multifaceted and I can easily apply it to writing. Students may forget the term I want them to remember, but if I infuse it with a baseball metaphor they remember better. You can vary the metaphor, of course, but it should be as accessible to students as the national pastime.

I make writing assignments for specific reasons, which I categorize under the headings in Table 2.1. I'll be explaining more about these in class as we practice them.

Portfolio

A portfolio system serves two purposes. The first is for collecting the written products of the class—daily writing, drafts, postwrites, note-taking—since writers cannot determine final value during collection. These artifacts comprise the working portfolio, analogous on a larger scale to freewriting or a first draft. The second is the final portfolio, which is a rewriting of select portions of the working portfolio. (More on this subject in Chapter 9.)

The two-copy requirement allows me to see the original assignment at the beginning of class or conference and the second as the impetus for student writers to begin rewriting during class or conference. I do not return my copy, as it represents only where the writer has started but not where she will arrive in a final portfolio. (I describe this process with more detail in Chapter 5.)

Offering Work

Writers must learn to accept deadlines for they make writing happen. I encourage writers at the same time I hold them to a deadline because recreating the context for writing at a date and time later than you planned will simply not work. As one student put it, "If a paper doesn't have a due date, what's the point of having an assignment anyway?"

Unlike a traditional publishing relationship between writer and publisher, the college professor is a fellow writer and editor. That last role, however, doesn't mean the professor edits the student work. I have been blessed to know and work with three excellent editors, and each one of them gave feedback so compelling that

Table 2.1. Categories of Writing

Category of writing	Stakes	Baseball analogy	Purpose for writing	Example assignments	Assessments
Unstructured	Low	Spring training	To think, to practice, to learn	• Daily writing • In-class writing • Planning • Postwrites • Workshop practice	B CONTRACT: Responses from professor and peers
Transitional	Mid	Regular season	To practice structured writing; to demonstrate learning	• Drafts • Working folder	B CONTRACT: Responses from professor and peers
Structured	High	World Series	To inform, to persuade, to express, to emphasize language	• Final portfolio • Examination	FINAL GRADE: Feedback from professor

I couldn't wait to rewrite. I covet that same rich experience for my students, as I'm sure you do. Since student written work is rewritable during the semester, college professors can be both writer and editor in soliciting work, setting deadlines, encouraging rewriting, and entering conversations about writing as fellow writers:

> I do not accept late homework because writing does not readily lend itself easily to make-ups.
>
> Therefore, all homework must be offered in person— being sure to make two copies, one for you and one for me—at the start of class or at the beginning of each conference, whichever applies. Conversely, dropping off homework, e-mailing it to me, sending it through a friend or classmate, and all associated submissions in absentia are unacceptable. If you're going to be absent, realize I cannot accept work ahead of time since we process together that first work during class or conference. That combination occurs only during class time!
>
> I argue aggressively in this course that growth in writing is a reasonable expectation when writers and their craft become accountable to all in one time and in one place. No one will defend, advise, promote, or argue effectively anyone's draft when its writer is absent. Please do not ask me to violate my own principles: therefore, work by deadline.

Absences

In courses where writing integrates into content courses, absences present special problems. It's always a pedagogical advantage for writers to practice their craft in class, where you can help them directly and without delay, so they practice their chops again in homework assignments when you are absent. This flipped classroom—where professors record lectures for students to play back later during homework time—can easily be adapted for use with writing. It gives you an opportunity to correct student misapprehensions or your own unintentional misdirections once you see what students are practicing. They also can question you right on the spot, which is tremendously powerful for learning. Thus, you establish common ground with students when you confess what they already know: you get sick yet you do not undercut your own principles:

> Of course, I recognize lateness and absences cannot always be avoided, that everyone becomes ill, suffers a family loss, participates in a critical sports meet or game, crashes a hard drive, forgets to buy an inkjet cartridge, or has some other Bad Day Incident at some point in the semester and cannot attend. I know I do. Like you, I face those circumstances every semester; I've had illnesses (my kids and my elderly father too!) that have pulled me out of school for a spell. I accept all of these situations (and countless others) as valid.
>
> To compensate for these eventualities, I have designed the course to incorporate as much of the human experience as possible and still have it retain its academic integrity. Therefore, I will drop two days of work—not two assignments but two days of work—from the first fourteen weeks of classes. These demolished days never erase absences from the totals in the B Contract, only assignments due. If you attend every class and conference, I will drop two days of low performance.
>
> Remember, late work is never accepted but may qualify as assignments to be dropped.
>
> If you play on a college sports team and you know some games will conflict with class commitments, take the time now to plan for those absences. My advice also applies to trips you're planning that interfere with the daily classwork.

Outcomes

With accrediting agencies emphasizing learner outcomes, it makes good sense to show you're following standards in your field and in writing. Every discipline has outcome statements for certain courses, and some colleges require that a boilerplate (word-for-word) be inserted here as well as in sections on plagiarism and academic standards. To safeguard your voice, continue drawing on the first person (e.g., *I, my, me*) and why you are using them.

Another option is to use L. Dee Fink's (2003) categories to define outcomes, each starting with a verb, as in this example from a rhetoric course:

Foundational Knowledge

- Remember the "first principles" comprising the canons of rhetoric.

- Identify the connections between ancient rhetorics and modern written argument.

Application

- Collect commonplaces.

- Write prolifically every day.

- Share your writing.

- Join with classmates in giving feedback.

- Apply rhetorical terms and concepts as ways to strengthen your own writing.

- Invent more content/material than you have time and opportunity to use in final discourses.

Integration

- Write and speak persuasively on topics—both assigned and self-generated—that are important to the communities in which you belong.

Human Dimension

- Become active and informed citizens in a democracy.

- Abandon myopic self-interest.

- Cope with ambiguous or paradoxical situations by pushing through to viable and peaceful solutions.

Caring

- Accept responsibility for learning.

- Enjoy writing, throwing yourself headlong into its fury!

Learning How to Learn

- Know how to pursue a writing project independent of direct instructor involvement.

- Create a learner portfolio that demonstrates and documents excellence in your writing.

How to Use the Syllabus

Here's how I use the syllabus on the first day, which you can adapt to your classroom and your own style of presentation. I'm pretty informal, especially on the first day when I ask students to read through the syllabus in class without my lecturing through it or, worse yet, reading it to them. After ten minutes have elapsed, I ask if there are any questions. Hearing the usual none—everyone is a bit nervous on the first day—I say, "Okay, let's have a quiz; everything off your desk but your elbows and a writing instrument."

Suddenly the room grows dark and sullen. I quickly distribute paper copies, and students busily set out to discover the right answer. This is the only multiple-choice quiz I give all year. (The Appendix contains one sample quiz.)

After ten minutes have elapsed, I ask if anyone believes he or she has all answers correct. No one raises a hand.

"But there were no questions!" I say dumbfounded, smiling a moment later. A few students snicker, seeing my point.

"Okay, in just three minutes, share with your neighbor-writer your answers and see what he or she selected. You may want to change your answer, but remember, it's your choice. By the way, you may want to introduce yourself, too, and get your neighbor's name and e-mail address."

Suddenly students burst with enthusiasm, nervous energy voicing to change answers, exchange names, challenge their new best friends in the class, and hurry about the task. It is here I have complete cooperation.

I walk around to see how everyone is doing. During my travels, I get questions.

"What does this word mean?" asks one, pointing to one on the quiz.

"I can't see it," I reply. "Say it for me."

"Sub-ord-in-ate," he utters, sounding out the syllables slowly.

"Have you ever heard of that word before?" I ask.

"Not sure," he replies. "Maybe in middle school ... "

"Did you ask your partner?"

He smiles.

Suddenly the partner chimes in with an answer. At this point, I can add to the answer or qualify it, but I want to validate that partner's viewpoint—the writer's prototypical, first reader in the class. It's an incomplete picture, but I am happy for a thumbnail of the reader–writer relation from the syllabus.

It is so invigorating to see processes slowly forming. "You're rewriting," I tell a classroom full of writers as they busily rehearse other answers with their teammates.

When you see such prototypical rewriting, you are witnessing an intricate, complex mechanism beginning to turn. Because you can acknowledge their contribution—their effort—you valorize the effort that is first necessary to any productive process. At that moment, you are beginning to develop a learning behavior that writing can bolster.

This opening exercise is all good-natured fun, too, and a tremendous stress reliever because student writers see what low-stakes work is all about. I time the exercise, but I expand the time if everyone is productive and working. I want the most throughput for the longest stretch of time possible.

"Okay, you have one minute to look up answers in the syllabus. Since your buddy and you both took the same quiz, you could be looking up one answer while your pal could be looking up another. By the way, that's called proofreading; you're checking the 'proof' for accuracy." This way, I introduce a term that I'll repeat several times this week as well as demonstrate. Using writerly terms helps writers self-identify because they know the vocabulary from usage in classroom dialogue.

Again, I walk around to see how students are doing.

After a minute, I give another prompt: "I'll take three questions from the class in the order I receive them."

Suddenly three arms shoot up. I pick on the first, "Number 6."

I next ask how one other group answered. Sometimes I say, "Who answered A for question 6?" More often than not, in simple quizzes like this one, I'll have at least 80% pick the correct answer. Then I say, "A looks like the right answer to me too." There's a quick rewriting among the other 20%.

When we're finished and the voices die down, I ask, "Why did I perform this exercise today?"

They think a while. If I get no answers right away, I ask students to write for one minute, nonstop, on why they think I sponsored this project today. I also write on the same question in my daybook, a required notebook (for students and their professor) devoted exclusively for writing. I get many answers, and they are usually good. After a minute, I ask writers to read what they wrote to their partners. Then I call on a few.

"You wanted us to work collaboratively like you said at the beginning of class."

"You were tired of lecturing." Everyone laughs.

"You said that all writing needs sharing. Maybe this quiz is a kind of writing too."

"You wanted us to know the syllabus."

"You want us to work with a partner, discuss what we write, check our answers, and then talk to you."

I pause over that last response.

To regenerate those kind of answers, I ask them to write me a letter or e-mail for homework that focuses on the syllabus. This opening exercise begins the written dialogue—oral communication to service written communication. I give a handout that always attracts great low-stakes writing on the syllabus.

These letters are a joy to read. They will be for you too, I think, because they really give you a sense of the writer within.

> Your Response to the Syllabus
>
> Compose a letter to me (800–1200 words) in which you answer the following questions regarding this syllabus. Some questions may overlap depending on your response.
>
> But don't give me an outline. Write a letter to me instead, a narrative, without bullet points or numbers. Please keyboard it, making two copies—one for you, one for me:
>
> Questions
>
> - What does my first section mean to you?
> - What do you think about my distinction between assessing and grading? Rewriting and revising?
> - Pick one point in the syllabus you like. Pick one you don't. Then tell me why you selected these.
> - What do you think might discourage you from achieving the outcomes listed on pages 1–2? How, specifically, can I help you reach them?
> - How might this class contribute toward your personal or professional goals?
> - What do you think of the attendance policy? The late policy? Do you understand the reasons for those

policies? What do you still have questions about?

- What do you like or find most reassuring about taking this class? The least reassuring?
- Tell me anything you would like me to know about you as a writer.

The next class, I receive their letters:

Dear Dr. Hafer,

This is my first college English class, and I will admit to being a little intimidated by all the writing we will be doing. Your opening statement, though, does help reduce the intimidation on terms of how you perceive and think about how things should work....

Dr. Hafer,

I'd like to explore my writing in this class by not just writing in the same style every time but by trying new ideas out. Your syllabus says that we are going to do exactly that, and that excites me. My father always says to me that writing is the key to any job and he wishes he had studied it more in college....

The syllabus need not be a dead or punitive document. It can be a lively, personal statement of your excitement in teaching this course and employing writing to complement that teaching. At the same time, it can converse with your audience, invite writers and new readers, and honor how writing is made with the disciplinary content that gives shape to the course. In effect, you emphasize the content of your course when you communicate effectively with your students, using a voice and structure they enjoy reading, you enjoy writing, and in turn, they enjoy writing back to you.

3

Open That First Class
with Writing

In the last chapter, that syllabus you explored in timed and focused freewriting now faces deadline. That means the time for roughing in the cut has passed and you must press the product into sentences that converse with the students who are about to enter your classroom for the very first time. Since they will see only the finished syllabus, you want their role to be deeper than most student readers. You want writers. For that reason, you can craft the syllabus as an organic document, a dynamic that invites students as writers to your course. It will also animate you as writer. You initiate that purpose by structuring your very first class.

This chapter narrates the way I incorporate my syllabus into the life of my first class. It is something I know you can do—better than any boilerplate or canned technique. Instead, your first day, like mine, springs from your convictions as a writer, a professor who has prepared for this course by writing a comprehensive syllabus and readied for the first day by enlisting writing in a central role.

So what do you do on that first day? I turn up early. Students haven't yet arrived for the very first class. I rearrange the room so we can see one another. Sometimes that means configuring the seating to a horseshoe and sliding my front desk to join them. A data projector's slide or a blackboard announcement anchors the center-front. I open my daybook.

Before uttering a single word about the required book in biology class or the term paper in philosophy, you can prepare students for that first class by tapping into the process of writing by simply inviting students to write. In other words, before you explain anything, show them how much you value writing by letting them see you do writing. To preserve that initial silence just for writing, I project one slide that all see upon entering: "Welcome to [class name.]" Then I skip a line and write, "Join me! I'm writing! Choose any topic about [some broad subject matter that the course will later investigate or choose nothing; students will supply content] and start writing." This technique I first learned from Janet Emig's work with twelfth graders, and it made such an impression on me in graduate school that I've been doing it in my own classes ever since (qtd. in Murray, 1968, 77).

Meanwhile, I'm freewriting in the front of the room. When students lumber in, they're puzzled and look quizzically at the overhead. Despite their confusion, most student resolve it: the very few who approach me ask what we're doing. I smile and point to the projected slide.

"Oh," they laugh and sometimes strike their forehead.

The opening is even more important in a nonwriting class because students don't expect writing to hold a place in a content class. To see you writing in the class when they first enter, however, means far more than anything you can say because you are showing writers a process for learning and learning writing in your course.

The First Minutes of the First Class

After a few minutes, when I think the whole class is assembled— everyone busily writing!—I advance to a second, countdown slide that signals we have five minutes left for writing. Sometimes I project what I'm writing directly from my desk or the computer, allowing the whole class to see my fumbling and false starts and long stretchy prose that show I'm busy at work but not too concerned with form.

If you're uncomfortable with that rehearsal, remind yourself that you're just doing what you performed in writing the syllabus.

Maybe that doesn't work any miracles in getting you writing nonstop, though. Then recall a recent professional event. Do you remember the last journal article in your field that excited you? Perhaps it was your recent conversation with a colleague. Maybe it's a new program launched in your department. Use one as propulsion into your freewrite: your writing-without-stopping.

Of course, you can rehearse the same act before the class meets and in the same classroom, too, if that helps you get started. In such situations, you're not doing violence to unrestricted writing. There's no harm incurred by a first rehearsal before today's dress rehearsal, for what you're doing is rehearsing your language.

If any students arrive late, I wave them to the front where I show them the original slide via a remote presentation controller I have at my desk—again, without speaking to them—before giving them paper. Once more, it's essential not to speak to the class at all during this time. This opening is reserved exclusively for writing. The spoken word occupies a lot of classroom space in a semester; give the written word first footing.

After doing a writing opening of this kind for several years, I've found it increasingly easier to spot students composing without stopping while still keeping my eyes and mind on the page. If I see a student not writing, I stop and point to the overhead with pen in hand. But those occasions are rare, especially on the first day. Students just know what to do without further prompting. They don't interrupt to ask about grades and goals and if they can leave early for spring break. If you open class with this scene, you defy many's expectations regarding writing in a course, at the same time allowing all to believe that this class will be special. Can you glimpse the opportunities that can stir students toward better performances when you open writing to rehearsal in your class, one that you practice?

When I open in this way, one or two students stop writing before the allotted time, for which I must *nudge* them, as Donald Graves (2001) calls it, ever so subtly back into writing. The nudge is just

1/10/2012

THE BEAUTY OF WRITING. HERE WE ARE
AGAIN, STROKING WORDS, FORCING THEM,
COMMANDEERING THEM TO FOLLOW THE
BEST THAT I CAN. OF COURSE THERE ARE
ALWAYS TECHNOLOGICAL GLITCHES, THINGS
THAT FORCE US TO RELY ON THINGS THAT
WE BELIEVE MAKE US BETTER WRITERS.
I'M THE FIRST TO SUBSCRIBE TO THAT
PHILOSOPHY. (THE SECOND STUDENT
ARRIVES WITH NO PAPER, THE FIRST
ARRIVES WITH A COMMANDING ATTITUDE
AND SOME WELL WISHES FOR A GREAT
SEMESTER. I AGREE—IT'S GOING TO BE
GREAT ALL 'ROUND, EVEN IF I CANNOT
GET THE PROJECTOR TO DISPLAY MY PAGE
FROM THE MACBOOK PRO — NOTHING
EXCEPT IN KEYNOTE, NOT EVEN IN MIRROR
DISPLAY — NO SIGNAL WHATEVER. SEE IF
THE SAME IS TRUE FOR C200 LATER. I
CAN CHECK THAT OUT. WE'LL SEE WHAT
HAPPENS.) SO ON THE FIRST DAY I GET
BACK TO WRITING MY BOOK — WORKING ON
IT THROUGH THE DRAFTS AND EDITS —
MORE PAIN IN ORDER TO BREAK THROUGH
TO PLEASURE. THAT'S THE ORDER OF
THE DAY, SEEMS TO ME. STRIP THE
GLOSS AND MOVE TO THE END. WHAT
A GREAT EXPERIENCE TO WORK THROUGH
WHAT NEEDS TO BE DONE. THAT IS THE
TASK OF WRITING — WHAT WE NEED

Exhibit 3.1. Freewriting

that: gentle persuasion. I always have another slide to show them
what I expect, or I pass them an index card:

Don't worry about what you're saying. Just keep writing.
Let your pen become your thoughts. If you don't know
what to say, write about that!

I do not want my new writers to finish prematurely, which will creep into even earlier finishes if I ignore them. Any professor can spot those who stop. Their inactivity telegraphs, "Help me!" Here is the time for a reassuring moment where you can advance the slide or flash the index card message to calm their anxieties.

After twenty-five minutes have elapsed, I give students a one-minute oral warning that they should prepare to conclude their work mid-sentence, with an ellipsis afterward to mark where they can return later. I ask them to stop as I rub my own hand and look at what I've freewritten (Exhibit 3.1). When they do the same, I make some brief comment about what I wrote. Then I turn the platform immediately over to them but not without another kind of rehearsal. I have them turn to a neighbor, introduce themselves, and then tell about what they wrote.

At this point, I ask them to summarize orally what they wrote, not to read their freewrite. In my experience, student writers don't know how to read aloud in class, at least not yet. They need some further time to practice, but again not yet. It's important instead to spread out the cognitive load, and I'm mindful of not overloading them on the first day. Students reading their low-stakes writing energizes the class too; it communicates that low-stakes writing is an asset in the classroom environment of scarce resources, just as rehearsals are important in shaping an artist's final performance. Students who read aloud enliven the classroom alive dramatically, and suddenly there's a learning community voicing their writing.

After a few minutes have passed, I ask a few at random what they wrote about in the exact same summarizing way. If I ask for volunteers, I may not get any, which is an immediate damper on that initial enthusiasm. Instead, I look for faces bursting with enthusiasm—"Call on me!" But if I just pick a few, cued by a bright face or some laughter or even a smile, I can keep interest high.

But before they answer, I ask, "Is it fair for me to call on you if you've already rehearsed your writing with a neighbor?

No cold calling." Heads nod in agreement, which is comforting to get on the first day, for students and you.

With some practice, I can probe some of their answers, but I always do so by asking more questions. "What made you think of this subject?" I can ask, or, "How detailed do you find the writing?" Of course, at this point I direct discussion so that it points toward processes of writing—inventing, drafting, rewriting, revising, editing, proofreading. I need to make students aware that they are writers, no matter the subject, and, particularly, writers in my class.

Others belabor this first writing; I assure them it's okay to have trouble. I ask if anyone struggled or spent too long on something or stopped midpoint. If someone raises a hand, I can let that person explore her writing before the assembled class: if she's willing, if I pause to listen and hear her before the class. Only then can I add my own stories of failure. Sometimes others chime in. I display a few pages of a keyboarded page like a schematic, complete with my handwritten rewrites and edits that are so full on the page that they compete with the typescript.

But these failures of both students and you have one common thread: they're high-stakes writing, where the price for failure is a poor grade, a lost promotion, or some gatekeeping penalty. The solution is to keep failing, but to do it with low-stakes writing, like you and your students just performed. That failed rehearsal or exercise is far better experienced—and learned from—when you make many low-stakes opportunities available to students, starting on that first day.

Ironically, stories of embracing failure in low-stakes writing can inspire other writers to stop procrastinating and fail now so they can make good later. The majority, however, are not that trusting, for good reasons. From later exit interviews, students tell me that they don't believe me: they believe professors never have any problems with writing and hearing otherwise is jolting. They don't see professors as vulnerable students of writing. Nevertheless, hearing those declarations on that first day empowers students to think that way and invites further questions, opportunities that segue into talking about the Contract for B. (See Chapter 10 for more details about grading.)

If you can initiate this opening, you can repeat it for the remainder of the semester. It's the ebb and flow of the class that weds writing into pedagogy: we write, we talk, we listen all in succession so we are commandeering associate things and not doing one thing too long, all of which keeps our attention taut and energy high.

What You Can Expect

After one opening session, I remember one student, John, volunteered his problems with writing to the class. He just stopped short of a therapy session, but I noticed other heads nodding in agreement as he explained how in-class writing made him think of grades and essay exams and, "well, punishment." I then asked if he had trouble starting today, to fill the page and "that sort of thing." When he said no, I told him he can keep telling himself, when he wants to stop or when he tenses up, that he is actually just starting again. If he stops starting, he will work to short-circuit his current writing with his past writing experiences—reengineering the starting mechanism while closing off an ending before its needed time.

If you substitute the *learning* for the *writing*, you will hear what problems John and other students expect to have in your course. For when you appoint writing for learning in your course, you will hear their unfiltered, raw experience when you open up the class discussion. That's one reason the subject of their writing is not essential to the exercise. You are really eliciting the structure of their learning, something you can never obtain directly, to uncover how students approach the unknown: the content of your course.

For John, as the course content unfolds so will his anxiety about exams and his reluctance to stay in the course. By giving John a possible solution to his take on the Writing Problem—his reluctance to write and to use the power of writing to solve learning difficulties—you show how failure is recoverable when students produce lots of writing, writing that will aid learning in the course.

After John's comment, others chimed in. Another started, "I have the opposite problem. Every time, I sit down, I stare at a blank page." That sounds like the same problem to me, but to her it's different because she sees the blank page as the cause for her apprehensiveness. Her responses are typical of students experiencing the Writing Problem; unsure of their writing—anxious about their success in learning—they hunt for language to express it, as in Emily's exchange with me:

"Okay. Did you have that 'blank page' problem today?"

"No, I don't think so," she said, still thinking about it.

"Why not?"

"Oh, well, I didn't think we were being graded on it." But she just as likely might have said, as others have, that "I could choose my own subject" or "It seemed different because you were writing with us" or "I was interested in taking this class as an elective, so writing here would be fun."

"So, could that mean that you've had a problem with the blank page—the same blank page all writers face—because you or another expected more than what you can give in a first draft?"

"Well ... maybe."

"Okay, what's your name?"

"Nancy."

"Nancy, next time we write in class, which I think, well, is the next class [laughs, followed by others], I have no expectations except one: that you fill the page with writing. Is that fair?"

She pauses. "Yes, I'll *try* to."

"Great. We can work from where you are today. And that's important, class. I want you to know, I work with you from where you are now," which, translated to academic language, is the bedrock of inductive teaching. When I hear students talk in this way about *trying* writing, such invigorates my pedagogy, my own writing, and my enjoyment of learning content. It is fundamental to growth in writing.

For many reasons, I believe the process will energize you, too. When you hear students' metadiscourse—what they say when they talk about their Writing Problem—you will find yourself advising students openly and honestly. After a few semesters, if you listen closely, you will begin to hear yourself giving advice that you could apply to your own Writing Problem. When you reassure inexperienced writers, you recall the fundamentals that all writers have to re-remember.

Here's an instructive moment where you're helping others and discover that you're also helping yourself. When I quote an economist, sociologist, a natural scientist, or any other writer who pops into my head at that moment to give reassurances to student writers, I recognize those writers—those professional people who write and count words—are helping other writers. Everyday we learn, we enter into the result of writing somewhere.

Every day we start with writing, we enter into the world of learning to find it is a world of writing. In the modern universe of merging fields, I see writing as a blended discipline that overlaps content. I recall one graduate of my college who was a biology and creative writing major and who finished law school to work as a lawyer writing detailed briefs for a biology company. These melded occupations are what our students will see in the workplace and should experience in our classrooms. Getting students comfortable discussing writing in the context of your discipline builds identity and purpose for writing in your disciplinary classroom.

I usually end this first day by saying this is the kind of writing we will do every day in this course. True, much of the workload is out of class, but we will always have quite a lot of work consumed in class, a workspace that cannot be skipped or neglected without impunity. That first day sets the paradigm.

At this point, I encourage students to keep a daybook, a notebook devoted exclusively for writing, and to have it with them always, every day, so they can gather or invent ideas when they occur. I tell students that if I did not keep a daybook with me at all times I would lose ideas; they would be unrecoverable, as I can never remember them in the same way, in the same context, as before. Yet the daybook is not a dictation machine either; it may start in the shower or in the middle of the night but the daybook gives it a harbor from which to sail out into a larger ocean. It's primarily a creative pathway to make meaning.

If you spend a few minutes showing students various notebook sizes and styles, you can steer them away from expensive pens and lavishly covered journals. That kind of opulence gets in the way of freewriting that purposes to march forever forward and not in neat lines and beautifully correct sentences. Encourage instead sketches, lists, and fragmented first drafts, that trifecta common to the writer's craft. I tell writers to find a handy daybook that works for them and to boast how cheaply they bought it. Buy at least one for yourself, too. Some can even be positioned to work with the digital phone camera so that writers can take a picture of what they have written for the cloud while still preserve the tactile experience.

"This notebook," I repeat, "is only for writing. Call it a daybook from now on."

This starting point for writing in your first class meeting can forge a template for the beginning of every class meeting. In this way, when students come to class they know they must write, which in time calms their trepidation. Opening with writing has another benefit. Here is a solution for the lingering problem of unprepared students practicing their fear before class officially begins, fidgeting with their cell phones and digital media, or cramming because they haven't done the reading. They know that they will write upon entering class and they know that the writing may fail, but they also know that writing can prepare them for class, that they can bring their experiences and merge them with the experiences generated in the class readings, lecture, discussion, and even other writing experiences. Still, they need to find their voice and subject each time in class, to read aloud to a fellow writer, and to offer their writing to me. Occasionally, I ask a few to report what they wrote in class, but only after they've rehearsed what to say with a partner immediately beforehand; there are no cold contacts. Students must know these will always be constants in the classroom.

You must inform perpetually late students that they are at risk. The subtle touch is often enough. Throughout the semester, I sit with students and write with them. Late arrivals feel uncomfortable because all are quietly busy while they are trying to close a creaky classroom door, unsnap their backpack, and stumble into a seat. I glance at these students good-naturedly and return to my writing. If they persist in their lateness for next week, they will miss the writing prompts that fade from the class's view after the first two minutes of writing; they will remain with the students now who sit uncomfortably and fidget as spectators watching the class of writers move past them. Within another week, they react in one of two ways: they either have dropped the class or have begun showing up on time. It's far kinder to make *trying* an early demand.

Is placing writing into a prominent place in your classroom worth this effort? Absolutely, for the first week sets the pattern, like the written syllabus before it, for the rest of the semester.

After the First Week

After a week, I suggest composing prompts that build student responsibilities as writers in the class. For instance, I may want to reinforce the importance of reading the assignments during the first week of class; I start with something like this on the overhead, with the *I* referencing the student writer:

1. I read the assignment thoroughly—I digested it—so that I can write about what I read (or ate).

   (a) Yes (I'm lying—no credit)

(b) No (half-credit for honesty)—I'll catch up by next class.

(c) Yes—I read it *and* can write about it.

ONLY if you answered (c) above may you answer one of the next two questions:

2. What ONE significant thing did you derive (chew) from the reading assignment that is due today? (Five minutes of freewriting—keep the right margin wide and unoccupied.)

3. Cite any ONE thing from the reading that puzzled you or contradicted what you thought you knew.

Again, write this assignment with students in your daybook so they can see you investing your own composing process after the first day. At the end of six minutes, ask the writers, like in the previous week, to discuss what they've written with their neighbors. In my experience, peer pressure presents a silent force in embarrassing the unprepared. Low-stakes writing is still important; students shouldn't treat it as if it doesn't matter because it does. I never met a good coach yet that allowed her players into the big game if they hadn't been to practice and worked out their failures.

If that experience is not enough, I discretely ask to see those students after class; they are easily spotted as the silent members in the neighborhood or the quick finishers. If I miss any, I locate them while the class is conversing about what they wrote; I ask all for the white, top copy so that I can quickly scan the responses. It does not take much effort; the scan tells me immediately who is doing the reading.

I am sometimes asked if students decline to give me what they've written. I have never had that happen, but the question intrigues me as to why it has never happened. In some way, it involves an established trust writers have from that first day, evidenced in how willingly they share their struggles with writing. You can accomplish that camaraderie, too, by showing your own writing from class, even when it's taken a nasty turn, especially when the prompts become more reflective. Again, rehearse freewriting before class if you think you'll be stymied, but try *not* to. For then you will experience what students go through in their experience with the Writing Problem and the power of writing to undo it in reflective learning:

> Richard Rodriguez draws sharp lines between private language and public language. Account for similar distinctions in your own language by telling at least one story that illustrates difference. (Freewrite/5 minutes)
>
> Explain how Apple's drop in stock price reflects market conditions or an aging company or some combination of the two. (Freewrite/5 minutes)

After a few minutes, I walk around the classroom, glancing at their answers, to form a profile of the responses.

When peer discussion wanes, I call on a few students to share the substance of what they've written—not a read-through, however. I want them to summarize. Since they have already rehearsed their answers during the previous peer discussion, I'm not making cold calls because I've already scanned their work in my walkabout. I know on whom it's safe to call and am assured of a reasonably strong answer.

This quick review keeps students active. Those who did not do the reading realize they have suffered a hit, but all is not lost. They can learn through failure, as you've been telling them; you still can work on the reading by recording what others have said and so benefit from doing half the required work. Such students have imposed their own silence, hearing others converse in ways they cannot. Yet, through failure, there is always the promise of next time.

Thus, students use writing to learn in several ways. They learn to articulate what they know in answering prompts. They reduce confusion by articulating their feelings and thinking in a mode (writing) that is purposeful and even can be pleasurable. They also use writing when they take notes on what others say in the ensuing class discussion as well as when they copy models and terms you have placed on the board. By the end of class, they leave a writing community with a fuller and calmer sense of what they know and what they need to know.

Making Two Copies

In class, you can use carbonless packets to receive a fuller reading of student work. (See #8 in Appendix A.4.1 for details on making these packets.) Each unit contains two sheets: a top white-lined writing sheet and an unlined yellow one underneath, bonded together, three-hole, and punched at the top. Students write on the top white sheet, which records a copy on the yellow one below. The times I've used them is when students finish their brief writing. At that point, I ask them to pair-and-share with a neighbor while I collect the writer's top copy, glancing at the writing I gather until discussion subsides. It gives me a better sense of what to emphasize in the class discussion.

During discussion, students take notes in the margins of the yellow sheets. By the end of class, students archive these *yellow* writings and jottings in their logs and organize them chronologically. I also organize their collected white sheets for easy later retrieval if I need them. I bind the white sheets with a rubber band, label the date and class on the uppermost one, and file them quickly in an office drawer that contains vertical dividers separating the number of weeks in the semester. I don't need to store this work or to comment on it since this initial work has expired—a *first draft*. Students have already added and subtracted to them, based on the class discussion, on their yellow sheets, rendering the *white* writing obsolete. All I need is a file drawer and a set of dividers organized by semester weeks for archiving. It's accessible, if I ever need the originals.

Lately, I've been digitizing the white sheets with an affordable sheet-fed scanner. On the preprinted white sheets, I've added letter blocks, like table cells, for which I ask students to print their name within. I highlight the blocks that the scanner can index as a keyword for automatic filing and retrieval. Thus, with a digital filing cabinet I have instant access to any student's first exposure work in writing.

Moving on to More Focused Freewriting

As students display greater facility with the opening writing, you can introduce more focused freewriting. The goal remains the same, however: to give writers something meaningful in your discipline to write about that leads to an ensuing discussion. In other words, you provide the opening structure that gives students the circumstances to explore content. For instance, you may prompt students to "Explain one way sunspots contribute to radio propagation that you remember reading." Or you can ask a reflective question: "What difficulties are you having understanding the theory of motion I outlined in the class today?"

You can even touch on nontopic writing behaviors that interfere with larger projects. For instance, if I am teaching an upper-level sophomore course where students are apprehensive about their research papers, I can start with an opening stretch before the exercise that involves writing. I have students fill in the empty slots of a sentence I project on a slide:

> In the next five minutes, I will freewrite, starting by completing this sentence—"Writing is like … " and then trying to support it. Join me by doing the same. Again, I plan on freewriting for five minutes, starting with this first sentence.

When time is up, I switch to the next slide and plan to write for five minutes again:

> I need to complete this sentence—"Writing is NOT like … " for five minutes. Join me by doing the same.

Last time I used this prompt, I wrote, "Writing is NOT like riding a bicycle," and explained in my paragraph that my wife and I started riding on the town's bike path; for me, it was a twenty-year hiatus since my last peddling. The metaphor illumines my own thinking about my relationship to the research paper and communicates that relationship to students through a common experience.

You can easily alter such generic prompts to your discipline, too:

Writing for a sociology class is like ...

and later, alternately,

Writing for sociology class is NOT like ...

or don't reference writing,

Physics is like ...

In responding to an assigned reading, I can propose an open-ended prompt:

Deborah Tannen observes how her husband responds to a waitress as one way to explain how men relate to women in our culture. Develop a similar example from your own experience. Don't worry about interpreting it. (Freewrite/fast, 5 minutes)

Look back to an argument or disagreement you've participated in where the words just came out wrong. Maybe you even prepared for that encounter, but when you had to deliver you just didn't achieve what you hoped. Recreate the dialogue, as you remember it. (Freewrite/fast, 5 minutes)

Having writers discover these notions for themselves or recalling a reading with their own content can go a long way toward reworking mechanisms that keep writers from their tasks: writer's block, fear, anger, self-loathing, a harsh fourth-grade teacher named Ms. Grundy, and so forth. Here again is an opportunity to show writing as a complex but manageable and even enjoyable activity, one not to be feared but to bring under control as writers transition from low stakes to high stakes. After all, students can easily reason, "Here is the professor, ransacking through possible ideas in front of the class—he's using low-stakes writing. That's something I can do in private … maybe even better." And before long, after talking to a neighbor about their writing and then discussing writing in the classroom, they may even conclude, "I'm sounding like a biologist!" or "I'm sounding like a psychologist!" or simply, "I am beginning to understand."

First Things Freewriting

If students are searching for a topic, say, for a research paper, you can use this first things freewriting so they can locate a topic, revealing each step only after the preceding is completed.

1. In your daybook, select a clean page and date it.
2. Place your pen on paper and write for ten minutes without stopping. Start with one object or thought uppermost in your mind and explore just one with which to begin, using your pen as your brain. If your writing strays after the first line, let it. Then pursue the stray.
3. Keep writing; don't stop until the ten minutes are up. Don't look back, read, or cross out—just write.
4. Return to your writing after class—but today!—and try to freewrite for a longer period, say, twenty minutes.
5. After incubation—hour, day, week—look back on what you wrote: Did your writing take an unexpected or puzzling turn? Is there an unresolved conflict present? These are seeds for a topic to grow. Bring them to the next class for germination.

Here's another variation. When students have a rubric for an assignment or criteria that professors will use in evaluating their writing, they can work backward—from criteria to freewrite—by addressing each criterion or rubric in a freewrite. Instruct them to take ten minutes for each one, much as in the previous exercise, with one exception. This time, for #5, see what insights and questions emerge that they can work out in time before the final draft is due.

Beginning Again

Remember, you are rewriting the first day every time you begin a new class. Each time the community of biology students or chemistry students or literature students convene, they come together as writers. That you procure writing for your classroom means you reinforce what you believe is essential in your discipline and what you want to impress upon other writers in this community. Each class becomes a workshop; each class, an opportunity to learn content through writing.

I like what the Benedictines record at the beginning of their prayer book, "Always we begin again." When I apply this motto to writing, I add an initial comma—"Always, I begin again"—for I want to pause on the *always*. Every time I write on the first day and in the first moments of all succeeding classes, I face my Writing Problem with a deluge of low-stakes writing—always, I begin again.

That cycle is never rote or tiresome, for we are new writers each day, with different experiences and varied thinking even from the day before. I know, too, slowly and over the course of the semester, that my working students will begin to pick up this habit. The recursive action of starting again in writing takes on a spiraling motion, encircling ever inward but in closer paths to meaning. That perpetual motion keeps teaching fresh and writing tight as the spiral collapses inward, matching writer to meaning.

At the beginning, students ask me how I can always begin again when I've been writing for so long. "Haven't you overcome the Writing Problem by now?" they ask sincerely.

I used to ask myself the same questions until I settled on a comfortable but puzzling knowledge: no writer's triumph is permanent or her struggles unique. Now when I begin again, I recall my past starts. I may always start with the same blank page as my students, but I know from practice how to populate it. Perhaps that alone differentiates the expert writer from the novice writer when initiating writing.

That first day, looking out at the community of writers assembled in my classroom, I see their nice clean daybooks that they have retrieved from their new backpacks and slings. I pick up my bargain-bin daybook. Soon we are all writing and finding that those initial freewritings are unkempt but purposeful. They have spilled onto the page and, in time, will effect an unexpected cleanliness in our thinking. We are explorers, whether in your 7:45 weekday morning or the postlunch 1:00, from what started as just ten minutes of, "Join me; I'm writing."

4

Daily Writing: Practice Before Polish

In the following two stories, what similarities do you notice?

The first occurs whenever a first draft for a major project is due. No matter how clear I thought I had been about low expectations for their first efforts, I always have a few students submit rough drafts as if they are consummated, finished pieces. Whether they like what they've written weighs little; to them, what matters most is that they're finished. Like a final examination, they believe their writing is executable only at deadline. One in particular stands out in my thinking.

"I'm no good at writing," came his first objection after he met me after class in my office. "Working longer at my writing won't make any difference."

"The writing, you seem to be telling me, is a final product, like you 'lost the case' in the courtroom when your work was presented," I countered. "But how good are you at practicing? For instance, how often do you practice your writing?"

"What do you mean?"

"Do you write, oh, once a month, once a week, once a day?"

He looked at me as if I had hurled a boulder in his direction.

"I don't know," he sincerely replied, dodging it. He then scrambled for an answer. "I have a draft of a psychology paper due next week!"

"OK. So how do you gear up to write it? Do you freewrite? Do you draft an intro? How do you work on it every day?"

"I haven't started it yet."

We both paused; I refreshed in my mind the one response I have given the most often.

"Try this," I said. "Write every day on this paper, preferably at the same time every day. Pick a place that's comfortable for you to write and claim that spot just for your daily writing. Keep a routine and log it. Map what instruments you will use that day too. Keep to the routine for one week and report back to me at this same time and day next week to let me know how you're doing."

"But I'm no good at writing," he emphasized, returning to the initial objection.

"Then practice. Practice your writing. Every day. Now go do it. And log your efforts."

Next consider this example, occurring during this same initial period, when I spoke with a colleague in his office. He is a writer, but someone who hadn't written anything for some time. This day, however, he said he had a "new writing project."

"What kind of project?" I asked.

"A book," he said.

"Do you know what it's about yet?" I asked. I recognize that exploratory writing means the shape and focus of writing can change as the writer processes it.

"Sort of," he replied snappily, and then he gave a short formulaic description of the book.

"Well, I better leave and give you time to write it," I said.

He growled, concluding that I hadn't been listening. "I didn't say I was writing. I'm just thinking about it," he confessed, not looking me in the eye.

The answer to both dilemmas is to write every day—both students and their professor. The initial enthusiasm students and you exhibit for first-day freewriting in the classroom is the same for us when we start on a new disciplinary project that involves writing. That writing experience creates new expectations of where writing may take us. Similarly, students anticipate a consistent experience with your courses throughout the semester. Daily writing is that constant.

But how can we write *every* day? We already recognize that students need to make their writing habitual; this way they will stay fluent with language and will produce enough writing so that later we can take on other habits, like polishing: rewriting and revising. Yet we, too, need daily writing for the same reasons.

The Same Problem?

What else is common in the two opening situations? Many aspects, but I want to focus on three.

The first is so obvious that we all forget it sometimes: nonwriting never leads to writing. In the two situations, the writers speak of their writing as an idealized state, where writing is only the product that is publishable. Similarly, thinking about writing is not writing. When we speak of all writing as thinking, we have lower expectations that help us start writing.

Another similarity in both situations is that the student and the professor cannot produce the one kind of writing they desire: high-stakes writing. That condition is true for most of us, most of the time. The structured writing we all desire does exist within us, but only the end of a process, as final drafts, can bear the intense scrutiny of examiner and editor.

A third similarity is that, since such structured writing cannot be produced at will, writers produce it infrequently. It is an academic predisposition for the difficult to remain in that unchallenged state for as long as possible—perhaps forever—since faculty are under pressure to publish and students, to produce edited English by deadline. Both also acknowledge high expectations for their writing—nosebleed high—that dissuades them from starting.

What we need is an accessible, reliable approach so we can achieve high-stakes, good writing. In most circumstances, good writing is a result, an ending achievement of a process. Yet even when writers create a process they may need to succeed with a good product. As Don Murray was fond of saying, good writing is accidental; it cannot be plotted or mapped or fit into an equation. As true as I find that aphorism in my own writing life, I notice over the years that good writers have more accidents than others simply because they drive more frequently than others.

The only way for these two writers in my opening examples to have accidents is to shift their cars out of park and into drive. The power to move these writers out of the garage—yours, mine, and your students'—is learned through daily writing.

The Benefits of Daily Writing

In the last chapter, I outlined the immediate benefits of starting that first day with writing that will continue if you can devote five opening minutes to it in every class. At least five other benefits result when you sponsor daily writing as preparation for your more formal, high-stakes assignments.

First, it reminds writers they need a way into their language and the course, to get loose in writing, just like exercise. Daily writing is always available to the writer because it is unstructured and unrehearsed. It relies on the movement of the pen and can be produced without forethought, planning, or mapping. What it offers students and you is a presence of mind to develop experiences and generate thinking (low stakes) on the way to making meaning (high stakes).

A second benefit is that sometimes daily writing can lead to larger, finished projects. But what it always leads to is greater fluidity and facility with language. It prepares the mind and hand to work together. What matters most is that daily writing foregrounds a practice, a habit of mind, a how-to discipline. In fact, there can be no real polishing work—rewriting, editing, revising, proofreading—until writing is produced and given opportunity to mature. The best way I know to hurry maturity is through writing daily.

Third, since daily writing allows experimentation with craft, both students and faculty can use it as a platform to make their language meaningful. As students begin to trust this low-stakes writing daily, they see your practicing along with them as creating a learning community before high-stakes writing appears in the course and in your scholarly responsibilities. In a study by Ramirez and Beilock (2011), the researchers found that students who wrote prolifically before high-stakes performances, like examinations and final papers, significantly improved their performance on their final work. As the researchers discovered, it mattered little as to what the subject of their writing consisted; just writing about their emotions or their anxieties before a high-stakes performance was good enough. Ramirez and Beilock call the practice effort *offloading*. It wasn't fluff or wasted time in the classroom for students to get centered—and, I would argue, centered on language moving.

Fourth, freewriting can be tremendously effective in energizing students, indirectly, to engage content, even if they use writing for offloading. I can understand why instructors dislike students' familiar style in daily writing because they believe such informal, student language trivializes the subject of the course. We all know there's little time in the classroom as it is. But the language of daily writing is an entryway for students to learn new material with its own disciplinary vocabulary and expressions, merging it all with something they already know—informal language. This merging encompasses a feature already common to effective writing; some stylists point out that effective sentences typically have old information positioned at their beginnings and new at their ends. Writing to learn content is similarly composed, but on a much larger, discourse-sized scale.

Last, daily writing helps us all confront the Writing Problem each day by making writing the solution. And it's simple: we must write each day. As a result, we make writing accessible and available to all.

To reach competency or a public proficiency for any kind of discourse—to prepare for those final forms that folks call good writing—students need to participate in tons and tons of low-stakes writing to bring about the accidents of good, high-stakes writing. Daily writing also helps faculty: to reflect, to plan, to search for ideas. It takes the daily rehearsal to reach the far fewer and better final performances. The practice of daily writing yields greater and more meaningful experiences as writers trust it to bring about new connections and new understandings. How much more powerful is this approach than the paralyzing alternative: truncating writing to high-stakes alone, making it impervious to the writer's will and available to infinite postponement.

After the very first day, and therefore first session of daily writing in all my courses, I always reflect on why I ask students to start class in this way. I also ask students to reflect on why they think I provided time for this writing at the beginning of class. "I'm not sure," one student reported. "But my mind was jumping all over the place until class began. I settled down in the course once I started writing."

Once this writerly behavior lives within students—that is, daily writing—they will begin to recognize their own voices, compare them to other voices that are privileged in your field, and begin to solve their own writing problems.

How to Start It

My daughter used to complain that she loved art but hated art class because the teacher would talk the entire class time and they "never had time to finish a project because only ten minutes remained at the end of class." The art of writing needs opportunity to happen in the classroom, too: not to talk about it endlessly or to wait for it or to assign it for homework but to make it happen in the classroom first, as outlined in the previous chapter with freewriting, and then reinforce writing with similar assignments outside. I suggest starting small with those outside assignments, such as requiring a ten-minute freewrite on nonclass days. These assignments can be focused or unfocused; they must be nonstop writing, recorded in their daybooks, from this day on for the rest of their lives.

I find a number of students anxiously question what you expect in daily writing. They want definitions. How long should each entry be? Do weekend days count? Can writers use *I*? What should be included? Must the course subject be addressed? Does spelling count? Will the instructor read the writing? It's fine to steer students past these concerns, gently reminding them that these questions spring from structured, high-stakes contexts; you are asking for low-stakes writing. All of these questions and concerns are important, yes, but not until daily practice is established and built upon.

Once initial inertia is overcome on the first day, you can continue daily writing throughout the semester. Even on essay exam days, I encourage a *getting started* daily write, following the mantra, "Before Writing, Write." I urge them to get limber with language first. Flex those muscles! Get a workout before the deadlined work starts! When students practice daily writing in the classroom, their anxious questions fade, too, and they concentrate on readying themselves to make such writing truly daily, extending it into their private lives outside the classroom. That process brings students an awareness of voice within the universe of discourse.

You will undoubtedly find new spaces for low-stakes writing where instruction was problematic, which students can use outside the classroom. For instance, a modern language teacher wants her students to experience how difficult translation can be, so she assigns them each a passage from a bad translation that she wants rendered to a better form. When completed, she conducts a class discussion. What's hidden in this assignment is how students went about translating the selection. Since translators have to make all kinds of decisions about meanings in text, students can reflect on the decisions they made in the short piece. The writing could even be a narrative: what they did first, how they compared the selection they were responsible for with the larger work, and how they chose one word where several others could qualify (a sort of reflection on connotation). This exercise—short translation, short reflection—could launch a better class discussion on how translation is both like and different from writing, plagiarism, and intellectual property. Plus, the teacher can see the thought processes of the whole class, not just the speakers, by opening the class to low-stakes writing opportunities.

Since daily writing takes just five minutes of class time, plus a two-minute reading with partners, other opportunities open when direct instruction falls flat. The unexpected pregnant pause, the afterword following a particularly difficult lecture, the notes students just summarized without reviewing them—these are the teachable times when a quick daily write is an indispensable reinforcer. Every professor has felt that sinking feeling after posing a question to find the raised hands with enthusiastic responses fall far short of the answers they expected. Instead, "Let's just stop for a moment as we all spend two minutes to explore this question...."

I'm not a Luddite, but I encourage students to have a physical daybook just for writing and a favorite pen or pencil. As of now, tablets do not present the same tactile experience and obvious gains over paper the way the word processor did over the typewriter. Writers are more apt to distribute working memory resources to planning during freewrites with paper than with digital media where more effort is required. Perhaps that will change with succeeding generations who learn keyboarding at even younger ages; I'm not sure. What I do know is that I don't want any electronic distractions: just physical interaction with the page for our students. If you use a projector, you can easily place a countdown timer on a slide or use a smart phone to mark the two-minute mark. Encourage student writers to date entries and, when finished, to read what they wrote—unedited and rough—to a neighbor writer to give them a sense of audience and to hear how their writing sounds. In daily writing there are no worries over grammar and punctuation—you just want to increase the flow of language from them and from you.

You can then call on anyone after that brief explosion of enthusiasm to keep the energy moving. It sets the opening of class with writing and gets people into the course for that day.

The most critical part of any daily writing rests with you. I keep introductions very short—just what we're doing in class today—and then I move to the daily writing. You must participate if you want students to follow. I plant myself at my classroom desk, retrieve my daybook, and begin writing. After the first couple of weeks, I move anywhere in the classroom and freewrite. The whole process can take seven minutes—preparation, writing, reading aloud with one partner—and can lead to a class discussion if you are using focused topics for the freewrite. When your class has an odd number of students, yoke with the stranded student writer during the reading aloud. I love it when I'm partnered with another student and I read last; if I'm prolific that day, other students in the class finish before I do and they hear some of what I've written. *Wow! Hafer really does write with us.* Imagine how you can become a colleague of your students in that situation.

Later, and as you grow more comfortable with daily writing, you can spend a few minutes at the end of class reflecting on how the class worked, perhaps when students are postwriting. What was successful? What wasn't? Where do I need to focus the next class? What did I forget to mention, or what miscues did I make? Such reflective practice is becoming more commonplace among professors. Professor Matthew Liberatore (2012) takes a few minutes after each class to reflect on the class he had just taught. This reflection unifies his thinking on the class in ways inaccessible to the nonwriter. I frequently find material for the next class just in those few minutes of reflection after class, something I cannot recreate with the same accuracy outside of this time and space.

In time, you will find ways unstructured daily writing leads to structured, formal, high-stakes writing. For example, Liberatore is freewriting in his after-class reflection; however, he noticed that the organization of his class improved, and so did the work of his students. I notice that students who habitually freewrite begin to use that strategy in preparing drafts of formal papers, particularly with organization because they can go back and cherry-pick ideas from their prolific, low-stakes writing. Out of chaos comes order. Out of daily writing comes structure.

Inventing Metaphors to Help Writers

One way to connect students to doing freewriting on nonclass days is through metaphor. Here's how I do it, something you can do—probably better than I too!—with very little planning.

Two of them, coffee-drinking and baseball playing, shout loudly in my ears whenever I consider daily writing. I'm happy to share that work ethic with my student writers since—whether they understand it or not—they depend on practice. Students consistently tell me that their previous teachers who assigned a lot of writing, as well as their current professors who believe they should enter the college as college-level writers, describe boilerplate scenarios that supposedly produce clean manuscripts. In sharp contrast, I tell my students daily writing is the most important means to furnishing that clean product; it's a slow train arriving at the station, but it does arrive. (And, no, that's not one of my metaphors!)

In my first metaphor, I tell students I think of daily writing as my morning caffeinated coffee; it awakens me to my routine and, as a teacher of writers, to the need for each student to develop at least one helpful writing routine. If I avoid my routine, like my morning coffee, I miss the opportunity writing offered for just that one day.

Like many writers, I work better in the morning and, since this is second nature for me, I can fool my brain by expanding my morning coffee throughout the day as a viable metaphor that carries my writing throughout the day. That means finding small spaces to write, small time blocks between classes, while I'm waiting for a student to come for an appointment or right before faculty meetings. Sometimes when a student and I finish early in an office visit I ask if we can freewrite continuously for two minutes about what we just discussed and then read those responses to one another. As writers cultivate writing in these brief times, they can begin to establish best practices for them. It is those very practices that eventually carry me with new material, both good and bad, that I can later judge ready for rewriting and, finally, for publication to an audience.

It's always good to motivate students to discover their own metaphors for writing, from hobbies, sports, and family situations. On days when class does not meet, I encourage students to find their own space in the cafeteria or the campus hangout but, once there, to locate a safe spot in a dark corner no one inhabits to get started on daily writing. If they see me in the library or on campus, they should see me with my daybook, just as art students carry pads for quick sketches. When class meets, students can experience the exhilaration of pulling out their daybooks to see how much they wrote between classes. The daily exercise made into a habit—and illustrated by metaphor—confers power, voice, and shape to all their writing.

Admittedly, my metaphors are idiosyncratic, but they help to open students to that wonderful routine of daily writing. My intention is to provide metaphors and stories as powerful reminders of what we all must do. Choose yours with similar goals in mind. (You'll have to wait for my second metaphor.)

Misapprehensions and Daily Writing Outside Class

Far too often, students come to us believing that their writing is powerless because they've accumulated evidence from failed paper starts and poor grades. They think their failures come because they must have everything worked out before they record a first paragraph and, when that doesn't happen, they collapse before the looming deadline. They want to write what the teacher wants, a beginner's appreciation of audience, but end up inventing a voice that doesn't sound like them or anyone in the discipline. They believe the shape of their writing comes from them, whereas it comes from the instructor and established genres in the field, which they can experiment with if they have made daily writing a habit.

So many classrooms and movies depict the act of writing occurring in perfect environments with large blocks of available time. Those situations are unavailable to most of us, but especially for student writers facing all kinds of constraints, imposed from many quarters. Writing practice squeezed into unexpected places and opportunities on days class does not meet—even if they are just corners of the cafeteria—make writing less threatening, spontaneous contexts providing opportunities for good starts. This daily habit of finding writing available everywhere is essential to establishing groundwork for the better writing later on.

In sharp contrast, the daily writing, particularly outside the classroom, allows them to explore those three—power, voice, shape, indirectly and inductively—they can start wherever they are and without penalty. They can experiment. The daily writing tells them it's safe to write, and in that space there is growth. The more students write independently, the greater the capacity for good writing.

The Subjective and Daily Writing

Some instructors worry that student discourse, even when under the aegis of a content-laden course, will be too personal, too subjective. Others fear that such daily writing may initially be useful only to the writer because it is such a writer-based form and will persist in that form throughout the course.

I don't think those situations materialize. The subjective need not be at war with the objective. When we speak about writing, we can get into trouble when we work from the objective into the subjective. The deductive approach is similar to what happens when professionals argue *what works* in a given field as if it "implies the speaker has solutions that will be immediately applicable" to everyone in all contexts (Tanner, 2011, 329). It is so tempting to look at laboratory studies and falsely conclude we can import whatever works there wholesale into our classrooms.

Writing teaches us we must make all content subjective; to learn it ourselves, we must make that emotional attachment for learning to happen. Similarly, in daily writing, the grammatical first person encourages students to learn in their writing. If they are free in this low-stakes daily writing to relate to content, they can be free to translate content of the course into expository prose later when they have a greater measure of reading experience in the course: a better sense of disciplinary vocabulary, concepts, ways of expressing findings. At the point when they relax in the position as writers, you can legitimately expect (even if they don't) bursts of readable prose or effective editing, say, in the rough first draft of a report because the necessary and personal connection to their text occurred, making the next draft transition even more fully into the language of polished, structured prose. Those transitions work to harmonize the subjective and objective rather than eliminate one or the other. There are no guarantees for success, obviously, but at the very least we can help students spread the cognitive workload more evenly across their drafting to find out what works for them.

Subconsciously, all writers, no matter their proficiency, are emotionally attached to their writing. Even student writers who hate writing feel vulnerable whenever they are compelled to write. They swell to praise and bristle at criticism. I know I hated getting referee feedback on essays I submitted to professional publications where the referees seemed more interested in demanding changes than in improving the writing. When we identify students as writers, we can better understand their struggles because those struggles are our own. We can better appreciate the emotional attachment they have to their writing when we recognize we too are hardwired in the same way. When others disapprove of our writing, we hurt, too.

Low-stakes daily writing gets students writing because we expect less. As anthropologist Barry Schwartz points out, the key to happiness is "low expectations" (2004, 85), something we all need to keep in mind when we compose our daily writing. If we can lower expectations for greatness in any first effort, we can then create some breathing room and push the ceiling up a bit. The transfer from the messiness of our minds to the pristine demands of structured writing can prove debilitating. However, if we can change the chronology—that is, instead of procrastinating we lengthen the writing process—we now can set intermediates that assure that we start early and finish only at deadline. Start small; finish big. Bring such a perspective into your teaching and your own writing practice, particularly when you and your students are having trouble starting. Daily writing gives us that needed push.

After Beginning

What other advice about daily writing do student writers need? Not much. I tell them to start a daybook and to think about when they can practice writing, encouraging them to set limits, such as at least ten minutes. Everyone has at least ten minutes they can find each nonclass day. Then begin to move to longer and more complex projects with daily writing as the starter.

It sounds silly but I suggest students schedule *reward times* when they can gift a movie, a TV show, or a chocolate bar to themselves for persevering through a particularly tough writing day, some reward that will return them to writing the next day. They should also share what they discovered through their writing by telling me in an office hour or to a classmate what they wrote about each week or through some other public exhibition. I may ask them to read an entry for a particular day at random after they've rehearsed one with a partner. If they know they must write every day, they will be on the lookout for ideas from lectures, readings, and everyday speaking. When such happens freely, the formal requirement fades, and the writer emerges.

Invariably, students ask if they become better writers through daily writing. Yes, but that daily writing cannot conclude the writing process or halt at semester's end. It must grow into a longitudinal study of habit that leads them to a lifetime of better practices, which in turn, brings about even better practices. Better writing is far more likely when students are less stressed yet better prepared for the pressures of high-stakes writing.

Daily writing is like baseball for me. (Here's that second metaphor.) Even the major leaguers need daily practice, for they realize that is the way they qualify as team members and the way they improve their game. There is no off-season. They need sit-ups and squat thrusts, even though they think they will never use such in a game.

Students don't need to become professional writers to recognize this similarity. My children's Little League coach always tells the team as a whole and as individual members that they had a good practice on any given day, and I'm positive he means it. In viewing from the bleachers, I could view that same practice as a critic: I could cite dropped fly balls and in-the-dirt pitches. What about those missed swings and the overthrows? Every fan would say I'd be wrong to emphasize finality at that point when I should be witnessing causality. I'm supposed to be the spectator to a process; during practice, there are no umpires on the field. It's okay to strike out during spring training if I am actively working to improve my swing.

We learn far more from our frequent daily practice if we view it as the cause for our periodic game days.

5

Make Long Assignments
Manageable for Everyone

After daily writing is established in your course, it's appropriate to design your high-stakes assignments. The advantage to front-loading these writing assignments in your course—taking some extra time and effort to design them up front—is a reduced workload at the back end when student papers are due. This strategy especially helps faculty who teach large sections or have a lot of content to cover. This front-loading also means you compose assignments that briefly and clearly communicate your expectations to an audience of student writers in your course. You can also identify higher-order processes that low-stakes writing at best only faintly addresses: the purpose for such an assignment and an audience, a critical dimension that helps define what makes *good writing*.

In designing any high-stakes assignment, we face a dissonance. We all know that students frequently misinterpret our assignments or underwrite what we expect them to perform. We also know there are no guarantees for universal understanding with any technique or scheme we orchestrate to bring students to complete a high-stakes assignment. Yet if we take special care in designing our high-stakes assignments, we make effective writing more probable.

When we require student writing, we mirror that process in the way we design the assignment. There are added benefits, too. When we write out our assignments, we suddenly anticipate problems in ways hidden from us in oral delivery. We can also resolve these problems more readily by specifying in writing what we require.

To help us explain "what the prof wants," we can again enlist low stakes. For example, if we know from past experiences that students struggle with writing thesis statements in final drafts, we can require students to write three alternative statements as hypotheses for their first draft so that they can compare choices, in writing, so we do not lock them into a commitment to one thesis they are not ready to make. At the same time, we have them thinking about thesis in having them write three alternatives. I use this same strategy when I'm struggling with an article. I'll have a colleague look at three alternative hypotheses that I've tinkered with—all correct grammatically but with different emphases—and ask her to pick the better of the lot. I tell my colleague what I'm looking for, and she tells me the degree to which one delivered on my promise more readily than the others. By comparison shopping, I have a closer rendering of the meaning I hope to capture for my article. Students can seize the same opportunity with us as their colleagues.

Similarly, if we know that students spend a lot of their time checking the grammar of their first drafts when we know, in sharp contrast, that their papers lack development, we can adjust the requirements. For instance, we can postpone the editing requirement for first drafts so that we can distribute the cognitive workload throughout the semester and the writing process. I am absolutely convinced that writers need the freedom to explore what they're trying to find out before correcting mistakes in sentences that may not even show up in their final versions.

Other benefits accrue to us when we write the assignment requirements. When I gave my first high-stakes writing assignment to a college class, I found a line of students outside of my office wanting to see me about it. Each wanted to meet me separately, which resulted in my repeating the same assurances and advice twenty times in separate meetings. Writing an assignment carefully can circumvent the time wasting of misdirected office visits and repetitious comments on papers. There are no guarantees, of course, but odds are that a carefully constructed writing assignment that articulates its requirements, in writing, diminishes students' anxieties because it anticipates its audience's questions. In such cases, you are harnessing the epistemic power of writing to illuminate your own understanding of how student writers go about their assignments. When we compose those assignments in writing, we can review our language choices and rewrite for brevity and clarity—two features we demand of students and they of us—before any students hear what we require.

But suppose students *still* don't understand what you want? Then construct a one-page handout that describes the purpose of the assignment and what you want. Circulate the handout as a first version to students, asking them to read it in class and to ask you questions about anything that is unclear. You can take notes on the kinds of questions they ask and respond in class, but be sure to give them a rewritten second-draft handout by the next class meeting. (I explain more about rewriting in Chapter 6.)

High-stakes writing assignments also give us a chance to review what we're teaching our writers in class. We can use disciplinary vocabulary and theoretical concepts from the course to show students we expect them to understand how we are using this language, and if they don't know, to find out from the textbook or in class discussion. The more times we can integrate writing assignments with our own teaching, the more we make their learning stronger and deeper. It's like the automobile buff who is constantly checking the oil in his crankcase: the more times we call up those terms, in context of our course, the more confidence we have in communicating key concepts to our students.

Therefore, we must write the assignment cogently before receiving students' writing.

Writing the Long High-Stakes Assignment

The long researched writing assignment is a typical stress builder, even for experienced student writers. It overwhelms students even as they deliberate about what to do first. Their frustration escalates when they realize they've been through this process before in other school settings yet still have the same questions: *Should I go straight through in a fast draft and then come back for rewriting? How much time will I have to pick a topic? Should I outline? What is the professor looking for?* If the professor furnishes unsatisfying answers, students will return to those same questions again.

If we step back and look at the long assignment, however, we find the same characteristics as the short assignment. Student writers still have to invent a subject, even if it is assigned: They still must make it their own. They must explore the subject, or develop it, for an audience. They must place that material in a structure established by a disciplinary field. They must find a voice that invokes their audience and conveys credibility and approachability. Their sentences need to be crafted clearly and economically. Their conventions—grammar, punctuation, usage, and the like—should show they are competent writers who care about communicating without error.

Wow! Now I'm overwhelmed.

So to keep from feeling overwhelmed, writers need to take the writing assignment and break it, no matter how large or small, into yet smaller chunks. You can facilitate that breaking in the way you assign long projects; I call these components *briefs*, as in lawyer's briefs. They are manageable and scaffold in complexity; they will become, in a final version, a sum greater than all of its parts. In a sense, by making briefs you develop sequenced assignments for students—a structure or shape—that reduce overhead pressures. In other words, you start high-stakes assignments with elemental components that move your student writers to more complex components of the assignment later on. That process has the added benefit of making your requirements transparent to students a bit at a time and thereby reducing those what-does-the-prof-want? moments.

For example, in a researched high-stakes assignment you could first construct a series of briefs (assignments) that gradually become more complex as your student writers familiarize themselves with the writing project. At first, I make light cognitive demands that require equally light *yes–no* assessments. These tasks students undertake (not underachieve) as citizens of learning in your classroom: tasks they should be able to do by good faith effort. As the semester progresses and their level of understanding increases, you can raise the expectation to greater achievement and supply some preliminary evaluation. For instance, you could require a sample *thesis statement as one sentence*—a task—but by midterm *a sentence with a predicate that makes a point.* In old-fashioned pedagogy, these transitions used to be called drills, which require students to achieve some benchmark that can be proven to the professor. Drills also have the potential to move students from low-stakes to high-stakes writing.

The alleged drawback with drills, of course, is that they can be rote recitals that disconnect learners from applying their knowledge. Yet drills can provide students incentive to *acquire* the background knowledge necessary in a field before they can hope to apply their knowledge to contemporary problems in that field. It may involve history or a technical knowledge; it may mean knowing the periodic table or cultural codes or who Karl Barth was. This knowledge is a prerequisite to understanding and can be stored in long-term memory only after it is automatic. Drills work to accomplish just that.

Similarly, writers need background knowledge of some writing processes—like writing a thesis statement in the previous example—to relieve working memory of the complexities of writing for the new knowledge that will enlarge their craft. Your writers will perform better on assignments, too, as their working memory becomes open for the assignment itself when it is not occupied, for example, with how to do freewriting or some other writing processes. If you give students credit for knowing that milestone and can repeat it (task), you can concentrate on students preparing a quality product (drill). For example, in first drafts I transition students from the task of "I tried to write 1000 words … " to the drill of "I wrote at least 1000 words.… " The signal for me to make that change occurs when I find that 80 percent of the class has succeeded in the task or after we have repeated the task at least three times. This pattern avoids needless repetition and allows the class to proceed at a pace that most can follow. Those who don't I can see in group conferences during office hours and review their work. (See Chapter 9 for more details on conferencing.)

One Way to Plan for Brief Assignments

Stepping backward through the semester calendar, you can scaffold assignments so they funnel into polished final versions. By plotting these planning assignments ahead of time, you spread the cognitive workload across the entire writing process, which benefits students and you. For students, an impressive workload is simplified and more illustrative of how real writers work through long assignments by sequencing a series of short assignments instead. For you, a dispersed process permits you to assess one writing operation at a time and substantially increases the chances for better final papers from students near the end of the semester.

To begin, I design the first draft as the platform for student writers to take their initial step toward meaning-making: making the assignment their own, determining what they want to say, processing and applying background knowledge. In scheduling such a project, I know the final version will have to come near the end of the semester because I want to avoid receiving first drafts that masquerade as final drafts. I therefore schedule the final version deadline on the fourteenth week.

I also want to praise students who make that genuine initial first effort—a good faith effort—so I'm really looking to validate writerly behavior because that effort sustained until the end informs the final draft. In addition, I want to reward meeting mini-deadlines that I set on the way to completion since these efforts are instrumental to improving their work by the end of the course. That said, I know these briefs—what Robert Marzano calls "nonachievement factors" (2000, 37)—are really rehearsals for good writing.

Yes, I know these first efforts in and of themselves are not necessary causes for good writing because there are no necessary causes for good writing. There are associated causes, however. Honest first efforts, for example, construct background knowledge, a storehouse that accumulates the experiences of the most successful college writers. These nonachievement factors for writers are commonly referred to as *craft*. As a result, with the whole semester schematic before me—a manageable cognitive workload throughout the semester—I then require the first draft to come in at exactly the halfway point (the seventh week) as I work back from the final fourteenth week.

Again, I want the first version to be a genuine groping toward meaning, getting students to wrestle with their topic in a prose style early. I seldom get that without having a proposal first from students, a paragraph or two (no longer than a page) pointing out their topic to me and due on the second week.

I plan on giving students feedback in a short conference so I can hear them talk about their writing. (I develop more on the short conference in Chapter 8, a strategy that is more effective and less time-consuming than paper grading.) I can do that the same week the first draft comes in since I'll have students bring the draft to me in conference. Consequently, I schedule a first draft on the seventh week—with a conference—to see what ideas students have invented.

To check progress, I schedule a second draft workshop in class on week 10, about two-thirds of the way toward the final draft. If there was scanty research on the first effort, I expect a greater supply here. The researched writing assignment has four deadlines in the sixteen-week semester (Table 5.1).

The reason I don't need to see all students for a second draft is that I want to teach peer review to accomplish my goals for the

Table 5.1.   Deadlines for Sixteen-Week Semester

1		9	
2	topic idea	10	second draft
3		11	
4	topic decision	12	
5		13	
6		14	final draft
7	first draft/conferences	15	
8		16	

second draft. Yet I still need to see what they've done and rewritten in their second drafts. I therefore make conferences optional and only after peer review. Dedicating, at most, one-quarter of a class period to the second draft, I have students bring their drafts with two copies. Then during class I have students read one copy of their papers to one another while I quickly scan for common problems in the other copy they handed me at the beginning of class. Maybe it's a sentence or documentation problem. In the second draft I'm still working higher-order concerns like thesis and development, but I also talk briefly about documentation style. I can show a good example from the stack—put it on the board or type it on a slide for the projector—and have students work on their own. While they are checking them or rewriting, I walk around the class and see if they have any specific questions.

"Is my thesis statement too broad?" asks one.

"My first sentence sounds blah. How can I make it better?" asks another.

"Do I have to have parenthetical citations in every sentence on this page?" asks a third.

These are the times when you refer students to what you taught earlier.

"What words make you question whether the thesis is too broad?" I ask.

"Do you need the first sentence?" I ask another.

"No, but in what other ways can you show the audience you're using another's intellectual material?" I ask a third.

For each question, I try to return other questions, probing their background knowledge and their new learning. In doing so, I'm also trying to make their memory stronger by calling on it frequently and at different intervals and on different occasions in the course. At other times I'm pointing out how to apply this or that point, again calling up previous memories. In each encounter with students, I'm looking to see if they offer me work from their examples to the greater principle. That is the way writing is learned and relearned, from the example to principle: inductively.

Yet how do you show students explicitly what you expect in each draft?

The Checksheet

The checksheet is a single keyboarded page I prepare and distribute to all students in the class. It lists the tasks I expect them to complete for each draft. Writing a checksheet geared for each draft, I can front-load the assignment by specifying exactly the features and commitments for each draft: *what the prof wants*. Students can then check off the boxes as they complete them or after they finish their assignment so they acknowledge what's required.

Checksheet items resemble rubrics, sets of scores that measure student performance in the hope that grading can be made consistent and reliable. I have lesser expectations for my checksheets, however, because I do not believe I can ever lock writing assignments into a comprehensive, irreducible set of writing features that can never be added to or subtracted from. Writing is too complex—an array of linguistic, cognitive, and metacognitive functions—for such reductionism. Rather, I contribute reminders for student writers: they take their previous low-stakes assignments they rehearsed and place them altogether into a larger framework—a discourse, a sustained piece of writing. It is like taking background knowledge and applying it to the assignment at hand. Once again, I am giving students a structure or a shape for which they invent an infinite number of ways to place content.

I first started using checksheets when I noticed checkboxes creeping into the back envelopes of electric and credit card bills. "Is your check enclosed?" and "Did you write your account number on the check?" and similar questions prompted me to borrow this strategy for student writers. I wanted to reduce the number of submissions that needed to be returned because they didn't make a good faith effort, as I describe it in checksheet tasks. Additionally, like the utility and credit card companies, I want my audience to acknowledge what I require and to meet these items in their essay submitted to me. I know students can check off anything at the last minute. Regardless, I notice the quality of drafts and final versions improve immensely because the checksheets make the writing assignments transparent *by task*. The same is true for bill collectors.

Thus, checksheets are also teaching tools. I can use terms from the course freely, and I can reference obscure points with page numbers from the textbook. Since I want students to concentrate on the most important matters early, I allocate the requirements among five analytic areas. The global areas affecting whole discourses are at the top, like focus, and require the most planning since they affect the entire piece of writing. The most discrete and local are at the bottom, like conventions, which I work into play late in the composing process. I adapted these five areas from Janice Lauer to stratify tasks and drills clearly for my writers. Thus, in a first draft I populate requirements in the first two areas (focus, development) the most. As writers get deeper into the writing assignment, I populate more of the remaining areas (structure/organization, style, conventions). In the final version, I weigh all areas equally.

Each checksheet also has several sections. First is an opening paragraph that lists the purpose for the writing, the audience, and the deadline. After that, I itemize tasks that prepare writers for working on the five analytic areas. In the first draft, I use verbs of effort—*I tried* or *I attempted*, and the like—because I want students to experiment, to apply their learning. Gradually, I convert those verbs to confer degree of successes. For example, in reading their first drafts I discover that 80 percent of the students have already written a thesis statement with a stance in its predicate; now I can require them to write such a thesis statement in the second draft. (The 80 percent is my base number for comparisons: the Contract for B.) In all checksheets I keep to the first person point of view, which also transfers ownership to students: "I wrote a thesis statement that locates the insight in the predicate."

I prepare the checksheets just before the drafts or assignments, sometimes deriving them from my daybook freewriting about the course. For instance, I want students to craft their introductions more carefully, which I noted in a daybook reflection, so I include an item in the checksheet that asks students "to compose two alternative introductory paragraphs." I write the checksheets into classroom language, capturing what I know students need to practice first. In that process, I can show (rather than tell) how I read their drafts, how one professional audience member looks at a piece of writing. These items become teachable moments in the class and in conferences, talking points of contact between student writers and me.

Exhibit 5.1 is an example you can freely adapt for your own course. Using the same assignment example from the previous section, I prepare a checksheet for the topic proposal.

Exhibit 5.1 Checksheet Topic Proposal

My assignment is to explore, through a proposal, possible topics for the argument essay, that genre that asks readers in my class to consider my debatable point on an issue. My deadline is the BEGINNING of my class — Thursday, September 5, 2013.

❑ I propose 2–4 possible topics, from which my professor will rank them.

❑ I met the deadline.

❑ I include this checksheet with my topic proposal; if I forgot it, I am still accountable for all the assigned tasks.

❑ I worked 2–4 hours outside of class on writing this proposal.

1. Focus & Purpose for Writing

❑ I include at least one sentence that lists the purpose for each topic I'm proposing.

2. Development for an Audience

❑ I used examples to show why I have credibility to write on this issue.

3. Organization/Structure

❑ I wrote using paragraph structure.

❑ Each topic I propose is no longer than one paragraph.

4. Language & Sentence Structure

❑ I wrote in a formal style.

5. Conventions

❑ I keyboarded the draft; I included my name.

❑ I edited the proposal on screen and on paper before printing a
   final copy.

❑ My proposal is no longer than one page.

❑ I kept the margins at about one inch.

❑ I made two copies and brought both to class.

I distribute the checksheet during the last five minutes of class, and then, standing in front of the class, I begin reading it silently. Others follow suit. After two minutes I'll ask students to read the checksheet to see if they have any questions during my reading, but I find just reading it myself tells them, by example, what to do, a pattern just like our daily writing.

After a few minutes, I ask, "What questions do you have?"

Then I wait, especially the first time I offer a checksheet. I'll wait until the end of class without a question if I have to.

Usually, at least one writer raises her hand. "So you want two topics. Do you want us to write two papers?"

Haven't I been clear? Is the student just looking for reassurance? Is the student trying to fill empty class time? Has the student read the checksheet well enough to answer her own questions? If I pursue an investigation of any, I lose confidence in my own checksheet.

Instead, I involve the class, probably in the same ways you do in other aspects of your teaching. "Great question! Who knows the answer?"

Another pause. Someone in the back answers, "The first check-box says you are going to rank them. To me, that means we still get to choose, but we get your comment anyway."

"That's a terrific way to look at it," I respond with a smile. I return to the original questioner. "Does that answer your question? Would you like a follow-up question? Would you like me to elaborate for five minutes past the end of class?"

She laughs. That's the end of class and no one sees me about the assignment afterward.

For a first-draft checksheet (Exhibit 5.2), I concentrate a lot on effort, the kind of low-stakes tasks producing raw material that they can refine later. I expect unpolished versions this first time around, the writer transforming ideas into sentences and paragraphs before crafting sentences and grammar. I reference other writers who believe the same and to whom I've referred to in class previously.

Exhibit 5.2 First-Draft Checksheet

My assignment is to compose a first version of my argument that asks readers in my class to consider my debatable point on an issue. In writing my draft, I concentrated on completing higher-order concerns before working toward lower-level concerns. My deadline is the BEGINNING of my conference — Thursday, September 12, 2013 or Friday, September 13, 2013.

- ❏ I offer my draft to you now, not as "finished" or even complete, but as a work-in-progress that may turn into something completely other than I originally intended in a future draft.

- ❏ I met the deadline.

- ❏ I wrote, as Don Murray says, with "velocity[,] ... outracing the censor" that tells me that I can't do it.

- ❏ I include this checksheet with my draft; if I forgot it, I am still accountable for all the assigned tasks.

- ❏ I previously submitted at least two topic idea paragraphs; I'm using one of them.

- ❏ I worked at least four hours outside of class on writing this draft.

1. Focus & Purpose for Writing

- ❏ I understand the purpose of the genre in which I'm writing.

- ❏ My discourse exercise results from the in-class Invention activity and represents a modern interpretation of ARGUMENT, one common to the progymnasmata.

- ❏ I wrote my first draft discourse as a "discovery draft" (Murray), a "zero draft" (Zeigler), a "shitty first draft" (Lamott).

- ❏ I tried to write an arguable proposition as a thesis; I wrote at least three and highlighted them in my draft.

2. Development for an Audience

❑ I worked hard to explore a subject with which I have some experience rather than state what is obvious and broad and unmanageable.

❑ The writer and audience have a stake in the judgment of this discourse.

❑ I told at least one story.

❑ I made few inferences.

❑ I tried to write a compelling title.

❑ I used at least one common topic and one special topic.

3. Organization/Structure

❑ I tried to use classical Arrangement to organize my discourse — Introduction, Statement of Fact, Confirmation, Refutation, Conclusion — much like Boethius recommends.

❑ I identify with the audience's values, beliefs, or expectations (ethos) in some way in my introduction.

4. Language & Sentence Structure

❑ The level of style I attempted is low, middle, or grand (circle one).

❑ I wrote three versions of my closing sentence, as we learned to do in class with the aphorism.

5. Conventions

❑ I keyboarded the draft; I included a title, my name, and page numbers for all pages.

❑ I kept the margins at about one inch.

❑ I tried to make this draft between 1500–2000 words.

❑ I made two copies, stapled them into two packets, and brought
   both to the conference.

Again, I leave time at the end of class for reading and asking questions. If students flood me after class with questions, however, I answer on condition that they ask the same questions at the beginning of the next class. I take down any identical questions I hear and may even compose a rewritten checksheet that I can e-mail them quickly after class.

For the second draft, I expect greater precision: less seeking and more finding. It's time for students to penetrate other areas, so it's also a good time to remove some of the language of trying. For example, if students are writing good titles in their first draft, I require them to write a compelling title in the second. I also add additional requirements. The second-draft checksheet (Exhibit 5.3) reinforces what I have said and taught—in writing.

When students enter the classroom, they again bring two copies of their work and I scan them quickly for common problems. During the last ten minutes of class, I point one or two sentences and on the board without explaining what's wrong with them, and have them rewrite during class. I can walk around the classroom in a few minutes and ask one or two students, who have written better versions of the sentence to place them on the board, where we can copy them into our daybooks.

Exhibit 5.3 Second-Draft Checksheet

My assignment is to compose a second version of my argument that asks readers in my class to consider my debatable point on an issue. In writing my draft, I concentrated on completing higher-order concerns before working toward lower-level concerns. My deadline is the BEGINNING of my class — Thursday, November 7, 2013.

- ❏ I offer my draft to you now, not as "finished" or even complete, but as a work-in-progress that may turn into something completely other than I originally intended in a future draft.

- ❏ I met the deadline.

- ❏ I include this checksheet with my draft; if I forgot it, I am still accountable for all the assigned tasks.

- ❏ I previously submitted a first draft.

- ❏ I worked at least four hours outside of class on rewriting this draft.

1. Focus & Purpose for Writing

- ❏ I understand the purpose of the genre in which I'm writing.

- ❏ I wrote an arguable proposition as a thesis; I wrote at least three and highlighted them in my draft.

- ❏ I attempt to reach stasis with my opponent(s)/audience.

- ❏ I made my thesis an enthymeme.

2. Development for an Audience

- ❏ I worked hard to explore a subject with which I have some experience rather than state what is obvious and broad and unmanageable.

❑ The writer and audience have a stake in the judgment of this discourse.

❑ I told at least one story.

❑ I made few inferences.

❑ I tried to write a compelling title.

❑ I used at least one common topic and one special topic.

3. Organization/Structure

❑ I used classical Arrangement to organize my discourse — Introduction, Statement of Fact, Confirmation, Refutation, Conclusion — much like Boethius recommends.

❑ I identified with the audience's values, beliefs, or expectations (ethos) in some way in my introduction.

4. Language & Sentence Structure

❑ The level of style I used is low, middle, or grand (circle one).

❑ I tried to use one governing point of view and one verb tense.

❑ I tried to employ one periodic sentence and noted so in the margin next to it.

5. Conventions

❑ I proofread for any fallacies of form or matter in my draft, particularly the "either/or" fallacy; I alone carry the "burden of proof" (Textbook 63).

❑ I keyboarded the draft; I included a title, my name, and page numbers for all pages.

❑ I kept the margins at about one inch.

❑ I tried to make this draft between 1000–1500 words.

❑ I made two copies, stapled them into two packets, and brought both to the conference.

These scaffolding checksheets evoke truer final versions. What I mean is that students drill into the architecture of the previous versions so that they reconstruct their product. I find that students follow the assignment much more closely when they make multiple passes, just as all writers do, starting with their purpose for writing. Have you tried authoring multiple drafts for which you set increasing expectations in terms of features and adaptiveness to audience? It's a tremendously powerful device to complete full versions and return to them later with new eyes and new insights, your subconscious working on it in the meantime.

When students hand in their final version, the conversation is over, with student writers having the last word (Exhibit 5.4).

Exhibit 5.4 Checksheet Final Draft

My assignment is to compose a final version of my argument that asks readers in my class to consider my debatable point on an issue. In writing my draft, I concentrated on completing higher-order concerns before working toward lower-level concerns. My deadline is the BEGINNING of my class — Thursday, December 5, 2013.

- ❑ I offer my draft to you now, as "finished."

- ❑ I met the deadline.

- ❑ I include this checksheet with my draft; if I forgot it, I am still accountable for all items.

- ❑ I previously submitted a first and second draft.

- ❑ I worked at least four hours outside of class on rewriting this draft.

1. Focus & Purpose for Writing

- ❑ I understand the purpose of the genre in which I'm writing.

- ❑ I wrote an arguable proposition as a thesis; I wrote at least three and highlighted them in my draft.

- ❑ I reached stasis with my opponent(s)/audience.

- ❑ I made my thesis an enthymeme.

2. Development for an Audience

- ❑ The writer and audience have a stake in the judgment of this discourse.

- ❑ I told at least one story.

- ❑ I made few inferences.

- ❑ I wrote a compelling title.

- ❑ I used at least one common topic and one special topic.

3. Organization/Structure

- ❑ I used classical Arrangement to organize my discourse — Introduction, Statement of Fact, Confirmation, Refutation, Conclusion — much like Boethius recommends.

- ❑ I tried to balance the persuasive appeals in my discourse. In a nearby margin, I labeled one strategy for each of the three appeals I attempted to use — three total — even though I may (should?) have used more.

- ❑ I identified with the audience's values, beliefs, or expectations (ethos) in some way in my introduction.

4. Language & Sentence Structure

- ❑ The level of style I used is low, middle, or grand (circle one).

- ❑ I tried to use one governing point of view and one verb tense.

- ❑ I tried to employ one periodic sentence and noted so in the margin next to it.

5. Conventions

- ❑ The paper is carefully edited and proofread; I read the discourse to another reader to test how it sounds.

- ❑ I proofread for any fallacies of form or matter in my draft, particularly the "either/or" fallacy; I alone carry the "burden of proof" (Textbook 63).

- ❑ I keyboarded the draft; I included a title, my name, and page numbers for all pages.

- ❑ I kept the margins at about one inch.

- ❑ I made this draft between 1000–1500 words.

When writing your first checksheets, you create expectations in keeping with the whole writing process students will undergo. If you lower your expectations for a first draft, the more likely you can heighten your expectations for a final product. For example, if you transfer your expectation that student writers adhere to a grammatical correctness common in your field to the realm of final versions, the more likely you will have students' cognitive resources concentrated on more global features in a first version, like development and organization and working thesis.

One working writer I know devotes a workday to either three pages or three hours of concentrated drafting, whichever comes first. When it comes to revising, however, he works seven or eight hours without tiring.

The hardest work is getting something down first; the rest of the work is a refining fire, in which you can expect your student writers to work hard in shaping what they already have on paper. The checksheets make those expectations clear and unequivocal to students.

Conclusions About Management

By breaking long assignments into manageable units, you provide a framework for student writers to sequence their drafts and distribute the workload naturally across the writing process. You can more easily control that workflow—for you and your students—through checksheets and, in doing so, command more stellar writing by the end of that process. You also avoid much of the unproductive questioning and misdirection common when students don't clearly know what to do in an assignment. It also saves you from correcting language errors that more than likely would change anyway when students rewrite or revise.

As a result, you're commandeering writers with writing, appropriating the whole composing process in the classroom because you are doing what you require students to do. You compose the assignment and your expectations; students make the assignment their own when they know those expectations and apply their new knowledge to subsequent drafting. This practice can serve your own long writing projects too, assigning specific tasks to your planning and drafts instead of expecting everything to be completed in one swoop.

6

Prepare for Rewriting

There is so much confusing talk in our schools about the reasons students produce so-called bad writing. That confusion is paradoxical because, when we think of our own composing process, we all, at some point, produce bad writing. Maybe we're drafting a rough idea or just jotting ideas in a notebook or trying to find the right language; if anyone even glances at what we produced, we might be embarrassed that we churned out such turgid sentences. Sometimes I feel that way just looking at what I wrote. Other times, in a final version I've noticed a whopper I've committed only after a reviewer or colleague points it out. Maybe you've experienced the same gremlins creeping in unawares, ones the less sympathetic among us conclude is bad writing.

At least three different meanings are at play in school settings when we hear such characterizations about our students' writing. In one, bad writing occurs when students refuse a writing assignment the way you designed it. Their reasons can encompass a wide range of causes, willful and circumstantial. This kind of bad writing can be cleared up only with a student conference.

Another bad writing is because of assignment design: for example, when professors do not compose their assignments in writing for students or when a complex assignment has broken a strategy that would lead to greater precision and clarity in assignments. The checksheets, discussed in Chapter 5, are one way professors can clarify their expectations to students.

But there is another kind of confusion pertaining to the remedies for bad writing, one less visited and the subject of this chapter. This bad writing materializes when professors and students fail to distinguish between the close terms of revising and rewriting. Preparing students for successful, finalized work you expect often hinges on observing these distinctions.

Why Distinguish?

While some writers speak of revising and rewriting synonymously, we need to separate them in the classroom so we can more clearly communicate what we want. Revising transforms a piece of writing by refocusing its purpose or acclimating to its audience; very little of the original may remain. Rewriting, however, recasts sentences within paragraphs to discover what options in language are available to the writer, from which the writer can affirm a better version.

I have recognized this distinction for many years in my own writing. I know I need to revise when I'm struggling to find what I mean in the whole piece of writing, when I'm contradicting myself, or just when I'm trying to unify what I've written—often it's all of these when I'm revising. I also know when I need to rewrite: when I've nailed the piece I'm working on—the big picture—but haven't yet settled on the specific language, the details in the picture at the word and sentence levels. Yet I never made the distinction a pedagogical one until Ponsot and Deen (1982) emphasized it. You, too, can work that distinction into your writing and your pedagogy as solutions that all writers can enlist for their writing.

Like every other profession, writing relies on the right tools for the right job. Without these distinctions, students unknowingly grab the wrong one and perform the wrong job. For example, so many students come to my classes believing that rewriting translates into the professor making extensive corrections on papers with students simply transcribing them in a new version. Rewriting may bring about corrections, but that's a by-product: the real work is to construct clearer, more economical, cohesive sentences.

Both defining and sponsoring practice in rewriting teaches students how to rewrite, which can make a qualitative difference in the final product you receive from students and what you produce for others. It certainly has in my pedagogy and my own writing.

Revising and the Classroom

Revising is an opportunity for writers to see again. As students say, it's that vision thing, or rather, it is that re-vision that entails transforming a piece of writing from dreariness to engagement. When writers revise, they hold nothing back or preserve any segment of their original. They play at slash and burn, a full-scale destruction before launching forward to rebuild. Revisers alter global features like focus, development, and structure that effect universal changes in whole discourses. That change is complete. The original version is an ancestor that the writer genetically manipulates so that its descendant is substantially superior.

Revising is necessary when writers have misinterpreted the assignment or have achieved new insight into their topics. Either condition generates a renewed vision, or they will be unable to fulfill the assignment with distinction. Revising requires writers to cut into the skeleton of the draft and graft new bones; the original exoskeleton that protects content must be broken. This surgery is radical. The resulting new interior needs a reconstituted exterior structure too.

Has this ever happened to you? When I read my draft to find that my ideas are unclear, even to me, I discover my draft is a journey to determine what I mean. If I have the luxury of keeping the draft for a few days of incubation, so much the better, as I can then read the draft aloud or have my computer read it back to me. If the vocalization sounds foreign to my ear, as if someone else authored the piece, I grow suspicious and place checkmarks in the margin beside those passages that grate against my ear. Next I print the draft in a different font from the one I originally drafted to give me fresh eyes for the manuscript. When trusted and knowledgeable others are unavailable, these tricks give me a new perspective on my work.

Now I can look for two major weaknesses. First, I investigate for problems in focus; that is, can I write what I'm trying to say in a single sentence after reading the draft? Next I look for problems in development; that is, I play the role of my audience, saying "So what?" or "How do you know that?" or "Isn't something missing here?" If both kinds of problems are pronounced, I must first revise, such as composing a new opening section or shifting the middle of my first draft, before I do anything else. Sometimes I can see the revision only in hindsight. I start tinkering after asking those probing questions, and pretty soon I have a whole new section invented. When I stop to look at what I've done, comparing it to the first, I see only a distant family resemblance between them—now I know I've completed a revision.

I'm recommending that you offer revising as an option for writers, but in a content classroom you will probably not have time to sponsor revising activities directly in the course. But there are also affective reasons for avoiding it. Beginning and even experienced writers have a very hard time accepting revision when it is not self-sponsored. Otherwise, starting over can be even more painful and disheartening. No matter how much I encourage my writers, I find that revising is infinitely discouraging as an external motivator, so I leave them alone in cases where their assignment is finished but imminently revisable: I offer the revision tool but allow them the choice of whether to wield it. When it is part of a course requirement, revising occupies a huge chunk of time that instructors cannot accomodate in a disciplinary course.

We have all had student writers bring papers or assignments that misinterpret the required tasks so completely that nothing save a true revision will bring their submission into compliance. Sometimes writers just need time to clarify their minds by playing with language on paper—dress rehearsals—as long as they know they are not final performances. I tell writers it's never a waste of time to do such a draft—but they need to recognize it for what it is: a trial run. Otherwise they cannot decide to revise.

There must always be time, however, for rewriting.

Rewriting in the Classroom

In rewriting, the occasions for it are ever-present, under the writer's control, and essential for good writing.

Think of text production in this way. Drafting is a sandbox that writers manipulate with shovels and buckets, dry sand and wet; revising means they must smash their castles and rebuild from granules before the tide takes all away forever. In sharp contrast, rewriting substantially moves lines in the sand without disturbing castles. It subtly, but substantially, modifies structures to solidify them—a better mix of water and sand—without compromising integrity. The reconstituted structures emerge from recast words, sentences, and adjoining sentences.

For the busy, congested classroom, faculty will find rewriting less daunting than revising and, more importantly, teachable. Rewriting doesn't depend on students interpreting vague feedback. It doesn't focus on the peccadilloes of the professor either, such as split infinitives (whatever that is). Rather, rewriting builds on the universal need of all writers: to produce clearer, more economical sentences that communicate meaning better to an audience than what they originally composed.

We need to persuade students (and perhaps ourselves) that when writers draft they unconsciously manufacture placeholders—subjects, verbs, and their associates—for a discourse. Rewriting takes that action one step further by making writers conscious of the process and therefore better able to revisit their first drafts. Since choice is available only with alternatives, writers can experiment, through rewriting, those other words to fill those placeholders. In other words, they can find a better verb after they have written a weak verb in its placeholder. When writers generate such choices (rewriting), they can compare the better of the alternatives, an activity of greater precision than the impossible task of producing the best from scratch.

But as writers we need not stop there. We can also play with rearranging placeholder positions; we can open with a phrase or introductory word. Rewriters center on improving the clarity, economy, and cohesiveness of individual sentences as they interact with neighboring sentences. As a result, writers can see which is the better of their generated choices.

But the obvious power to initiate rewriting is nevertheless the most overlooked: rewriting is possible only when writers are disciplined enough to produce a rough version. A powerful benefit suddenly appears: when writers rewrite, they can address clarity, economy of expression, connection to other sentences in a paragraph and discourse, and correctness in new ways without directly purposing to do so. How much better is that effusive activity than fulsome error hunting that frequently breeds an even greater number of errors (Perrault, 2011) and a false equivalence of good writing with error-free yet deadened prose.

"Stop concentrating on the disease," I say to students and myself, "and look instead to the practice of wellness: rewriting."

You can also use rewriting as preventive medicine when your student writers are blocked to meaning as a way of rerouting them. In a conference, on a slide, in a handout, in a homework assignment sheet, you can show students by preparing a paragraph of really bad sentences—perhaps an introduction for a longer piece of writing—and asking them to do the same. Then have them go back and play with the placement of these bad phrases and words, voicing them quietly at their desks; spontaneously the bad becomes the better by shifting an ending phrase to the front or vice versa. At the same time, students can propose other words or phrases or clauses that better mirror the meanings in their heads.

But I stress to students that when I am rewriting, I don't know my meaning until I see it on paper or screen, until I voice it from paper to actualized word that reaches my ear. For writing to work, I must check it from sight to sound. With two or three options that I generate from my bad choices, I discover the better choice that fertilized from my originals.

Because of rewriting, I have confidence that I can return to my bad writing later with fresh insight. Thus, rewriting incentivizes students to get something down and come back, in rewriting mode, to generate alternatives for pivotal sentences that don't work yet.

Like the pulp editor who pays writers per word, you can tell students with all the enthusiasm you can muster, "Lower your expectations and get that writing down now!"

How to Start Your Rewriting

As professors, we always face minimal time so we concentrate on activities that deliver the maximum overall effect. Rewriting can achieve such a goal. But since all writers must learn how to rewrite, how do they become great rewriters in our classrooms?

I believe you can start by keeping it simple and valorizing what most experienced writers already do while drafting: frequent rewriting. I recommend you stretch students just a bit by suggesting they make a 60/40 split between these two tasks: 60 percent time drafting while 40 percent time rewriting.

You can keep that working ratio in mind when you're drafting a scholarly article or review. After a freewrite, in which you never look back or cross out, draft a first version that does look back as you tinker with word choice and sentence structure. Next move to the next sentence. Try an opening element in a sentence, pose a question, or invert the word order; by all means, test your alternatives out loud to hear how they sound and make changes accordingly. To teach yourself, try rewriting the first and last lines of one of your articles or essays, generating several alternatives. Then experiment with working on the first and last paragraphs, central sections for any piece of writing.

Here's an example from my drafting of Chapter 3. The first number signifies the paragraph order and the second the version number:

1.1. That syllabus you explored in timed and focused freewriting from the last chapter has a deadline. In other words, you need to polish that rough cut into sentences that you share with students. But students only see the finished product and participate in the process only as readers; you want more for them. You want writers, and so the syllabus guides you into a similar structure that begins on the very first day of class. /

1.2. In the last chapter, that syllabus you explored in timed and focused freewriting now faces a deadline. In other words, the time for roughing in the cut has passed, and you must polish the result into sentences that converse with the students who are about to enter the classroom on that very first day. Since students will see only the finished product in your syllabus, you will want their role to be more than readers. You want writers. So the syllabus must become an ongoing organic document, a dynamic that invites students as writers to your course. You complement that purpose by the structure of your very first class. /

1.3. In the last chapter, that syllabus you explored in timed and focused freewriting now faces deadline. That means the time for roughing in the cut has passed and you must press the product into sentences that converse with the students who are about to enter your classroom for the very first time. Since they will see only the finished syllabus, you will want their role to be more than readers. You want writers. For that reason, the syllabus must grow into an organic document, a dynamic that

invites students as writers to your course. It also ani-
mates you as writer. You engage/begin/start/initiate that
purpose by structuring your very first class. /

1.4. In the last chapter, that syllabus you explored in
timed and focused freewriting now faces a deadline. That
means the time for roughing in the cut has passed and
you must press the product into sentences that converse
with the students who are about to enter your classroom
for the very first time. Since they will see only the finished syllabus, you want their role to be deeper than
readers. You want writers. For that reason, you must perceive the syllabus as organic, a dynamic that invites students as writers to your course. It will also animate you
as writer. You initiate that purpose by structuring your
very first class.

3.1 This shows the way I build my syllabus into the
life of my first class. It is something I know you can
do—better than any boilerplate or canned technique.
Instead, it rises from your convictions as a writer, a
professor who has prepared for this course in writing the
syllabus. As such, you are ... ... /

3.2 This chapter narrates the way I incorporate my
syllabus into the life of my first class. It is something
I know you can do—better than any boilerplate or
canned technique. Instead, your first day, like mine,
springs from your convictions as a writer, a professor who
has prepared for this course by writing a comprehensive
syllabus and readied for the first day.

5.1 So what do you do on that first day? ...

In this example, I generated four versions of the first paragraph
that evolves slowly and experiments with placement, wording, and
structure. (Paragraphs 2 and 4 are unwritten because, as I describe
the experience, they're unavailable to writing while the openings

of paragraphs 3 and 5 are clearer in my mind's eye.) It is important not to erase or backspace over any paragraph because you may want to return to some aspect of it. Plus, having the history of sentences before you acts like a residue that builds your next version.

You can also focus your rewriting on keywords. In 1.3, I couldn't come up with a good verb when I needed one, so I quick-wrote the wrong one as a placeholder before generating several versions separated by a slash. This symbol shows me that, during my later rereading, I paused over some element to generate alternatives. I decide on what one I want later when I'm in finishing mode.

The ellipsis alerts me that there is an intervening paragraph I need to write, which is necessary because I want to invent a reflective paragraph first while I have an initial idea. The same experience occurred after writing alternatives to paragraph 3; I saw five as fixed, the place I needed to end up as a result of four paragraphs of rewriting. That bouncing around reflects the recursive nature of writing, one you need to seize in teaching rewriting to students.

Sometimes you may find that you want to draft nonstop when you can see the end of your essay or article in your mind's eye. In such cases, you have the focus of the article formalized and just want to race to get to the end. As you reach the proposed middle, you may be less sure, finding it harder to shape particular chunks of text into a presentable state. Yet this area is occupied with tentative words functioning as placeholders because you don't want to lose momentum by debating diction choices. When you reach the end, check the time you took to complete the draft; then double back and substitute the placeholders with stronger word choices and more cohesive sentences for 40 percent more time. Continue to test this 60/40 split in your own drafting time and adjust the ratio so it works into your final product.

How to Start the Class Rewriting

You can make your own rewriting the subject of a handout or a projected slide, giving students examples rather than just a precept. In this way, you are informing your pedagogy through your honed practice of rewriting.

The anxious and the nonwriters will want to know how many versions to produce, what words to use, what phrases to open with, and the like. The same group will want to know how successful can this approach be, given the innumerable sentences and contexts possible. Forestall such unproductive discussions by producing the handout or slide that records your rewriting work and a sample student sentence that is grammatically correct, together with several others. If you wish, you can show the original student sentence; this example is taken from a reflection paper and is unclear and ungrammatical:

> The best example to demonstrate my entire philosophy, and take of what I used to believe and hold true (whatever I was trying to be convinced of), and now knowing to judge for myself, learning on my mistakes and using my experiences to make the best judgment would be by talking about my hunting stories and how I have evolved.

Next, show the multiple alternatives, none of which indicate the order the student rewrote them, with all the choices grammatically correct:

1: I think what best demonstrates my entire philosophy is my hunting story where I take my mistakes and my experiences to show how I have evolved.

2: I think what best demonstrates my thinking is my hunting story where I discuss my mistakes and my experiences to show how I have grown.

3: I best demonstrate what I believe in the hunting story, where I discuss my mistakes and my experiences to show how I have grown.

In the handout, use directions identical or similar to these:

Circle the sentence that you believe is the clearest of the alternatives. (Hint: All of the sentences are grammatically correct.)

After the sentences, ask this:

Why did you select this sentence?

When students have finished—no longer than five minutes has elapsed—ask them to turn to a neighbor and see which she selected and why. This request brings a flurry of activity and disagreement and even laughter. After a minute or two at most, call on one energetic student and ask which he picked:

John starts by referring to the original sentence. "Shouldn't *stories* have an apostrophe?"

"What do the rest of you think?" I ask.

Tom calls out. "I don't think so. Stories doesn't own anything. Besides, the directions tell us that they are all grammatically correct," he says, reading from the handout.

"Well, I chose number 3," says Alice, returning us to my original question.

"Why?" I ask.

"Because it's grammatically correct," Alice replies, ultimately confident in her answer. She hasn't processed the directions or Tom's comment.

"But they are all grammatically correct," Tom retorts. "I think 3 is the best."

"Why?" I ask.

"Because it's the shortest, or it seems to be. In your words, it's economical."

"Okay. Does anyone disagree with Sally?" and another hand goes up.

You can continue as long as need be or until someone finally screws up enough courage to ask you, "But which do you pick?"

You repeat that all the sentences are grammatically correct—reviewing the directions once again—but that you like "3 as the better among the choices."

Now you judge comparatively: "I like this sentence better than that one because it is clearer to understand." Or, "I like this sentence better because of its emphasis—this word placed at the end of the sentence." If you read the sentences aloud to the class several times, you can test for rhythm and sound, as in "I don't like this sentence as much because the t's clash." Remind students that we use comparisons all the time. I sometimes tell students I like a particular chocolate cake better than another because the icing is sweeter or for the way it looks. You can easily substitute your favorite foods or restaurants in the example so that one emerges as the better one. That doesn't mean the others are necessarily incorrect or wrong—just less preferred. Then it's a simple sidestep over to judgments about the better options among even good alternatives.

In their first encounter with rewriting, students see the writer's original sentence. However, once students cross over to rewriting, there is no longer a need to show origins. I think it is always better, in using student sentences, to focus writers on generating valid choices so you can avoid prolonged discussions about correctness that don't lead to increased productivity. Instead, saturate writers' minds with equally correct sentences that bespeak the added bonuses of greater clarity, increased effectiveness, improved economy, and the like—a privileged sentence emerging that transcends mere correctness. In subsequent workshops, I lift correct student sentences from previous drafts with the names removed. If you spend just some class time with their valid sentences, they can rewrite some in their daybooks. Remember, you want student writers to choose among equally valid alternatives and to know why they made the choices they did, choices that delve deeper than notions of surface correctness so that you can explore the relationships that sentences and words have with one another.

Again, such a process removes them from thinking that the sentences you give them are wrong. Since you just identified them as correct, you are free to walk around the room while they're rewriting, glancing at their work; you gently remind those who are correcting what is already correct and that the task you are requiring is broader and fuller—rewriting.

"What I need to do," says the informed student, "is to produce other correct sentences so I have some options that might be more effective writing."

After all, if students do not have options, how do they know they have the better version? If you remove error hunting as the primary goal from such an operation, students will start looking for features you emphasized, emphasis and voice, based on your cues, that are easier to teach by example than by precept. When students start imitating the patterns they see on the board and on the projector, they begin making good sentences.

"Tell me again why you prefer #5," invites one student. Now students are repeating themselves—learning by repetition—instead of you repeating yourself, where only you learn it. In this scenario, they want to be assured of what they heard.

"I find #5 to be the clearer because its subjects are people. I've read a lot of research showing that where people, or agents, are the living, breathing subjects of their verbs, the writing is much clearer. Such passages also have fewer and better words, for which I point out one or two on the slide.

That whole process took ten minutes. I got students to talk about language options and argue about them and actually discuss writing. And I got students to get their focus away from error and toward making better sentences.

Sometimes I get a challenger, which makes the experience even more fun.

"Okay," sneers one, sitting to the side in the classroom. "How can you then discuss an idea or something like the Second Amendment? It's not a person."

"Fine. Give me a sentence. In fact, everybody, try writing three sentences with *Second Amendment* as the subject," I say, again working first from real sentences before moving on to the principles—bottom to top. Pretty soon, the whole class is writing sentences. I walk around and pick one or two and transfer them to the chalkboard or projector. "Look at these two. They have verbs that express actions. Here's Jenna's: 'The Second Amendment teaches...' By using verbs that express actions, she's humanized the subject since only living things can act." (Interestingly, beginning writers already believe all verbs express action, but if you compare *is* to *runs*, the vast majority of students will correctly pick *runs*. Students learn to rewrite by comparing.)

The challenger gets his second wind. "Yeah, but which of those two sentences is the better?"

The class and I both laugh, but I laugh last. I've gotten the class to learn what subjects and verbs are, how to rewrite for clarity and precision and economy without ever whipping out a handbook or reciting principles they never apply to their own writing. That isn't to say memorization is bad; it's just a far less effective strategy when instructors use it alone to start students in rewriting.

Building More Examples in Class

By the next class, you can give a more complex example of a student sentence with alternatives:

1. When I learned argumentation, I also learned to distinguish between claims and assumptions: the first, what we state; the second, what we infer.

2. I also learned that argumentation is how to distinguish between claims and assumptions: the first involves what we

state, and the second concludes what I infer from my earlier statement.

3. Learning argumentation means how to distinguish between claims and assumptions; in other words, I learned the difference between what I state and what I infer from my first statement.

When using sentences like these from my ancient and modern rhetoric class, I host a brief discussion, this time about the differences and choices in these sentences, such as using an introductory phrase. I also show them why I like parts of all the sentences. For example, I illustrate that less important material typically goes at the front of the sentence by pointing to sentence #1 ("When I learned argumentation, ... "). I also like the focus of sentence #3, or main emphasis, which appears at the end as is the custom in the best sentences ("my first statement"). I remind them how placing humans in subject placeholders works better, which #2 uses to its advantage. I then go back and ask them for needless words in the sentence and which ones cut just enough or too much or too little. We have a discussion about sentences and what they mean! With course content in those sentences, you can demonstrate certain disciplinary conventions like citation and verb tense when the writer cites sources.

At the end of class, I ask students to perform the same operation, but with another few sentences—and this is important—derived from the same original. I want to see if they can process the discussion I just hosted by applying the principles with similar content:

4. Argumentation distinguishes between claims and assumptions: likewise, I learned how to argue by differentiating between what I state from what I infer.

5. To learn argumentation, I had to distinguish between claims and assumptions, between what I state and what I infer.

6. To learn argumentation, I had to distinguish between claims and assumptions, between my statement and my inference.

7. By learning arguments, I also learned to distinguish between claims and assumptions: The first means what we state, and the second means what we infer from that statement.

(Chapter 7 shows how these student responses, or postwrites, form the basis for low-stakes writing.)

Yes, this activity does take more time, but it's worth it. If I want to receive readable papers from these students, I need to do the upfront work, and that means giving concrete examples. I can now show the interplay between principle and example in ways students can understand. Working from the bottom up—from their sentences to principles—inductive teaching makes the rewriting outcome possible. In my observations, students have twelve-plus years of school where they learned from top to bottom. It's time for them to learn from their own sentences.

It's possible to post these sentences in an electronic forum where students can debate their choices online and you can discuss the results at the next class. You can use this format when you're particularly pressed for time.

Gradually, you can increase the complexity of the task. For the next step, I take a paragraph—but no longer, especially when introducing rewriting—to show it's important that writers relate sentences to one another in a paragraph. If you want to stress line-by-line editing, you can reintroduce original sentences that may be ungrammatical. Just recognize that adding erroneous sentences to the mix makes the writers' task much harder, so offer such selections only to your advanced writers after they can argue consistently for better sentences. Here's an example from this advanced set:

1: I had the opportunity to give an interview with Mrs. Lisa Smith, ResLife Coordinator of Jones College. She explained how freshmen are paired with their roommates. Approximately 60% of incoming freshmen are paired by athletic coaches or by newfound friends at orientation sessions. The other 40% are determined by Lisa's office by reviewing questions listed in the Housing Agreement, and the office "relies heavily on student responses to those questions." Of all the "bipolar characteristic" type questions, Lisa finds two to be most important: "How important is it that your room be kept neat and orderly?" and "How do you feel about a roommate who drinks alcoholic beverages?" If two people respond on completely different sides of the spectrum, Lisa and her team will do their best to insure they are not paired. While she realizes that some matches aren't ideal, Lisa feels that the best way to make ResLife better would be to have students offer more honest responses. Lisa herself doesn't have any other responsibilities other than dealing with roommate conflict, but she recognizes that the Student Life Coordinators are also involved with the planning of campus-wide activities. When asked how many hours per week she was solving roommate conflicts, Lisa didn't give a definite answer. She explained how roommate changes are more common during the beginning months of a semester, but her job is slower now, except in emergency cases.

2: I had the opportunity to interview Ms. Lisa Smith, Residence Life Coordinator of Jones College, who explained how freshmen are paired with their roommates. Approximately 60% of incoming freshmen are paired by athletic coaches or by newfound friends at orientation sessions; the other 40% are addressed by Smith's office who reviews questions listed in the Housing Agreement, the office "rel[ying] heavily on student responses to those questions."

Of all the "bipolar characteristic" type questions she asks, Smith finds two that stand above the others: "How important is it that your room be kept neat and orderly?" and "How do you feel about a roommate who drinks alcoholic beverages?" If two students respond at opposite ends, Smith and her team will do their best to insure they are not paired. While she realizes that some matches aren't ideal, Smith feels that the best way to make Residence Life better would be to have students offer more honest responses. Although Smith herself also deals with roommate conflict, she recognizes that the Student Life Coordinators also help to plan campus-wide activities, even though those tasks are not her focus. When I asked how many hours per week she devotes to solving room-mate conflicts, Smith did not give a definite answer. She instead explained how roommate changes are more common during the beginning months of a semester, her job slower now except in cases involving emergencies.

3: I interviewed Ms. Lisa Smith, Residence Life Coordinator of Jones College, who explained how freshmen pair with their roommates. For approximately 60% of incoming freshmen, athletic coaches or new-found friends do the pairing at orientation sessions; Smith's office addresses the other 40% when it reviews questions listed in the Housing Agreement by "rel[ying] heavily on student responses to those questions."

Of all "bipolar characteristic" questions she asks, Smith finds two significant: "How important is it that your room be kept neat and orderly?" and "How do you feel about a roommate who drinks alcoholic beverages?" If two students offer opposing responses,

Smith and her team will do their best to insure they are not paired. While she realizes that some matches are not ideal, Smith feels students could make Residence Life better with more honest responses. Although she deals primarily with roommate conflict, Smith recognizes that the Student Life Coordinators also help to plan campus-wide activities, even though those tasks are not her own. When I asked how many hours per week she devotes to solving roommate conflicts, Smith did not give a definite answer. She instead explained her workload is more hectic with roommate changes during the beginning months of a semester, the exception being in cases involving emergencies.

In this sample, I can talk about formal language. I can address abbreviations. I can talk about professional titles, incorporated quotes, unemphatic information to the left of the subject, and the like. Whatever I deem 80 percent of the class needs I can address here. And, oh yes, I can now address error directly in the context of crafting overall better sentences.

Can you envision what you can do with rewriting in your course? You can offer other opportunities, whenever time permits. In any content course, you can host a seventh-inning stretch where you stop and ask students to take five or ten minutes in class to rewrite exclusively.

For additional support, you can make a homework assignment that builds on rewriting and directly benefits their work. For example, you can ask students to print a copy of their current draft in a font and size that differ from the on-screen version. You can do the same and show them an example. I frequently use Argumentum for composing on screen but Optima for printing on paper. Writers will notice all kinds of possibilities that they didn't see before: a better verb, a word substitution, a place where a gap and an example would be better. I'm sure there's a scientific or cognitive explanation for why this works, but it matters little if student eyes refocus on communicating meaning.

You can advise students to vary their posture, too, in writing. If I normally draft while sitting in a chair, I might go over to a stand-up writing desk or a laptop rest that works only when I stand. I find a quiet carrel in the library or a coffee shop to get me to see things anew. In the classroom, I translate this practice when I find a student desk, preferably right in the middle of the herd, and start rewriting.

In each case, I start with options so I can rewrite.

More on How to Deal with Error

My everyday practice is never show students an ungrammatical sentence and a grammatical one and have them to choose between them. If I did, I would be devoting at least 50 percent of class time to showing really bad sentences, which students dutifully copy into their notebooks and imprint into their memories. In such situations, the ratio of bad to good is at best 1:1; it's a small step away for students to conclude that there is only one good sentence possible, the one the professor corrects, for every bad one.

If the professor assigns incorrect sentences for homework, student writers become confused, falling back on their familiar, though flawed, practice of hypercorrecting sentences since they have plenty of previous school practice with correcting their teachers' artificial sentences. Faced with the unfamiliar, uneasy writers will choose the familiar every time, no matter how weak their past performances from those old practices. Inevitably, students imitate errors or introduce new ones into their sentences. Again, if you present real student sentences with errors for rewriting, students conclude something must be wrong before they can rewrite, just like the artificial sentences they corrected in grade school. As one student wrote reflecting on his inability to correct an erroneous real sentence: "I have lots of trouble correcting someone else's sentences. I just don't know what they mean." That kind of expertise takes years to acquire.

Asking students to deal with someone else's flawed sentences leaves little time for weightier matters, like emphasis and rhythm. Our students are not editors yet. First they need to become familiar with what good sentences look like as well as what options are available to them. The transition from practice with others' real sentences to their own prose will be easier if they dispense with error hunting and embrace rewriting sentences.

But it's going to take time to move students out of the error-hunting phase exclusively so that they can do real rewriting that moves correcting away from primary focus. For instance, near the end of one writing-intensive course, I noticed students were having trouble punctuating sentences, even after several lessons on punctuation. They stuck closely to the traditional period, but they weren't venturing into colons and dashes; they were playing it safe. So I gave them ten correct sentences that professionals authored, all with the punctuation removed. I next asked my writers to punctuate them as they believed the professionals would, stressing there were several correct ways but one better, more privileged way to signify a higher style. I repeated, in writing the directions, that there were no grammatical errors in any of the sentences, only punctuation omissions.

Five minutes into the activity, about half the class was hyper-correcting the sentences by replacing words, deleting phrases, or changing spelling. Even though I told the students orally and in the writing directions that the sentences were correct, they were programmed so thoroughly from school exercises that all they did was correct.

I was shocked. I asked them to think of punctuation as conveying meaning. Next, I required them to crumple that sheet and to start with a new copy that I now supplied them: punctuation only. They had never punctuated to clarify meaning before or to provide emphasis. Afterward, when I placed each sentence on the overhead and showed how the original looked with punctuation, we all started talking more productively about punctuation.

"Why use a dash there?" asked one student.

"Why a semicolon in that list of five things?" asked another.

"There are two dashes in that sentence. Could I have used a semicolon?" asked a third.

"Is the dash the same as a hyphen?" asked a fourth.

After answering those questions, I realized they first had to confront their previous experience, recognizing it for what it was—even repeat it—before they could move on. I smiled.

"Now you know what options are," I summarized. "Now you know how punctuation figures in rewriting."

What a splendid time, after such a conversation, to invite students to launch directly into rewriting! You could tell them to begin with punctuation or a difficult, opaque passage that you want clarified—anything so that they can narrate the rewriting process. Next you can teach them, comfortably and safely—without grading or penalties—to show them what options are available. When 80 percent of the class can rewrite grammatical sentences consistently—including alternates—you can drop sentence explanation as a regular reminder, inserting it occasionally as a part of retrieval practice. Those gentle reminders are powerful.

Then I give a quick postwrite at the end:

1. What was the most significant thing you learned from the rewrite exercise today?

2. Give me your original valid sentence and the better option of the three you generated.

After class, you can read through a stack of forty in twenty-five minutes or less since you've streamlined your reading to look only at the rewrites. You don't need to mark anything manually in your gradebook unless you note a student who made an extremely good performance. And you can correct any misunderstanding in the next class, so writing puffy feedback on their papers is unnecessary. For instance, if you notice a lot of problems with the comma, make a slide with correct student sentences, telling them there were problems with the comma but "here are samples of many correct versions." You are now free to talk about how the comma functions in a sentence toward meaning and creating understanding in the reader rather than theorize about commas. You may get some questions, which you can flesh out on the board or on the projector using a pen. If students ask you why a certain sentence in their paper is wrong, have them show it to you privately. The class sees only correct sentences.

If students are not copying down the correct sentences into their notebooks, remind them that whatever you write on the board—especially these fantastically shaped sentences!—they need to copy into their notebooks. When students copy the better sentences from the board, they are imitating, which is one of the oldest forms in learning to write. I like to remain silent until they finish copying. It's always a comfort to me that when I stop talking writing happens!

With the displayed sentences on the board, you can begin showing options, or inviting options from the class: an introductory phrase in the front instead of the back, eliminating unnecessary words, and the like. If you're not comfortable with that role, have students compose alternative sentences at their desks. In a few minutes, you can walk the aisles and ask a few to copy theirs on the board, ones you think are particularly effective and correct. Then you can add to their work with other alternatives. For instance, you can state that a semicolon would work in this instance, or "Did the meaning change when I put a set of commas here?" You can reread it aloud a few times to test the rhythm, a version with and a version without commas. Right here, you have a mini-rewriting workshop in the space of ten or fifteen minutes.

If there is not enough time for a mini-workshop, I may ask students at the end of class to demonstrate the rewriting task in a postwrite, a simple exercise that invites students to apply what they just heard or just began to practice:

> Consider the valid sentence from class today on the board. Copy it down on this sheet. Next generate three other options that are grammatical but begin differently or have different emphasis or punctuation.

Faculty always ask me how long this process takes. I think it's best if you give it a short space once and look for equally short opportunities to repeat a similar exercise in future classes. If you find an extra five minutes at the end of class or your class discussion wraps early, use that space for rewriting. Look for empty moments in your classroom times to fill with rewriting. And, of course, there are always online forums and bulletin boards where students can spend longer periods to debate choices and rewrite. Looking for class time to rewrite can tighten our own class management too. I remember the first time I viewed myself on videotape as I taught a class. I wasted so much time getting organized that I understood in a new way why I ran out of time so often. When I became aware of how I could use rewriting as a template for my class presentations, I found extra time at the end of class. Whatever the case, you use what time you have; a small investment really does compound benefits.

So start small. Those moments at the end of class are teachable ones for rewriting the content of your course. If you keep the next rewriting handout always with your course materials, then you can ask students to bring at least one draft with them to every class. When an unplanned extra ten or fifteen minutes appears at the end of a class, rewrite with them.

Conclusion

So these are the fundamental points I recommend for establishing rewriting in your classroom.

First, as in all writing things, work from the bottom up—from students' concerns and their sentences to the principles that knit good choices. We always start with student sentences (i.e., where they are) and build toward greater complexity (e.g., the final draft of a disciplinary writing genre). Later we build the universal definition. The way we mature as writers is identical to how students do: gradually becoming more aware of the sentences that are available to us. Rewriting attunes us to that process.

Next, from that vantage point you can posit correction, which is uppermost in students' minds, within the broader context of rewriting, which encompasses larger fields like clarity and economy of expression. Since there's no class time spent correcting erroneous sentences, you can get to things you know are important in your discipline.

Third, when students write in class, monitor their work as they are rewriting. Walk around for five minutes to see how they're doing, asking to see the original. If the groundwork of grammaticality is not there—a missing punctuation mark or a required placeholder like a subject or verb—you can suggest it at that teachable moment. You want students to start with a sure footing, formed from their own sentences, working from their experiences and then moving outward from there to effect rewriting. On subsequent passes in their aisle, you can ask, "Do you need help?" It's effective to whisper answers to individuals, appointed as hushed secrets passed from one writer (you) to another (your student). If your class is large, you can move quickly through the class, scanning for anyone who looks up rather than soliciting help to the many who are busy rewriting.

Fourth, when you see student writing in class or in homework, highlight particular clusters of sentences that sound and look better than the rest. Put them on the projector or smartboard or chalkboard or online forum by next class. Ask students to come up with three new versions for homework from time to time. If students are learning what good sentences are, you can tell them which ones you prefer, but only after they argue merits of one over the other. Remember, they are choosing only grammatical sentences, so you are persuading them to compare viable options instead of opening ungrammatical ones for them to replicate.

Fifth, after a month of occasional rewriting you can introduce simple terms like *noun* and *action verb*, or whatever you're comfortable with. In introductory classes, I suggest only those two function classes. The more you learn about grammar, the more you can share, but remember, the goal is a better style, one that is clear and accessible for you, their audience. If you bombard the class with grammatical terms without having good sentences first, their eyebrows will meet. Instead, pick out subjects and verbs that they have already written. Then they are prepared for rewriting.

But how are you, the professor, prepared to rewrite? Just now, as I'm rewriting this chapter, my colleague asks for help:

> I have to come up with a short, catchy synopsis for the back cover of my book. I can't get the wording right.
>
> How does this sound to you? I actually am allowed up to 200 words, but I'd rather have more room for endorsements from others. A dangling modifier? Maybe you can give me ideas at lunch. The book focuses on news stories, danger, raising children in an unsafe world, etc. I just have to turn this in when I turn the book in after classes get out. It should be something that makes people want to pick up the book and read it.

Sounds to me like she needs three alternatives! I'll work up three too! Only then we can choose the better.

7

Offer Feedback for Classwork

Writing feedback can be a chore. A *New York Times* article describes how one set of professors refuses rather than responds to student writing that is in the process of being made. One professor in the article resented the ten students in her class of fifty who sought feedback on their drafts within a few days of their research paper; they had e-mailed their first versions to her unsolicited. She bristled at having received such writing—writing where students were trying their voices in a field they had never entered before—as "presumption ... that I'll be able to drop everything and read 250 pages two days before I'm going to get 50 of these [papers]" (qtd. in Glater, 2006, A14).

For this professor and for many of our colleagues, the feedback workload is overarching. Professors are overworked and over-wrought over giving feedback, dreading the mother lode they will receive at deadline, weighing them down like Willy Loman's suitcases. I feel their pain. Certainly I was taught in that environment, so I naturally believed my students should work in the same conditions.

But there's a subtle irony here. In that particular article, the students said they received written feedback from the professor only at the end of the writing process, a time when they least needed it. After all, there were no opportunities to use feedback to revise or rewrite.

I am advocating, instead, that you reappoint the usual two modes of feedback—oral and written—so they correlate to where the assignment stands in the composing process. For low-stakes, formative feedback, choose informal writing and oral conversation.

For summative, high-stakes feedback, select oral alone in a writing conference, the one that precedes your receiving the final version and your assigning the final grade.

For assignments that will evolve into high-stakes writing, professors need to ask questions and get background information as to why students are making the choices they made in their first or second drafts. That inquiry is best accomplished orally, so for those few times I recommend conferencing, a place where students bring their writing to start a conversation about it. The commitment to conference is the biggest time investment you can make, and you will probably have to cancel a class to hold one so you're assured of enough slots for students. I recognize it is impractical for larger classes. Still, I recommend it in Chapter 8.

For low-stakes writing, however, I recommend lots of written feedback, specific to the writer. That does not imply, however, a huge chunk of unproductive time but rather quick feedback that serves as a steady, consistent source of help.

Responding to Low-Stakes Writing: The Postwrite

As you've seen in previous chapters, low-stakes writing can take many forms. It may be an element of a much larger assignment, such as an annotated bibliography that serves as the brief assignment on its way to the completed research paper. Narrow in scope, low-stakes writing requires you to make only short responses.

The most common and voluminous kind of low-stakes feedback occurs with the students' daily work. If you use quizzes, it could take this form. However, I would encourage you to look away from graded material and toward a more writing-centric approach, the postwrite, which asks students to put into practice some aspect of writing or content information that you're emphasizing right now in your course.

Your response is thus a guided reading of what students have written, which students seldom get to see before high-stakes writing comes calling. You can also design the postwrite so students rehearse answers to prompts on one side of their paper and reflect on their classwork on the reverse side. This way you establish a pattern for future postwrites: students first complete the short prompts that always ask students to apply their understanding; next, they turn to the back, for reflection. I always try to have a concluding postwrite in class.

For example, when I start a new unit, I expose students to a lot of new information in class rather than in the homework reading. Often, I use a lot of disciplinary vocabulary, particularly terms unfamiliar to them. Since students already know they must copy terms placed on the board or repeated in a mini-lecture, the information is archived. But the learning is incomplete. Other than students transcribing what's on the board, I'm doing all the work. I'm using the terms. I'm checking meanings. I'm finding examples that will relate to them. I'm delivering all the material. I'm doing all the learning! Yet what I really want to find out is how are students applying what they receive from me and the class?

Enter the postwrite. It permits students to rehearse what I presented in class and what they copied in their daybooks. Postwrites allow me to monitor comprehension, application, and reflection. Since they are ungraded, postwrites free students to concentrate on content and the writing, not the evaluation. And the responses I give on these postwrites can start a conversation that can last many sessions or for a full semester. Postwrites create a writing space for students and their professors to meet.

Managing the Workload with Freewrites

It is imperative to design good postwrites, ones that are manageable for you and dictated by the time you can make available for the response. In a class of eighteen, I allot twenty minutes total to respond. If I have more students, I find that it takes me even less time per student because I've hit a rhythm in my responding. Here is where you find your daily freewriting benefiting your fluency; after the first few responses, you'll find phrases springing into your writing while a natural cadence takes over. In essence, your feedback becomes low-stakes practice for you.

In postwrites, I ask just one or two questions up front, so I want to make sure they're good questions, slices of what I'm teaching today rather than the complete melon. For the first postwrites of the semester, I ask very open-ended questions that can be applied to any content course:

Exhibit 7.1 Postwrite

POSTWRITE.w1c2

Last name									
First name									

10 January 2012

1. What is THE MOST IMPORTANT thing you learned in class today?

2. **ANSWER ON REVERSE SIDE**. What is the most confusing or the most difficult for you to understand from today's class?

In subsequent weeks, I can ask for more specific questions or prompts:

> What kind of work do you think you will have to do to argue this issue at this level of generality and in theoretical or practical terms?
>
> List any social factor and describe what effect it has on intelligence.
>
> In a previous exercise, you formatted figures in class so that they conform to research journal standards. What are you considering emphasizing in the text portion of the formal lab report?
>
> Cite one reason that learning styles don't explain how people learn.

The postwrites show students how they need to think about researching their issue, since using course terms like level of *generality* and *multitasking* ask students to apply them to subjects. Designing good postwrites means looking beyond the superficial learning that yes–no types of questions produce to writerly ones that have students reflect, apply, or come to new understandings: all are deeper learning. Postwrites can also ask for metadiscourse answers, where students write about a larger, upcoming writing project, a portion of which, like data collecting, they perform in class.

You can quickly respond to these postwrites because you are responding to their rehearsal—their learning. You're not issuing grades, which always consume a lot of time and often contradict what you're trying to promote: learning. There is an energizing factor too. Since you are focused on responding, you're taking on the role of an experienced writer. When you try this out for the first time, you will be amazed how free you feel to address a student, in writing, instead of completing an administrative requirement with grading. (For more on grading, see Chapter 10.)

You also can set the context for responding so that it proceeds rapidly. I know it sounds silly, but I suggest making yourself comfortable when you respond. You'll enjoy the experience more fully. For instance, I find it best to respond immediately after class. I get a favorite beverage and place it next to my writing desk. Or I walk down to the Alabaster Coffee Roaster and Tea Company with a satchel of students' postwrites. I have an ample supply of my favorite pen with me, a Uniball Vision Precision in various colors. I release the postwrites from their rubber bands and thumb through the front sides quickly before responding to them individually on the backside.

I actually look forward to responding now since I know that, in designing and then distributing these postwrites in class, I have designed a manageable task for the time I have available and have asked questions for which I really want answers. I find myself smiling at their responses ("Lori summarized the lesson concisely") and sometimes saddened ("I really thought John caught on this time, but he needs a bit more practice."). Yet in each postwrite I get a more developed snapshot of my students. I frequently feel that I tap into some vast linguistic power when I'm responding, which carries over to my writing projects.

Over time, these response times seem to resemble much of what my daily writing provides. Occasionally I'm pressed for time after class and take postwrites home. If I'm completing them after dinner or late into the evening, I find that same power there: I want to keep going once started, like an engine leaving the train house that needs someplace to go.

Soon it's pretty easy to notice those occasions in other parts of campus life. When a guest lecturer or writer is on campus for an evening talk, I encourage students to attend and to take their daybooks to collect ideas. I always see a few at such events; I take my daybook to catch key phrases that I record next to some tangential idea it provokes in me. On one occasion, a colleague received an Artist of the Year Award from the Pennsylvania Office for the Advancement of the Arts; in his acceptance remarks, he thanked his wife. I took a daybook along and, when I arrived home, wrote a poem about my relationship to my wife, even though I hadn't written poetry in twenty-five years. It's a quick roundhouse transfer of energy from seeing, hearing, or experiencing others' writing before enlisting your own. (When you encounter student writing or campus colloquiums, open yourself to where such input can prompt your own writing.)

As a result, it makes sense to use metaphors to connect students from what they know to what they don't know and thus make the subject come alive (cf. Paul, 2012). For instance, when I'm discussing research I compare the resulting document to a chorus. The student writer's voice is important to the choir, but so are the other trained voices in their roles—the *sources*—which are just like the researchers' work. An academic essay needs support, I contend, and that support is enabled through these many trained voices. No one would mistake a choral for a solo performance or a trained voice for an undisciplined one. Equally, no professor would mistake an expository, researched essay for a narrative. If I use metaphors, students get the point without listening to me drone on and on about research and citations.

In the postwrite after that introductory class to the researched essay, I ask this question:

> How is the researched essay like a chorus? (two to three sentences/slow)

Students write responses, which I limit in length by description and physicality: a half-sheet. If I want a lengthy response where students have to explore an answer, such as when I suggest a metaphor but do not discuss it in class, they freewrite possibilities as a way to explore what connections they can find:

> How might the researched essay resemble a chorus? (freewrite/five minutes)

Normally, I expect brief postwrites, just a few sentences. I respond, always in kind (briefly), and use their names:

> Nicole, I'm surprised you didn't mention *solo*; did you miss this?

When I give praise, I center on effort because I want students to be committed to continual improvement, always trying to achieve more. I also offer personal help, framed as questions:

> Tom, you're really close. How would *choir* differ from *solo*?
>
> Alex, can you put some extra time in learning the terms? Do you need help with them?

On another, I urge the writer to listen more closely:

> Alice, did you miss this metaphor today? Your writing suggests you're guessing. Are you?

On one who answered perfectly:

> Josh, you are really working hard on your writing! Keep it up!

Again, my responses are brief: general in language for general questions, specific for detailed questions.

Tactile Learning and Responding

I also believe in that old technology for response: pen and paper. There's something cognitively different to have students take to paper in these postwrites. Many writers prefer to handwrite a rough draft and won't touch a computer until they complete one.

Although writers can be as superstitious about their craft as baseball players are about theirs, some research on print technologies show evidence of different processing than keyboarding (Jabr, 2013). Many years ago, Janet Emig hypothesized that writing provided a whole-brained approach to learning, with motoric skills as one of its modes (1971). (Researchers are just beginning to look at the brain areas that support reading and the motor areas involved in writing.)

Wonderfully subjective, handwriting supplies a warmness to the instructor's response. Addressing the student by name and by hand brings personality to the exchange. Such a mode rules out trite, cut-and-paste comments.

It's something I know you can do without much practice but with maximum benefit; here's the way I do it, but feel free to adapt it to your own classes. Response writing informs my own writing projects, too, as it will yours. It's the best training I know to learning brevity in a low-stakes writing situation because if I'm not concise I'm responding for hours!

To make sure my responses stay warm and not hot, I place a timer if I find I'm getting wordy or prolific so I can move on to the next postwrite. Sometimes, on the front page I ask for a summary of what we did in class today. There are always a few students who do this really well. In my personal response to the student, I just want to complement her writing effort:

> Alaine, I really like the way you structure your answers. Do you write the first sentence last in composing? I'd like to know. Your style really works well in capturing the other sentences in your paragraph.

I may want to show a sample of Alaine's good work on the projector next class time and explain briefly why I believe it is a good summary. Sometimes I'll ask students to explain more, if they are willing, in a future postwrite.

I also use postwrites at the beginning of class, after the daily writing, to see if they've read the assigned reading. I encourage students to use the daily freewriting as a warm-up, a *bell ringer* in grade school parlance, before the postwrite. Like the postwrite at the end of class, I start the semester issuing general questions:

> What was the ONE most important thing you derived
> from your reading of Chapter 1?

When I complete the front sides of the postwrites, I shuffle them and then look at the backsides to see with what they're struggling. I typically use a variation of this prompt, located in the footer so students cannot write below it:

> What is ONE thing you are finding difficult or are strug-
> gling with in the course? (Please record your answer on
> the back of this sheet.)

When I read the reverse sides, I don't see student writers' names, which appear only on the front side, and since I seldom recognize the handwriting I have only their responses to consider. I also see connections to what others have written in the class. Students often give elaborate answers on an uncluttered back page or short ones like this one that uses terms I'm using in the class:

> The differences between the three types of sentences are
> very confusing to me. Also subordinated versus unsub-
> ordinated clauses are difficult.

Since I just taught this lesson for the first time and know that this student will be exposed to the same lesson again next time, I respond in this way:

> Thanks for letting me know. Can you identify the subjects in each clause without confusion? Write back in today's postwrite.
>
> Keep trying. Does it help if I identify the subject and verb in the sentences here? Write back in today's postwrite.

This dialogue can continue for several classes, so the student gives me a running commentary of his learning. Since the writer stores these postwrites in his writing portfolio, he can always refer to them. I don't reply exhaustively to all the postwrites—many just want to vent for a minute or two, which is just fine. These back pages are analogous to e-mails; some require a quick reply, and some not.

After the first week, I ask this:

> What ONE THING from the reading is the hardest for you to understand or is the most confusing? (Explain on the REVERSE side.)

One variation that works well in a content course is to have students perform a daily write and then follow up with the postwrite. When students finish, you can say, "Turn to your partner and tell him or her what you wrote about in your daily write while I collect your postwrite." Then walk around the classroom to collect the postwrites, quickly scanning their first-page answers from the chatty students who are now centered on one another.

When the conversation dies down, I give students a synopsis of what I received. Or I can call on anyone in class to give a response.

I encourage students to record these best responses. If I write one or two of them in my daybook, it encourages others to do the same. After class, I have begun feeding completed postwrites through a scanner before I respond to them so I have a record that can be automatically filed in software. (Some online services even offer reasonably accurate handwriting recognition at very low cost.) Since we already had a class discussion of the first side, I can concentrate on the backsides before handing them back at the beginning of the next class or in a wall pocket outside my office.

I gradually increase the cognitive work throughout the semester, so my postwrites become more specific:

> Take two sentences from your draft and rewrite them so that they are different sentence types.
>
> What libertarian influences are present in the Republican Party platform statement?
>
> How did geologists prepare the way for Darwin's findings?

Here's one way to respond:

> Alice, have you tried using a variety of sentence types? I see a majority of simple sentences in your work. Let's talk about this next time you come for conference.
>
> John, have you confused the two major political parties?
>
> Emily, do you mean photosynthesis in your response?
>
> Tom, how is William James significant to this era?

Again, I write not lengthy comments but formative responses and even questions that probe for new understanding, in keeping with students' learning. I write in pen, and if I make a mistake I write something like, "Let me rephrase ... " which shows students I'm also rehearsing in my low-stakes response writing. Students want teacher commentary (Straub, 1997), but they don't need long comments that they interpret as summative (Sommers, 1982), which would close what should be an ongoing conversation.

Short responding is an energy-producing activity for all, especially as you see the least motivated really trying to communicate with you on the backsides of postwrites. In an introductory course, I had a month-long dialogue with a student about how difficult it was for her to rewrite. (Of course, she was rewriting her comments in several ways!) With (her?) his name only on reverse, I had nothing to latch onto except his diagnosis. At the end of each responding session, I continued to write a narrative about classroom communication in my daybook.

These short responses also become teacher reflections, which all instructors need (Hoffman-Kipp, Artiles, and López-Torres, 2003). Yet they have an audience greater than self in that they communicate with your students. Thus, when you write a response, you not only give student writers needed feedback but also supply them with opportunities to do quick-writing, which can warm up your own writing. As you give, you also receive.

Feedback in Mini-Workshops

After the quick response secures a presence in your classroom, you can work it into a larger structure: the writing workshop. Obviously, the workshop takes a good chunk out of a class meeting time, so if you're feeling you have little space for one you can still sponsor mini-workshops to handle specific problems.

For example, ask students to bring in the first typed page of their research papers that's due later in the semester. Assign them to read their opening in small groups, four or fewer, with their groupmates performing a two-minute freewrite on what they just heard, without comment and evaluation. When all have read and written, groupmates can take turns reading what they freewrote, ordered by author. In other words, John hears all the records composed by his groupmates before moving on to another writer in the group. As Ponsot and Deen (1982) note, this procedure teaches readers to listen; it also teaches writers what readers will notice in their prose. There must be time in the classroom to hear writing and appreciate it rather than always serving as a receptacle for evaluation.

As an alternative, you can build rewriting into the workshop by requiring writers to produce three different versions of an opening paragraph. For topic proposals, you can require three different subjects, a paragraph justifying their argument for each one. Authors can then read them aloud and have their listening groupmates argue as to which is the better of the three. This task teaches alternative ways of structuring an opening, picking a thesis placement, and other essential matters. It also will give writers a compass and not a straitjacket to finish the rest of the paper. Since listeners do not have a text in front of them to consult, they concentrate on *first things* such as cadence and meaning of sentences and are steered away from *last things* such as correction and proofreading.

Anytime you have ten minutes open at the end of class, you can sponsor a mini workshop on thesis based on what you know will be problematic in a first draft. For instance, if you find broad, generalized thesis statements are the norm, ask student writers to, right now,

> Compose ONE SENTENCE that identifies ONE SIGNIFICANT THING you found in your research so far.

Write this instruction on the board or on a slide, and give students five minutes to complete it. If you need to, reread the opening postwrites before the four-minute mark when you begin walking around the classroom. When I try this strategy, I see a growing restlessness if I spend too much time completing my rounds. I ask, wherever I am in the room, for two versions of the same sentence to give a different emphasis or better word choice. I continue my walk.

"Is that thesis manageable, say, in a five-page paper?" I whisper to one.

"Is there some element in it that you find most compelling while one or two others could be used for other papers?" I ask another.

These are the teachable moments for us.

If you use this exercise in an opening postwrite, you can pass out slivers of paper and ask writers to record their thesis statements but not to put their names on them. Collect them quickly, and, while doing so, copy three of the best ones on the board or type them onto slides. Ask students to copy them into their daybooks; you can do the same. Again, especially at the beginning of the semester, eschew poor models because students will most likely imitate them since they haven't developed the critical awareness that grows from context. Then have students share with one another, in which you can arbitrarily join a team. If any need further feedback than what they received in groups, they can see you after class. But the emphasis even then must be on students expending the most effort on their work.

Workshops mean work. Even with the occasional workshop, student writers who don't get help with rewriting will quickly lose interest. For my classes, partnerships in mini workshops work better and seem more accountable; writers don't need to move their chairs, and they speak naturally with their peer partner during class anyway. If I collect the work, I ask writers to attach their work together with a folded-over corner and address any comments to both of them.

Mini-workshops work well, but I still ask that you consider a full-class workshop when a major paper shapes the course. It takes about one hour. It is time well spent, even if you offer it only once. It builds a bridge between the individual conference and the more public classroom, and once crossed it secures a uniformity of method.

Reading Out Loud

Teaching in a workshop of any size is like performing improvisational jazz: it builds on the artist's familiar tropes of good practice. That is, it employs standards you've already introduced in the classroom—daily writing, rewriting to produce various alternative sentence versions, and the like. But it also requires your sensitivity to the moment. Teaching the poignant can't be planned: it springs instead from the student writer's workshop text alone, pointing out a great sentence in a student draft that inspires and energizes. It makes grammar real for student writers. Thus, student texts alone—all texts read by their authors without their written texts in front of others—form the workshop structure that urges participants to listen intently to texts. The workshop also invites its writer to hear it, perhaps, for the first time.

This strategy is deserving of class and homework time. When students first read their writing in class and in their own voice, they approach it as nonnative speakers do, working out their language timidly and awkwardly in public. That their texts are normally read silently (if at all) in regular course work should clue us in as to why student writers find their voice strange when they read. (I encourage students to read just what's in their texts—no embellishments, voicing errors and all.) Vocalization works in rewriting, too; when I'm writing, I'll frequently write a sentence aloud and then quickly rewrite the next version that sounds better.

Over time, I discover that students who regularly vocalize their writing can produce more readable prose if they become familiar with how it sounds. Students who are voracious readers progress quickly because they are rehearsing the scripts they have picked up from their reading. Even students who listen to audiobooks will get some benefit when they need to read their own prose.

The benefits of hearing a student text read are obvious, but they are seldom realized and practiced. Students don't describe what they hear very often; they're asked to judge their peers' writing and without the training necessary to make sound judgments. They may be even required to *peer edit*, a fine workshop activity but often premature since writers are not finished with the larger issues of thesis and development, for example. The success of any evaluative practices in workshop can be built only on a strong foundation of proofs: descriptions of what they observe in a text.

When I assign a report, I prepare students for the observation work required in that genre by having them write observations (Ponsot and Deen, 1982). Bringing a Red Sox bobblehead from my office, I have students come to my front classroom desk, daybooks in hand, and make lists describing it—no observations. (You can use almost any object; sometimes I bring in a bat bag that some enterprising student has to unzip to observe what's inside. There are so many variations—e.g., a knapsack, a gym bag, a cosmetic bag, a lunch bag, a beaker, a lab coat, a twig.) When three minutes have elapsed, I lead a class discussion to ask what their individual observations are. I list their answers—*wavy brown hair, spiked shoes, wrinkled skin* (observations)—but I steer them away from *old, handsome,* or *tall* (inferences). Students don't need training to write inferences—they do so naturally—but they have a much harder time writing what they see without concluding or inferring.

But why would this skill be important in any field and in, say, a sociology class? Mastering this skill in observation, students have a much better sense of how to read one another's texts just for the value of reading so they can hear the voice of the writer emerging out of the page and into readers' heads. That skill of listening is akin to observation writing, necessary before any can profitably advise and evaluate one another's texts later. In freshman classes, I sometimes don't get students to advise and evaluate until, at best, the last weeks of the semester because consistent, repeatable observations are the groundwork that needs to be firmly set so that they can evaluate competently later. This skill is beneficial in all learning.

Working Group Workshops

Again, the ideal is that every student should read his workshop before the whole class, but usually this is not feasible in large classes. Therefore, I recommend working group workshops. I use these whenever I want the class to hear their work read, using their own voice.

To teach students to work in writing workshops and groups, I create homogeneous writing groups of four or five, except for one group that represents the most hard-working writers; I call this singular group a *model*. Within the first week of any writing assignment, I hand the class a list of how to process their drafts in a workshop:

1. One writer reads her text so that others can hear. (If we can't, we stop her and ask for a louder volume. That means only the writer is reading; everyone else is listening. Listening means pens down, eyes forward.)

2. When the writer is finished, everyone in the group writes descriptions of what they just heard: no judgments, no criticisms, no advice on what to do. I ask the whole class to do this, and I write too. Nothing is too apparent or superficial for us to record or repeat. Since everyone is freewriting these descriptions, the product will be rough. That's okay; it's genuine.

3. After this one-minute freewrite, the next writer reads.

4. One-minute descriptions follow as before.

5. After writers have read their writing aloud, each member takes a turn reading what he or she just wrote, as ordered by writer. In other words, all members read their observations of John's writing before moving to reading the next writer's observations.

6. When all are completed, the writer can ask anyone for a repeat of anything any member read.

7. All in the group now write for one minute about what they will do next in a rewrite—for example,

change the focus, switch to the first person, research the bare generality on p. 2 of his text. It can come as a result of what was just read or what springs spontaneously from your subconscious.

8. When finished, I ask everyone for responses on the group's performance.
9. All groups workshop #1–8.
10. We all rewrite: a bit in class, a bit for homework.

Reading a list and making a good workshop differ immensely, however. For that, we need modeling to prepare writers and readers in the classroom.

Preparing Writers and Readers

Here is one way to prepare students for a model workshop and for the tasks required in working groups.

On the week before the major first draft is due, ask each class member to type and print one copy of her draft for a working group that will convene next class. At the same class, prepare a model group of four, however, to stay briefly after class: four students who are hard and enthusiastic workers. Ask them if they would be willing to form a model group to work through a workshop for the entire class. Reinforce that it's better if they give you imperfect drafts to that workshop, those not completely worked out, so they can mirror the kinds of incompleteness with which the rest of the class identifies, making the rewriting task more reachable.

The rewrites we have rehearsed informally in class become an underlying structure for the workshop; we are looking for the workshop to show alternative versions of our texts. But first we need to listen and observe. The writer needs to know what others hear in her text before she can judge what could be more effective or clearer.

This preparation is all background for the next class in which you rearrange the classroom chairs so that the model group sits in positions facing one another, with a circle of the other classroom writers sitting outside their group. There are no second rows, with you seated in such a way that you can eyeball everyone in the class.

When classmates arrive, they should sit on the outside circle to see how the model group processes the workshop—that is, how they workshop each writer's text in the group. Each student reads her text, followed by groupmates who compose one-minute reactions that describe what they just heard. When all writers have read, with one-minute observations in turn after each reading, all participants read their writing, ordered by each author, so that writers can hear what participants heard. For instance, John reads, followed by all others writing observations; the remaining members Sally and Alice repeat John's lead. Next, Sally and Alice read their observations of John's reading and so forth.

If you tell all students in the class that you want them to see how this group processes a workshop, you do not need to give elaborate instructions: just ask them to describe what they hear from when other writers reading aloud. Student writers quickly come to attention to do their own additional observation: to watch the model group.

Now it's time for the modelers to take over the class. One begins reading to the rest of the group, the remainder of the class eavesdropping. When the writer finishes, the modelers freewrite for one minute without stopping about what they just heard; since you have already briefed the modelers but not the class, the latter are still in the dark as to what the modelers are doing, which keeps intrigue high. Again, try to disallow judgments and criticisms, and if the modelers fall back on those responses nonetheless deal with them later in a review of their performance. I want all group writers to center on what they heard, not on what they inferred: "The writer started with the first person," or "The beginning starts with a point about the beginning of the War of 1812." I'm not looking for great prose here. I want students to listen first so that when it's time to draw conclusions they can discern the difference between the two and thus offer observations as evidence for those judgments. I cannot emphasize this point enough.

Whenever I use modelers, I am intensely interested in producing discerning readers and writers, and that can come only through writing observations first. A colleague recently told me that she finds in teaching primary texts from other centuries that students need first to put the author's text in their language as a way for them to begin understanding meaning. Without this intermediate step, students cannot approach the text with any appreciable understanding. Writing observations performs the same translation.

True, listening of course avoids the *everything is good* (or the reverse) kinds of generic comments students make because they have no other behavior to fall back on. Observations have their own embedded critique that is far more effective when coming from students. Group members who report that the writer has "used the word *often* more than five times in the first minute" is a meaningful description that signifies something greater to its author. In a later class when writers workshop a near-final draft, it's okay to ask for printed texts, but those copies should be turned over or undistributed until the very end of the session, after all have read and all have responded in the one-minute (or perhaps longer) freewrite.

When the model workshop is finished, distribute index cards to the class members, but not to the modelers, asking the classroom students to answer two questions that you pose on the board or slide:

1. What ONE THING did the group do well?

When most have finished, I then ask for answers to a second prompt on the opposite side of the notecard:

2. What ONE THING does the group still need to work on?

The limited space on a notecard ensures tight, controlled responses. Collect the cards after five minutes and ask the class to assemble their assigned homogeneous writing groups to workshop their papers in the same way. In the meantime, ask the original group to join you in a corner of the room, with your backs all facing the wall and with a full view of the class. Read aloud through the cards, but softly to the group to see their reactions. Sometimes one member will agree or disagree vehemently with what someone wrote, but usually the group members as a whole are surprised at the class response—some discussion is always generated within this tight group and they take great energy from that experience. Finish this episode in less than ten minutes, after which you invite the model group to view the class during their individual workshops from their seats in the corner. Ask the modelers to see if they notice the same strengths and weaknesses that were just identified in their own group.

After twenty-five minutes have elapsed—groups usually finish around the same time—have the modelers write observations about what they just saw. It's best if you do the same.

When you're all finished, there's a kind of relief, as if students have just completed a marathon. When off-task chatter dominates, distribute another set of index cards to the workshop participants and ask them the same two questions in slightly modified two-part form:

1. What ONE THING did you identify in the model group as a strength? Was that also a strength in your group?
2. (On the reverse side.) What ONE THING did you identify in the model group as a weakness? Was it a weakness in your own group?

After five minutes, ask groups to reassemble in a circle that dissolves the writing groups into a larger identity for a whole-class discussion. Review their self-evaluation notecards that identify strengths and weaknesses. If you have time, record them on the board or ask a few class members to record them in their notebooks. If you have a class rule that requires students to copy everything that appears on the board, they are already copying them in their daybooks.

After some discussion, ask all to compose a five-minute freewrite that self-evaluates: what they learned that day about workshops. When they are finished, call on individual class members by name, since they already rehearsed, in writing, several general questions, as in, "John, what did you write about workshops today?" This pattern of writing and response, within the context of reflective learning, reinforces the writing as the means to improvement.

Before dismissing the class, remind writers that the workshop provides a structure to review and rewrite. It is that structure that guides them into making choices.

By the next class, tell writers your goal is to rewrite based on their previous workshop, incorporating all the strengths and avoiding the weakness we identified. Repeat the same scenario with the model workshop group: through the index cards, the secluded model group consultation, the simultaneous group workshops, and the final discussion evaluation.

Next, ask the whole class what has changed in terms of the workshop from last class—for example, attitudes, efficiency, quality of observations. Record these responses on a slide or the blackboard, asking if any new disagreements or topics about writing appeared. Discussion ensues, after which we work on incorporating those qualities in our own drafts. (I bring some uncompleted piece of writing I'm working on or just started so I can practice, too.)

What is important now is to model some of this advice on the projector and report, "Now turn to your own drafts—perhaps one you believe is near finished—to see if you can strengthen it anywhere with these techniques. I'll be around in a few minutes to check with you."

If you allot time for another workshop, you can speed up the process, enlisting your modelers again by assigning each member a separate group to join. When you reassemble as a class, you can ask for a report to the whole class on strengths and weaknesses in the writing and what the workshop needs to still work on.

A Structure for Learning Rewriting

A difficult way to teach course content through writing is by showing professional models and ordering students to write like them. They cannot do the deduction alone. Instead, give them the gifts of the postwrite and the workshop, together with the responses they need, to initiate rewriting.

They don't need to hear exactly what's wrong and how to fix it; writing's not like that. They need to hear what you and a classroom of writers see in their writing; they need to figure out how to make even better choices in their later rewriting. At the beginning, students may struggle before they see benefits so you have to capitalize on peer incentives. As one student told me, "I thought rewriting was a pain until I realized we all have to do it." By the end of the course, however, the same student devoted a whole section of his portfolio to show how he rewrote a history paper.

When students compose descriptions and postwrites, they take steps to becoming reflective learners and better rewriters. When you, in turn, reflect on their learning in your feedback, you are tapping into a low-stakes writing opportunity that can get you back into writing language, a practice all writers need.

Giving Feedback During Short Conferences

With two ingredients, you open communication with your students: the syllabus and first-day events. Your communication simmers during postwrites, your responses to those, and the daily writing. It all comes to boil with checksheets for the bite-sized assignments that turn into your major writing assignments. Then you simmer and stir with workshops.

So how do you test for doneness? How do you communicate to student writers the quality product you expect them to concoct? Simply by giving student writers an overview of the mixture: through sampling feedback you provide in the short writing conference.

Writing Conference and Workload

Of course, when faculty hear of writing conferences, they envision long lines of disgruntled students checking their phones and chatting while they impatiently wait for their professor to be free. "I simply don't have time for conferences!" my colleagues echo in their defense. I have great sympathy for overworked faculty who work diligently on their teaching and can't see how conferences can help them.

When I speak of mandatory conferences, however, they can't imagine anything other than that harrowed vision. One terrific young faculty member, someone who has earned several teaching awards, spends an average of thirty minutes with each student in a draft conference four times per semester.

"Do you grade their papers at your conferences?" I asked.

"No. They're just drafts. They are still working on them."

"Do you ever cancel a class to hold conferences?"

"Never," he vowed.

"Why *so long* a conference with each student?"

"They have so much that needs fixing!"

I paused. "Aren't student writers overwhelmed with all your attention and your 'fixing'?"

It was his turn to pause. "I guess so . . . . "

I could see from his expression that he was also overwhelmed. The long conference tempts professors to take over tasks they've given students to do. Like my colleague, they feel somehow if they don't address every fault and error they aren't doing their job. It's hard to control one's hands when you have unfinished papers for too long a time; the brain starts editing others' writing and stops teaching others. By electing long conferences, professors take ownership of student papers. With professors correcting every fault and error, the student now becomes the transcriber, copying what the master scrivener has laid out. Isn't that the wrong path if we want students to become better learners and writers?

In conferencing, our goal is to offer options, to give a nudge and not a shove to our fellow writers. We are aware of the conflicting roles as teaching professors (Belanger, 1985; Meikle, 1982), but those don't need to enter into conferencing if we acknowledge that students own their own texts. We can be both teacher and writer as we work with other students to improve their higher-level concerns, working to establish a good focus and develop content that converses with an audience. We can't adequately address lower-level concerns, like conventions, until student writers take care of more global matters like thesis and development. We cannot lose sight of students as fellow writers, especially in conferences, or else students will interpret such marathon conferences as sessions to fix what's broken in their writing.

The short conference, like the brief assignment, is a remedy. It ensures there won't be time to delve into minutiae and micromanage drafts. In short conferencing, you take those unproductive hours spent appropriating another's text and shorten them into productive minutes with the learning writer. Here you use language—written and oral—to get the conversation started about their drafts and to finish with one thing they can accomplish on their own.

The Necessity of the Short Conference

Short conferences form a backbone that sustains writers in your classroom and furnish them the support to grow. Unlike middle and high schools where teachers, because of imposed high-stakes testing, have just enough time to give a two- or three-word flourish to a graded response, we at least have the conferencing format available to us. We can also use it not only as a feedback strategy but as a setting for two writers to converse about writing in your discipline. I would further argue that short conferences are necessary because they are singularly effective in bringing about better writing and better teaching through writing. Short conferences open communication between writers and you, extending your pedagogy to individual needs.

True, so much of the writing problem can be addressed in the classroom. Are students handing in unprepared work? Schedule deadlines for multiple drafts and use checksheets to guide their composing. Disheartened with unprepared students who expect you to do all the work? Segment the long assignment into manageable, brief ones that add up to a long assignment. Not sure students can rewrite? Practice in class through mini-workshops and postwrites.

But how do students appropriate what finishing work is yet needed for their written project? Conferences furnish the spontaneous, opening the best give-and-take venue; it's also a place for immediate dialogue that's unavailable through terminal and marginal comments. By loading as much preparatory work into the classroom as you can, you can open short conferences to formative feedback that can be handled only personally between writers: instructor and student.

Preparing Students for the Conference

The key to making short conferences manageable is to prepare students in class beforehand for the focused work that you design exclusively in conferences. For example, Table 8.1 shows a sample outline again for a sixteen-week semester course with one extended research paper, together with process markers.

During week 2 in a conference-based system, you can ask students to type three possible topics for a researched paper, each a paragraph long, that identifies what they hope to find out by writing this paper. You can even ask student writers to pose a research question, one that starts with *how* or *what* to avoid superficial *yes/no* answers later on. When you review these quickly, in the same manner as you do with postwrites, you can pick the strongest of the three if one contender emerges. In a subsequent class, you can even show strong topic selections to students on the projector by scanning the originals. That way, students can see models, not to copy but to identify so they can resubmit a better topic idea. Again, you are using comparison as a way to improve their initial submission.

Students then have until week 4 to get a suitable topic to you. If you require an annotated bibliography first, you can ask students to do that immediately after topic approval.

Table 8.1.   Sample Outline for Sixteen-Week Semester

1		9	
2	topic idea	10	second draft
3		11	
4	topic decision	12	
5		13	
6		14	final draft
7	first draft/conferences	15	
8		16	

At week 7, you can require students to bring a first draft to a fifteen-minute conference. You want them to get something substantive down on paper rather than having all the problems worked out, which would compromise the effectiveness of any feedback you give them. In fact, they won't know many of the problems confronting them in their topic until they commit to a first draft. I typically have students in a Tuesday/Thursday class submit the first draft electronically to a service like turnitin.com by 11:59 P.M. on Tuesday night so that everyone's paper is due at the same time. Students can then schedule one conference on Wednesday, Thursday, or Friday; I can cancel my Thursday class if I'm crunched for available times. That one conference, students tell me, made a huge difference in their vision of the paper, so I don't hesitate to cancel one class in the service of delivering better pedagogy.

To steer the draft they bring me to *first things first*, I compose a checksheet.

Exhibit 8.1 First-Draft Checksheet

My assignment is to compose a first version of my argument that asks readers in my class to consider my debatable point on an issue. In writing my draft, I concentrated on completing higher-order concerns before working toward lower-level concerns. My deadline is the BEGINNING of my conference — Thursday, September 12, 2013 or Friday, September 13, 2013.

- ❏ I offer my draft to you now, not as "finished" or even complete, but as a work-in-progress that may turn into something completely other than I originally intended in a future draft.

- ❏ I met the deadline.

- ❏ I wrote, as Don Murray says, with "velocity[,] ... outracing the censor" that tells me that I can't do it.

- ❏ I include this checksheet with my draft; if I forgot it, I am still accountable for all the assigned tasks.

- ❏ I previously submitted at least two topic idea paragraphs; I'm using one of them.

- ❏ I worked at least four hours outside of class on writing this draft.

1. Focus & Purpose for Writing

- ❏ I understand the purpose of the genre in which I'm writing.

- ❏ My discourse exercise results from the in-class Invention activity and represents a modern interpretation of ARGUMENT, one common to the progymnasmata.

- ❏ I wrote my first draft discourse as a "discovery draft" (Murray), a "zero draft" (Zeigler), a "shitty first draft" (Lamott).

- ❏ I tried to write an arguable proposition as a thesis; I wrote at least three and highlighted them in my draft.

2. Development for an Audience

- ❑ I worked hard to explore a subject with which I have some experience rather than state what is obvious and broad and unmanageable.

- ❑ The writer and audience have a stake in the judgment of this discourse.

- ❑ I told at least one story.

- ❑ I made few inferences.

- ❑ I tried to write a compelling title.

- ❑ I used at least one common topic and one special topic.

3. Organization/Structure

- ❑ I tried to use classical Arrangement to organize my discourse — Introduction, Statement of Fact, Confirmation, Refutation, Conclusion — much like Boethius recommends.

- ❑ I identify with the audience's values, beliefs, or expectations (ethos) in some way in my introduction.

4. Language & Sentence Structure

- ❑ The level of style I attempted is low, middle, or grand (circle one).

- ❑ I wrote three versions of my closing sentence, as we learned to do in class with the aphorism.

5. Conventions

- ❑ I keyboarded the draft; I included a title, my name, and page numbers for all pages.

- ❑ I kept the margins at about one inch.

❑ I tried to make this draft between 1500-2000 words.

❑ I made two copies, stapled them into two packets, and brought both to the conference.

I would encourage you to make first-draft conferences mandatory because it's at a place where you can deliver the most help to the most people at the most critical time. You can judge whether others fulfill that same criteria, such as when students first envision (inventing) the paper, when they revise or rewrite (second draft), and when they *near finish* so you can edit one paragraph with them (revised or rewritten third draft). Most of us cannot schedule conferences for all, but in one drafting cycle for a content course I like to sponsor one for the first draft. Of course, I offer follow-up optional conferences during office hours, and I do attract a few students who want to do well.

On the Tuesday of week 10, I hold a brief workshop in class on the second draft, prompted by another checksheet. I'll have students bring in two copies—one for them to workshop, one for me to see what work they performed—and we'll work on openings or conclusions and maybe devote some quiet time in class for rewriting. The second draft is their ticket to the workshop: no ticket, no admittance. I'll craft the checksheet to reflect those concerns and give full credit only if all items are completed. This gateway prepares students for the second draft, where I expect a more refined expression and a far better opening than I saw for the first draft.

Exhibit 8.2 Second-Draft Checksheet

My assignment is to compose a second version of my argument that asks readers in my class to consider my debatable point on an issue. In writing my draft, I concentrated on completing higher-order concerns before working toward lower-level concerns. My deadline is the BEGINNING of my class — Thursday, November 7, 2013.

- ❏ I offer my draft to you now, not as "finished" or even complete, but as a work-in-progress that may turn into something completely other than I originally intended in a future draft.

- ❏ I met the deadline.

- ❏ I include this checksheet with my draft; if I forgot it, I am still accountable for all the assigned tasks.

- ❏ I previously submitted at a first draft.

- ❏ I worked at least four hours outside of class on rewriting this draft.

1. Focus & Purpose for Writing

- ❏ I understand the purpose of the genre in which I'm writing.

- ❏ I wrote an arguable proposition as a thesis; I wrote at least three and highlighted them in my draft.

- ❏ I attempt to reach stasis with my opponent(s)/audience.

- ❏ I made my thesis an enthymeme.

2. Development for an Audience

- ❏ I worked hard to explore a subject with which I have some experience rather than state what is obvious and broad and unmanageable.

❑ The writer and audience have a stake in the judgment of this discourse.

❑ I told at least one story.

❑ I made few inferences.

❑ I tried to write a compelling title.

❑ I used at least one common topic and one special topic.

3. Organization/Structure

❑ I used classical Arrangement to organize my discourse — Introduction, Statement of Fact, Confirmation, Refutation, Conclusion — much like Boethius recommends.

❑ I identified with the audience's values, beliefs, or expectations (ethos) in some way in my introduction.

4. Language & Sentence Structure

❑ The level of style I used is low, middle, or grand (circle one).

❑ I tried to use one governing point of view and one verb tense.

❑ I tried to employ one periodic sentence and noted so in the margin next to it.

5. Conventions

❑ I proofread for any fallacies of form or matter in my draft, particularly the "either/or" fallacy; I alone carry the "burden of proof" (Textbook 63).

❑ I keyboarded the draft; I included a title, my name, and page numbers for all pages.

❑ I kept the margins at about one inch.

❑ I tried to make this draft between 1000-1500 words.

❑ I made two copies, stapled them into two packets, and brought
both to the conference.

So here is what I expect when I see students in the second-draft class:

- Checksheet

- Two copies of their second draft, typed

By the time they leave the class:

- *Momentum*, as Alan Ziegler (2007) calls it: one major task they will accomplish first in rewriting or revising

- A working thesis

- A clearer idea of how one reader (you) will read their paper

During the quiet time of composing in class, you can quickly scan the papers to see any trending (major) problems that you need to address in class. This stack you never return; they comprise an archive that evidences *working really, really hard*, which I discuss in Chapter 10. I know my attendance record for that day cofirms who submitted a second draft. I simply note any who fall far short of what I asked them to try, as defined in the checksheet.

How to Do Scheduling

In a conferencing system, student writers must know from the first week that the only way they will receive individual feedback is through a short conference. By contrast, classroom feedback is frequent and corporate: a word of encouragement, a smile, praise when a great line is read, the occasional workshop. Conferencing offers the most intense, the most personal, and the greatest way to offer help for the developing writer.

In planning for the conference, students do the most work and you the least. Remember, it is your goal that they learn how to ask questions and figure things out; you offer assistance but not surrogacy. You are a resource but not the writer or their editor. It is always useful to remind students of what hat you wear in the conference—a coach sometimes; a confidant at other times; a fellow writer all the time. As a result, you will tell them neither exactly what to do nor one way they must do it.

I suggest scheduling conferences in fifteen-minute blocks, one block to a writer. For instance, with three sections of twenty-five students each, I can schedule three days of conferences at the end of one week—Wednesday, Thursday, and Friday. As stated earlier, I require the draft to be submitted electronically by 11:59 P.M. Tuesday so that the deadline is the same for all students. If I cancel Thursday's class, I occupy that time with conference slots; if I hold Thursday's class, I make it a brief workshop that focuses on one or two higher-order concerns, like research or unity in a paper. With conferencing, it is true you will have a lot of contact hours. But it is also true that time marches quickly on those conference days; when I reflect in my daybook after a day of conferencing, I am amazed at how much we accomplished together. Since conferences mean no class preparation, I can devote myself to the conference with a clear head, scanning the student paper as its writer arrives. I do not get sidetracked with trivial issues at the conference; there isn't time. And I never take papers home.

With fifteen-minute slots, I also schedule at least fifteen minutes off every two hours plus thirty minutes for lunch and a brief walk. I hold just a few slots back in case I need to accommodate someone at the last minute.

You want to streamline the mechanics of scheduling conferences as much as possible. If you bring a paper conference sign-up sheet to class to distribute, recognize that students will double-book over their chemistry class or forget they were going home early on the weekend. Plus, some students just forget to show up.

I've found that a far better scheduling method removes your direct involvement. Electronic booking sites like youcanbook.me and doodle.com offer free appointment services too that are built on electronic calendars you may already be using. Students can sign up, cancel, rebook, and be reminded of their conference appointments without you serving as ombudsman. These sites send them reminders, too. I love the sheer simplicity of conference days when I open my smartphone to see my conference schedule of the day and without my middle-managing the enterprise.

I love conferences days. I arrive at my office early and spend a minimum of ten minutes freewriting before my first conference participant of the day arrives. The focus of my freewrite always gravitates to what I want to reinforce at the conference. But then I stop. This freewrite inevitably turns back on me. It calmly reminds me—through writing—to listen first at each writing conference and to let my ear guide my speaking.

"I Don't Have the Time for Individual Conferences!"

Perhaps you're saying, "I get your point about individual conferences. There's no way with my schedule that I can see students individually. What about group conferences?"

Group conferences are much like workshops, and you can import ideas from that venue. There are differences, of course, because you have a definite role. With groups, you can't schedule short conferences though you can still use youcanbook.me or doodle.com to set up thirty-minute slots where no more than four can sign up at any one time. When students arrive, you can seat four students in a small working group, with you forming the fifth. You have several options with the itinerary. If students have trouble with openings, for example, have all students read their opening and compose observations. Then you can infer from their observations the kinds of work that rewriting can center. Reserve at least five minutes for doing rewriting in the conference.

Another option is to have students make two copies. You can have a postwrite ready that asks them to comment on their writing process and one thing they need help with. While they are postwriting, you are scanning their drafts. When everyone is finished, you can ask students to report on their progress briefly—one minute—and then you can comment after each with some general comments when all have reported. At the end, have all students freewrite on one thing they will change in the next draft. You can freewrite during that final time on the inferences you made in the conference.

In still another option, you can have students freewrite on questions they would like answered or problems they're having. Then have each read them in turn and answer them. Then spend time rewriting, using you as a resource until fifteen minutes are up.

Group conferencing is a compromise, of course, and functions more like a mini-workshop. But sometimes there are few good choices available and the group conference is the best option. At least in the group conference students will receive more direct feedback, far better than the boilerplate responses they are accustomed to receiving when they complete the final draft, the kind that never find their way into students' composing processes.

But if humanly possible, make space for an individual short conference at least once in the semester.

How to Arrange Your Office for Conferences

The real work in conferencing is twofold: to review quickly and fairly the student writer's work, which he has just brought to you or posted online, and to solicit student response to that work.

If possible, meet your writers in your office. It offers a place away from the classroom that you can conference without distraction. Consider this environment for group conferences too. If you have a single-occupant office, so much the better.

After much trial and error, I have found an arrangement that works for me because it allows for greater collaboration. I have students sitting beside me, sharing a desk or two desks facing in the same direction along a wall. Since no desk separates us, I find it to be an easier environment to convince student writers that we're both writers sharing work. Since two copies of a text are always available—either two physical copies that the student brings or electronic versions—there's never a reason to share the same text. They can take notes on their draft independent of mine or do so electronically, as some do, using an iPad. No matter the media, students and I have our own copies. If I use groups, I can bring some movable desks in from the hallway or use clipboards to make a tight circle.

When we're doing close editing during individual conferences, I show students ways to edit, using proofreading marks the way an editor would proceed. But as a teacher I must do more, reading their text aloud so they can hear my misreading, stumbles, and joys in my inflected voice. They can transcribe token corrections onto their copy as I solicit suggestions from them, which I also record. *I can show them exactly how one reader reads their writing.* They take notes more often on ideas that suddenly occur to them rather than transcribe anything specifically that I say.

If I have a conference to flesh out ideas for a paper, I have the option of facing the student directly so we can converse. For example, I have a rectangular office with a long desk that stretches from one wall to the doorway on the long side. Perpendicular to that I have a comfy chair for students with a movable writing desk alongside. I give them a clipboard, too, if they prefer to write using that. It may seem puerile, but it's really helpful to have a wall clock located directly behind the student chair; it's critical to keep my commitment to fifteen minutes.

Physical space is important to conferencing. However you configure yours, make sure it is conducive to the kind of work you want to accomplish there.

Conference Routine for First Drafts

The first-draft conference is a great way to get started in conferencing for the first time. Let me show you one way you can do it that is easily adaptable to your needs.

When students arrive for the first time at conference, I want to welcome them, show them their seat, and ask them to complete a postwrite after they hand me their draft and completed checksheet. (If the checksheet is not completed, I patiently wait and do nothing until they check the items. No matter how unprepared they are, we will still finish in fifteen minutes.)

At the beginning of the semester, I prepare working folders that contain all the work students bring to me in conference. Along the tab is a printout of the student's name and section, the printed output from my electronic gradebook. When students arrive, I have their file folder ready, arranged in chronological order of the day. I also have a log sheet that I've placed in their folder on the first day of class; it is laser-printed on cardboard stock. This log collects my notes for each conference—appointed or drop-in—and guides my response. If you prefer, use an electronic or online gradebook that permits direct or shortcut text entry. But I don't get hung up on recordkeeping. I'm here more for the writer. Recently, I only use my daybook, a one-minute-or-less freewrite with the student at the end of the conference. I've also begun using electronic filing for the working folders, either through turnitin.com or Evernote scanning, which lessens the paper load tremendously.

In a fifteen-minute first-draft conference, I quickly rediscover that I have to concentrate on the highest-order things first. There simply isn't time to sort through lower-level processes, like comma placement, that often are addressed or discarded when the student reworks the draft anyway. So time management becomes a friendly reminder to address global concerns and not final matters like editing. Similarly, even though students submit drafts electronically ahead of their conference time, I don't look at them ahead of time so I don't slice and dice them and foil the whole conference exchange. Again, I find myself looking forward to these times, learning from my writers what they have been thinking. There's a kind of urgency in the conferencing office: friendly but on task. There's also a comfort in reading drafts in consort with their writers, something I was never able to gain when I took working drafts home.

The postwrite during the conference becomes an interactive experience for us both. While I'm reading the draft, students are reflecting on her learning, prompted by one or two questions on the postwrite that they answer. What a splendid time it is, too, working toward the same goal. At the beginning, I keep the questions open, just like during the in-class postwrites:

What questions do you have upon submitting this draft?

Student writers typically list their frustrations, problems, and even roundabout questions that are difficult to articulate orally. But once they are given a chance to write about them, they pour it on. Usually, I finish reading before they finish writing, so I go back and review the work quickly on a second pass and may even jot a few notes. But I stop as soon as they are finished.

I ask for the postwrite, which I can read in about ten seconds. For specific questions, I repeat them aloud for both of us and do my best to answer them in ways that leave work for them to do. For instance, if a student is unsure of her thesis and lists it on the postwrite, I ask where the thesis is in the paper and how she arrived at it. I may ask if she can tell me what qualities belong in a thesis. I ask questions that require more than yes–no responses. As time goes on, I want to encourage thoughtful question-posing and self-reflection as precursors to any feedback I might give. I find it advantageous to focus on matters the student knows are problematic rather than on areas she knows already require rewriting.

Conference Patterns

The weakest writers won't ask specific questions, of course, and want me to tell them if the draft is any good. I resist such a definitive role since in most composing projects they won't have such an evaluation. Besides, the composing process is not finished.

Instead, I ask them a question. "If composing occurs in stages, at what stage would you characterize the present state of your writing piece?"

"It's pretty early, pretty rough," replies one student.

"Ever been to the hospital or seen a hospital drama on TV? The nurses always want you to assign your pain a number on a scale of 1 to 10. Suppose I invent another number scale, say, 0–10, that identifies the degree of finalness, not pain. Is your draft what Alan Ziegler calls a zero draft—a get-it-all-down draft—or a 5-level draft, since you said it's still pretty rough?" (And yes, I really do cite sources during conferences!)

The response can often explain much about how writers see their task. In introductory courses, I often list common responses for drafts with brief adjectives—rough draft, minimal draft, careful draft, risky draft, zero draft—as they proceed up the scale. (I think risk is a sign of writerly growth.)

"A 2," Susansays, who reveals in her answer that the draft is not ready to be graded. "So what about my ending?"

"What about it?" I ask.

"Well, I finished it early this morning, and I don't think it sounds like it belongs in the paper."

"I agree. What can you do about it?"

"Cut it?"

"Yes. Tell you what: if you give me three versions of that ending paragraph, I can point out the better of the three for me as a reader."

"That's great," Susan says. "When should we do it?"

"At our next conference. Or come to my open office hour, and I'll be glad to talk to you about them. Just make two copies, so I have one for my files. Now, let's freewrite for one minute on what we both discussed in this conference." I play timekeeper, read mine to her, and she reads hers to me. We part.

I leave the responsibility with the writer, who may find something more pressing when she gets into her rewriting later and thus delays the conclusion rewrite. That's okay, as long as they are about the process and business of writing.

If you develop a conference routine and sponsor several, you'll see patterns develop. Tiffany from my advanced rhetoric class, for example, always appears in the doorway timidly, just as she does for every appointment. "Hi," she says, and walks straight in and sits across from me. "I'm really having trouble coming to focus," she says, not demonstrating that deficiency in her address to me.

"Okay, let's write about focus first."

She and I push away the postwrite, and we both freewrite for one minute on focus because she always has an agenda—no postwriting needed to get us on task—and I'm more than happy to accommodate.

I reach for the folder, record the date, and read her first draft. She laughs less nervously. I really am thinking about what she wants from this conference, and I admire her new openness about writing.

"What is it you're trying to say?" I ask.

"I'm not sure. I think I'm saying a lot of things."

"Okay, what are the various things you are saying?"

"Well, one is about the wilderness and the need for solitude and ... "

"So you know at least one subject. Now that you've written this essay, what are you trying to say about one of those subjects?"

She thinks for a while as I read the essay quickly. After a few minutes of healthy silence, I say, "What about this description on p. 5? You spend a lot of time developing this image. Do you think this may help focus the essay at all?"

Her face shines. "I just noticed that, too," she says, and she begins describing how she can better lead up to the insight captured there. Soon time is up.

"So, what will you do next with this draft?" I inquire, already anticipating the answer, but I want her to articulate her commitment.

"I'm going to move the description on p. 5 to the introduction and break the structure for the reader. I want to return to this image at the end."

"Will you try rewriting the intro and conclusion first before recasting the body of the paper?"

"That's a great idea!" she exclaims. Another student appears at my doorway. "I'll see you in class Tuesday," she states emphatically and she picks up her backpack and leaves hurriedly.

The next week, I ask Alice in class how her focusing work is coming. She smiles.

Of course, not every conference is productive. Sometimes it takes months (years?) for student writers to get over their blocked and hypercorrective habits in writing, ones learned after their life-time of schooling. I know I had the same problem.

I know, too, that such is the case with Mark, who always knocks on my door and takes a seat on the couch without looking me in the eye. "How are you doing?" I ask as I retrieve his folder from my desk.

"Okay, tired," he snarls beneath the rim of his baseball cap. He still won't look at me. He seems to arrive at every conference intending to do battle from bedside.

I remain silent.

He looks up before speaking: "I had a lot of trouble with this paper."

"May I read it?" I ask.

He hands one copy and checksheet to me while he works on the postwrite.

"What kind of trouble?" I ask after reading his draft, which is just three pages.

"Getting started," he states and hands me his postwrite. I see that it's hurriedly completed and the only question he lists is about how to get started.

"So how did you get started? You obviously were able to finish it," I say, trying to sound satisfied.

"It's no good."

"Why? You were able to finish though."

"Yeah."

"So how did you accomplish the finishing?"

"I sat down at my computer after our last class and just stared at the computer screen for a couple of hours, trying to get a beginning."

"So what you're telling me is that you did find a way to begin, just not a very productive one. Are you asking me for a better way for you to get started?"

"Yeah, I guess, because I'm always staring at the computer screen."

I take some notes on what he has told me. "Well, I can give you some options. Suppose I list a few and you try one or two and report back to me next time on how it worked."

"Okay," he says, only now opening his daybook.

I give him options, the most obvious first: "Try turning off or blackening the computer screen. In that way, you can't go back because you can't see what you're writing."

I next describe how he could start at any point in drafting where the image in his mind is the most clear—any part that seems the most defined and then work back and forward as his vision of the paper clarifies. Alternately, he could try writing in his daybook instead of the computer to cure the blank paper syndrome that seemed to plague his writing time. Or I suggest he might try standing to write. I tell him about the bandshell at the city park where I have freewritten, a place just a block from campus. I then talk about varying his routine or time of day for writing. In short, I give him options.

I then look at his draft. It's a mess, all over the place looking for meaning. "This looks like freewriting."

"Yeah, I spent almost the whole time trying to get started on this abstract."

"Is there any part that you really want to emphasize?"

"Yes," he says and points to the third page and last paragraph. Even though this passage appears at the end, it is not a conclusion but a claim without evidence.

"Suppose you use this sentence." I circle my copy. He looks at it, too, and circles his copy. "Then try moving front and back from that point in your writing. We don't know yet if it's in the exact middle, halfway in the middle, or at the end. It will take some revising to tell that, but start with anything but the blank screen again." I pause. "What will you do next with the paper?"

He repeats methodically about starting with the one sentence, almost not believing it will work. Then I ask him what strategy he will try and, if that doesn't work, what backup one he'll use for getting started on the revision.

Now he is forced to pick one. "The park," he says, and I record it. When we're all finished, I reserve the last minute for the student and I to freewrite on the conference, summarizing or stressing what the writer will do. We read to each other and depart.

I'll check how that worked out next time. Did I spot a faint smile?

Conferences always intrigue me in the way they seek the heart of the matter, a surgery unachievable in the classroom alone. Although conferences are labor intensive, they are fun as you create a community of writers who come to you with all their varied inexperience and hang-ups with coursework, life, and writing. Conferences have a way of generating good feedback from students on what works for them in the course. At the end of the semester, I always receive comments from students in my class evaluations that show they enjoy them—"The conferences were helpful" so much so that "they should probably be longer."

Supporting Student Writers

Carolyn See (2003) recommends that writers *hang out* with people who support their work. When I offer support, I want to underscore it and write only in big caps: I'M FROM YOUR FAMILY

AND I'M HERE TO HELP YOU. When I see students arrive in conferences who only want a better grade, I stop them and offer supportive options.

When I first started holding the short conference, I found that students misinterpreted those options, but I didn't find out about the misinterpretations until I received the evaluations after the course had ended. For instance, one student reported that "Hafer is not as smart as he thinks he is in conferences," followed by another student saying I was "too critical." Or sometimes I receive ones like this: "The conferences were helpful, but I did not feel he got me on track with writing—he just told me what I was doing wrong." Others stated the opposite: I'm not directive enough.

All these indicators told me I need to emphasize options I'm giving writers—I'm giving reader feedback—and not knowledge, commandment, or legislation. Questions can clarify much. For example, I ask, "What problems in organization did you have and how have you resolved them?" instead of declarative statements like "I see some problems in organization here." Or I can let the questions in the postwrite do all the work.

Yet I don't always succeed. I recognize that when I think I am doing otherwise, and purposely plan such, my plans may be overshadowed by students' negative experiences with the writing problem. Not only can I not resolve them all, but I also may never find out these pockets of resistance until my teacher evaluations arrive. Sometimes students' past experiences with writing cannot be overcome in one semester or even a longer period of time without constant injections of writing successes. That said, writing does not often work with predictable successes; sometimes writers learn more from failure than success. Hardened, beginning writers sometimes cannot comprehend the reality that will make their writing stronger. There is a positive pedagogy available in writing failure.

I try to let writers do most of the speaking in conferences because I want the focus on their writing. I know I'm in danger of violating my own principles when I leave my conferencing day and find my voice is sore. That tickle in the throat alerts me that I'm talking too much, that I haven't let student writers talk enough. It's a bit like therapy sessions: if I'm doing all the talking, I'm being directive and consequently unreceptive to writers' need to monologue.

Incorporate your own style and manner of opening up to students in conferences—asides, anecdotes, references to class. Whatever approach you choose, you do best if you keep your comments short and unified, their success measured in the eagerness they instill in student writers to discuss their craft. Even though checksheets help keep you on task, conferences are where you and students finalize what their next task must be. This isn't your glowing opportunity to teach apostrophes—that's best for a different venue, and only if needed. Instead, conference times solicit individual problems of the student writer seated here right now in your office and develop options for her to choose. The goal is to get them working on at least one thing after leaving your office.

What about the students who don't want help? Tell them that the writing enterprise is based on soliciting help and feedback from those around them, including you as mentor and coach. That's what writers do.

Alternatives to Conferencing

I'm frequently asked, "Isn't there a better way? I get the short conference idea, but I like to write comments."

"Great, " I say. "So do I. I write comments on the student papers that they give me during conferences or in a digital notebook. But I keep those in my own file; students write comments on their own."

I don't know about you, but I need to restrain my editorial mode when student writers need to learn how to correct, to cite correctly, to model the kind of public language features. After all, that is one hope I have for them in taking this course. In a traditional classroom collection and return of papers, that comment workflow cannot be realized.

A new psychology professor lamented that her return of student research papers were greeted by students disowning them, a flippant flopping of their papers into the trash can on the way out of class. She was horrified, having spent days correcting usage and pointing out flaws in logic and format. Didn't they know how hard she worked? On top of all that, she had done an excellent job of documenting the grade. She then reported to our workshop that such an experience made her reconsider her grading and response strategy. It was a justifiable reaction: she was motivated to change her grading ritual so she could survive.

She had the wrong personnel involved in the right activity. It can come about so easily. All the comments she had written and all the corrections she made were valuable contributions that ought to be made, but by student writers and not by the professor. In this situation, it was the professor who learned the most, spending days laboring intensely over a paper, writing helpful comments, consulting reference works, and becoming an accomplished stylist. She was entirely successful, too, successful in wrestling control away from students to the extent that they no longer could acknowledge the work as their own. She had gifted their papers back to them, but they no longer cared. Such cold grading assured student writers that they could walk out of the classroom *without* their papers.

Instead, you need to keep the fire hot for your writers, or they will end up missing from action. The best way I know to keep the fire roaring is through short conferencing.

9

The Finals: Portfolio and Conference

It's an achievement to rethink your course, especially when writing takes on an instrumental role for learning course content. As we all know, given academic constraints and even our best intentions, it isn't always possible to implement fully the strategies and activities I advocate in these pages. Certainly I wouldn't advise any faculty revise a course wholesale and relaunch a new program overnight; like students, we all need time to learn new strategies and to deal with new obstacles. As teaching professors, we also need time to make a particular pedagogy our own, especially when we are teaching others our content specialty. We must also preserve the instinct that protects us from overwork whenever a new perspective on teaching alters our course obligations. I have always tried to keep workload uppermost in my advocacy for this approach; a method cannot be better if it burns its champion!

Just positioning a course to receive writing as a way of learning, however, is a cause for rejoicing. It means you are seeking a more integrative role for writing in what you teach. It all begins with rewriting the question all faculty face, "How will I teach this content?" with the recast "*How* can I use writing to teach this content?" Adopting just a few connected activities signals you've made a change in your thinking, one situating writing as less a subject the English department teaches than about the best way to reach your students with your subject. You can feel good about that.

Throughout this book, I've given you the bellwether, the ideal, for a course that responds to a writer's sensibility with the kinds of activities and strategies that can bring about greater learning. All along I would be doing you a disservice if I had not given you something for which to strive. This chapter is no exception. It may prove the most challenging to implement because it summarizes where a semester of using writing for learning can lead. The finals I present here represent capstones for a long process that emphasizes *how* to learn throughout a semester but presents *what* was learned at its end. Nevertheless, the finals are natural and necessary outcomes for the approach I've espoused throughout this book.

As you import some of these writing activities from previous chapters into your course, you may interpret the final portfolio and its associated conference as idealistic rather than the ideal. I want to reassure you that these two finals are available for you. I have used these capstone tools for over twenty years, and I continue to refine them as dynamic instruments to offer more complete assessments. I believe you will discover that the final portfolio and conference show the merits of postponing the grading of student writing until it is ready: at its natural deadline, the end of the semester.

The finals also have bearing on your own writing life, particularly with portfolios. They are increasingly required to demonstrate professional credentials and to document performance to colleagues, administrators, accrediting agencies, and public media. Mere listings providing in curriculum vitae will no longer suffice. Increasing demands for deeper student learning must be met with better documentation of faculty credentials that go beyond the traditional tropes, such as reflective essays on teaching philosophy, technique, and learning. Portfolios pull these artifacts together to show diverse readers what faculty teach, much in the same way portfolios bear witness to what students learned in a course. The final conference is not unlike the informal writing process colleagues use in showing the first draft of a scholarly article to a colleague, receiving that feedback, and revising or rewriting to better the writing before submitting it for final review.

In like manner, these two finals serve as a testimony to what students and you have learned and are still learning. Now that the semester has concluded, students are the most prepared they will ever be in your course for a summative evaluation. The final portfolio and the supporting final conference are its measures.

The Finals Defined

The final portfolio and conference are agendas to receive writing that most closely resembles what writers experience. It is similar to the situation in which professors compose portfolios for teaching, promotion, and job interviews: a testament to colleagues as to what they have gained and discovered through the product itself and by reflecting on that product. Although many types of student portfolios document learning, I'm arguing a special place for students to prepare a product portfolio—one that showcases final, better versions as a result of a reflective process—that they can present to the professor on the last week of class. It is also the depository for the one and only grade for writing in the course.

Remember, the freewriting, drafting, and postwriting in a course comprise its formative measures. But at the end of the course, what have students done with those assessments? Have they worked to improve their understanding of the course material, for instance? Given the opportunity for more learning that delayed grading provides in writing contexts, what improvements can students document? A summative evaluation provides answers to those questions, and a final portfolio and conference are the mechanisms that provide that feedback.

The final portfolio can be composed of any number of final pieces. The writer should, however, select these pieces from the variety of genres or writing assignments you've assigned in the course. For example, a writer preparing an introductory biology course portfolio might select lab reports, reaction papers, and a literature review, all previously assigned and now rewritten for the portfolio. As a result, the portfolio should record what students learned in the course. It also documents that students can prepare final works.

You can engineer this final system during the very first week when you introduce the final portfolio, describing it in the terms of formative assessment. (I describe this in light of the Contract for B in the next section and in Chapter 10.) But writers need to work up to that final portfolio: hence, the working portfolio, a collection of everything students do in the course—drafts, feedback, and some middle-of-the-way rewrites. The working portfolio is the low-stakes practice for the high-stakes final portfolio. Throughout the semester, it is organized simply, by chronology. In the opening week, I show some slides depicting some working portfolios that my previous students have completed.

Housing the working portfolio is also simple: loose-leaf notebook, accordion file, or the binder. I care less about the type and more about what students collect, for writers should be great collectors, not knowing the value (yet) of what they accumulate. I don't even care if students do not bring their working portfolios to class—by midterm, they might need a wheelbarrow to haul them—but I do ask that they maintain them and bring them to a final conference.

Some professors are rightly concerned about how early, midterm, and final examinations might fit into this approach, especially since a growing body of research shows that cumulative examinations enhance learning (Khanna, Brack, and Finken, 2013; Lawrence, 2013). From a writerly perspective, you can also interpret these examinations as drafts. For instance, in the history course Europe of the World Wars, the second exam might focus on the scholarly debate regarding the causes of World War II. Student writers' responses depend on their grasp of the unresolved conflicts in the Treaty of Versailles, the focus of the first exam. In such a course, you can even weigh the individual examinations differently, treating the earliest as a first version, the second as a second draft, and the last as a final draft. Only the last is a summative assessment, the letter grade.

Self-Assessments

By the fifth week of class, you have the option to ask students to complete a brief self-assessment, based on the formative work students have completed thus far in the course. They can compile this evaluation in reviewing their working folder. In a very real way, this fifth-week assessment is a first draft of what you can expect by the fifteenth, the last week of class. For these assessments, you could ask for short answers to questions you pose, a reality check to see if student writers and you are reading progress in the same way. For a tenth-week self-evaluation, you could ask nearly identical questions without being needlessly repetitive because the class needs reminders about what their obligations are as writers in the class. This one is a second draft, formative like the first self-assessment but more developed and cognitively more challenging, as it lies closer to the final. (The Appendix contains sample self-assessments for weeks 5 and 10.)

By the tenth week, students should have some formative pieces available as candidates for the final portfolio. Perhaps they completed a postwrite that was fragmented, but now, with a better understanding, they can articulate what they misunderstood. Or the second draft that they handed in has a final section that still needs rewriting, a skill they're building into their repertoire. Or perhaps they freewrote on a particular point in a lecture that they believe they could develop into a short essay. These possibilities are available to developing writers, and they should be the ones to choose. As Reynolds and Rice (2006) note, the final portfolio takes a central role once writers have the power to select.

By the end of that tenth week, you need to address writing quality in your class, what your standards are for superior writing. Although I explain the contract in relation to grading more specifically in Chapter 10, the contract also has implications for writing quality even though it measures only sustained effort.

The Contract and Writing Quality

As students expend much effort, as I define it in the contract, that effort impacts the quality of their writing. Professors have a reasonable expectation that there will be results from all that effort, and that is something students expect without explanation. At the same time, there are no guarantees. Whether that effort is sufficient to raise the quality of writing above B is indeterminate until the end. By deadline, writing must communicate to its audience. Although effect on any audience is hard to measure or predict student writers are communicating solely with someone they've grown to know (and, I hope, to love) during the semester—you. By the end of the course, you are grading the quality of the writing for one audience—you—which is the fairest measure available to both.

Throughout the semester, I remind students that grades of B+, A–, and A are based solely on the quality of the rewritten (or revised) final portfolio. As a result, the final portfolio is the final performance: a showcase, a pheasant under glass. I reiterate that they must concentrate on achieving what Elbow calls *writing excellence*, a term I also reference in class and in the self-evaluations. By the end of the course, I have the quality of students' portfolio writing to grade, especially rewarding for student writers who have kept the contract and are working hard for the grades above B. Since grades above B measure actual performance—not trying—I can concentrate on reading student writing instead of making corrections that they will never use in the portfolio.

Final Conference and Contract for B

To emphasize writing as an effective way to learn, I make grades above B based solely on the final portfolio. I believe that if students have learned the content of the course they should be able to write about it competently. That is my perspective, not only as a teacher of writers but also as a writer myself who cares deeply about students communicating clearly and accurately the disciplinary content of their studies.

To help students achieve writing excellence, I sponsor one last, optional conference during the last week of classes. I make myself available for those who want more feedback and specifically feedback for final work. All of my teaching during the semester turns on preparing students for the last conference, too, a culmination of all others and all coursework. Moreover, this final conference is a rehearsal, a place where students can present their completed portfolio for a trial-run review. Here we can discuss it using specific criteria—articulated and practiced throughout the course, summarized by me in a final portfolio checksheet, and prepared by them at the end of the course.

I require students who have successfully completed the contract up to this point to sign up for a trial-run conference. I debated this point quite a bit over the years, but this last year I've come to require final conference attendance. The deciding point for me was simply the practice common to most writers I know. I would never think of submitting a manuscript or an article without consulting another writer first. Writers I know derive such help from a sympathetic reader's work, and such has saved me several red faces and apologies for my own gaffes. As a professor, you no doubt want to reach at least minimum competence in a draft before handing it to a colleague for good feedback. The ensuing conference with a colleague should help you find your readers when you've lost those companions in your writing, even when you don't know you've lost them! I've served as a reader for other writers and find I'm helping my own writing in the process because such responding alerts me to things I'm doing in my writing too, both good and bad. We want our students to benefit from those same rich experiences, so there's good reason to integrate the final conference into the contract.

For those not keeping the contract, I make the conference optional. It's not that they are second-class writers either; they can still earn a B in the quality of their final portfolio. At the end, those who haven't worked hard during the semester are working harder than everyone else now and don't want to be interrupted with feedback that repeats what they already know; I tell them they don't need to sign up for the conference. I know that at particular junctures I don't want any feedback if I'm in the midst of some tough rewriting, no matter how sympathetic the coach is. I leave the decision with them.

Making this conference optional for those who have broken the contract also spares you from students who continue not to work hard or refuse to better their work. Nothing is so irksome for student and professor than to read unprepared work, particularly from students who have not worked hard. Forcing students against their will to produce better work—something they refused all semester—rushes them to make judgments in their writing that they are unprepared to make and can actually make their final portfolio worse. I found in the past when I required them to attend that many contract breakers did not show up for their appointments anyway. I believe in giving the most help to those who have worked hard all semester and just want a little more time with me. On average, about 80 percent of my students not only sign up for the final conference but also come prepared.

Trial-Run Conference

If student writers have their portfolio ready for a trial run—all parts complete, as defined in the checksheet—they can bring it to a thirty-minute conference, at which time I give them a preliminary portfolio grade evaluation. At the beginning of that conference, I conduct a quick interview to see if the portfolio is complete. I use the front page of the checksheet (Exhibit 9.1) for that purpose.

Exhibit 9.1 Final Portfolio Checksheet, Page 1

Writer's name

Your Phone number

I am submitting my final portfolio …

1. so my professor can review it for a "trial run" during week 15,

2. to meet the FINAL DEADLINE — Monday, April 22, 2013, 12 NOON at Dr. Hafer's office, D314.

I have …

MY	HAFER	GATEWAY TASKS
_____	_____	(a) included this checksheet, with the first column on this page "checked" to show I am prepared for my portfolio to be graded;
_____	_____	(b) employed a theme or metaphor to guide the reader and his/her reading;
_____	_____	(c) supplied a complete table of contents, with essay titles, genre labels, and the initial page number where each discourse appears;
_____	_____	(d) numbered all pages throughout the portfolio;
_____	_____	(e) forma!ed all the essays in a keyboarded* standard and/or academic documentation s"le, depending on the genre;
_____	_____	(f) featured an introductory reflective essay after the table of contents;
_____	_____	(g) showcased "best works" essays from my working folder: three–to–six genre assignments I selected and any other assignments taken from the structured genre or unstructured (prolific) writing assignments;

MY	HAFER	GATEWAY TASKS
_____	_____	(h) applied rewriting and editing to my final versions, based on what I applied as a writer in this class; and
_____	_____	(i) "published" and designed my portfolio carefully within a portfolio that contains pockets (no stapling or clipping of papers).
_____	_____	(j) uploaded the electronic version of my final portfolio to <www.turnitin.com> after a "practicing upload" file. (Class ID: 6244025; password: GoRedSox30.)
		I understand that the final grade is
_____		(k) based on the grading policies in the syllabus.

*Obviously, figures illustrating handwritten freewrites from class, editing, and the like have power only in their original forms because they are snapshots of your thinking at the time. You may, for example, want to show how one of your ideas originated so to trace its evolution through your drafting. Having the original image adds strength to your argument because you have the original written record.

If incomplete, we can chat about the gateway requirements and they can ask me questions, which usually take less than the thirty-minute appointment. If complete, I can tell so almost instantly with a quick scan of the portfolio and thus dismiss them for about twenty-five minutes so I can read their portfolio uninterrupted. They close my office door when they leave, so I'm undisturbed in reading their portfolio.

"When the door reopens, I'm ready for you," I say.

Using what we studied all semester, I read quickly over their portfolio, noting patterns of strengths and weaknesses that I emphasized in the course. You can do the same, and you'll be amazed at how quickly and expertly you can read. The rapidity of this reading experience is similar to what some colleagues describe when they read essays for advanced placement tests. The similarities, however, end there, for we're still looking to help students improve for the final evaluation.

Because I've seen their papers in previous versions, I recognize any changes they have made. I make checks in the margin and maybe one correction per significant problem—a squiggly line if I have to reread a sentence for meaning—so I can show writers exactly the kind of weaknesses I still see in their writing. I do the same for strengths; it's important for careful writers, those who have worked hard at their writing all semester long, not to tamper with what they've done well. The symbols I make look less like corrections and more like cues for discussion with student authors.

I do not know ahead of time whether I will discuss all of these points until I finish reading the portfolio at the end of each session; each time, I'm looking solely for patterns that aren't evident until I'm well into the portfolio. My notations are summarized on the second page of the checksheet (Exhibit 9.2), along with a simple scale (see Chapter 10).

Exhibit 9.2 Final Portfolio TRIAL RUN

	EXEMPLARY 4	3.5	PROFICIENT 3	2.5	DEVELOPING 2	1.5	UNFINISHED 1
Reflective Introduction							
Rhetorical Knowledge							
Understanding & Application of Genres							
Design and Appearance							
Conventions & Craft							
Style							

Name

Kept B contract? _____

You may stop work now with a final grade of _____

If you continue rewriting until deadline, you can achieve a grade between _____ and _____.

Continue rewriting/revising? _____

FINAL GRADE _____

Back from Exile

When student writers return after twenty-five minutes, I point out these patterns of deficiency or excellence. Next they face one of several possibilities.

If the portfolio lacks uniformity in rewriting, it breaks the contract and I send them back for more directed rewriting until deadline: for me, that's the Monday of final examination week. Therefore, they *must* rewrite to keep the contract. This time, however, I can give them real examples from their own work because I have the best work they've done in the course so far. If they refuse, I award a final grade based solely on the final portfolio, since the contract is broken. If they rewrite, I can assure them a grade of B or higher.

The vast majority of students give me a consistently rewritten portfolio after having completed the preliminary portfolio work and thus aiming for a grade higher than B. Here is where we can see how dedicated students are to their work. If the final grade I award them during the trial run is lower than they expected, are they willing to work a little longer for the chance to achieve excellence in their writing?

"So what would you like to do?" I ask. "Would you like to stand pat with the current grade assessment—say, B+ since you kept the contract—or continue on for a higher grade? If you decide to take the portfolio and continue to work on it until deadline, I guarantee that you cannot earn lower than B+ when I reread it."

Only at this moment will both of us know their commitment to achieve beyond trying to arrive at the better writing, which means grades above B.

To give them the tools to reach these higher grades, I show examples from their own portfolio: all the problem areas that fall below writing excellence and those that rise above. I again want to reassure students that if I find additional problems during a later rereading—as I always do because I have more time to do a slower reading—I will not incorporate that critique into the final portfolio grade. I want students to concentrate on the items I point out now, ones that consistently work against them en masse rather than their missing a few gremlins of proofreading that creep in.

If any students elect to rewrite and resubmit their portfolio that Monday of final examination week, they must include that same checksheet with all my notes because without them I must begin the grading process anew because the only record is lost. (I have yet to have any student lose that checksheet and notes!)

On the few instances where student writers coming to the final conference are unprepared for a trial run, however, I don't turn them away. I present two options for the twenty-five-minute session. One, I offer to edit, with them sitting beside me and sharing a desk, any one page of their rewritten portfolio; I also narrate what I edit. "Here I think the two sentences could be combined because the end of the one is the start of the next. Let's see what it sounds like … " and so on. The only stipulation I make is that the page must be rewritten from the first draft I saw, which is surprisingly easy to ascertain since I have a working folder from their previous conferences on hand. But I rarely need to check. I have students' attention at this point—a teachable moment where they can follow the examples taken from their own work.

A second option is to ask me specific questions, such as "Do I need a new paragraph here on p. 8?" But the list of questions expires quickly. In my experience, unprepared students haven't thought about questions or rewritten any pages, so we're finished in fifteen minutes or less; the burden of proof in showing improvement is still with them. Regardless, they still have until the final deadline on final examination week to complete the portfolio.

No matter which option they qualify for or decide to take, the total conference time is no longer than thirty minutes. If you adopt such a scheme, allot one conference opportunity per student; after that one, make clear that they are on their own in preparing for the final deadline. There simply isn't any more time left to formation; the instruction period is over. They now have to take full responsibility for their writing.

Typical Problems and What's Humanely Possible

Each conference should take thirty minutes. If you fall behind, you probably will have at least one in the lineup with an incomplete portfolio or a no-show, so you can catch up but don't rely on that happening. Most students want to see you this last class week and on time!

For latecomers, I do the best I can: what I say is humanely possible (weak pun intended). Again, I cannot do a full trial run if they arrive late, but I can answer at least some of their nagging questions. I cannot reschedule either, since I would have to offer the same to all, but I can edit up to a page of their finished portfolio or answer detailed questions. In short, I focus attention on what we can do with the available time if they haven't met the gateway requirements specified in the checksheet.

Table of Contents in the Final Portfolio

There are three irreducible components of the final portfolio.

The first is the table of contents, which lists all the parts, just like a book. Writers need to include a contents page for several reasons. It reminds them to include all the required parts. It identifies those parts for you, the audience, which, depending on the original assignment, may be ambiguous. Sometimes students include extra sections, like appendices or optional assignments. For example, if students are showing changes from one version to another, it can be hard to discern which the writer intends as the better if both are unlabeled and missing from the table of contents. A contents page also allows you to move quickly around the portfolio, to dissemble it for rereading sections and to reassemble upon completing it.

I find increasingly that students are unaware of what a table of contents is. They don't use them in their textbooks and thus don't even recall what one looks like. In class, I have student writers turn to one in the textbook. I show at least three different formats, not only from student portfolios but also from different books; sometimes we rank them in class to see which is the better, the easier to read, and even the most accurate. In advanced classes, I ask students to explore the reasons that there might be different tables of contents page for a single book—for example, an analytical table of contents and a chronological one—which leads to a brief discussion of their varying purposes and structures.

The Reflective Introduction in the Final Portfolio

The next irreducible part is the introduction, which serves as a preface to the final portfolio in three ways. It is the only finished piece you will not have seen in any previous versions. Here you discover what students can do on their own, using their own resources, in preparing final versions. The reflective introduction is also the first discourse—a sustained, monologic, and complete piece of writing—you will see in grading the portfolio. It is a work that announces what rewriting students performed so you can see the evidence (i.e., the rewritten essays themselves) in the body of the portfolio.

When students reflect on their writing, they should choose an overall strategy that highlights the way they think about their writing and charts ways their writing has improved. The goal is deeper learning because they are analyzing and evaluating what they did throughout the semester. To draft a reflective introduction, they should lay out their work from the semester, captured in the working portfolio. Ask them what patterns they see. Is there a particular theme they've traced in many of their essays? Maybe a writing strength? Maybe a weakness?

Since the final portfolio includes only finished, rewritten pieces, the introductory essay should spotlight student writers' best work, speaking to what they applied in the course. They should focus on their performance—their work product—and not on their effort. Remind them again, as part of the Contract for B, that their efforts have been taken into account as learning and cannot be counted twice in the final grade.

Sometimes it's helpful, especially in introductory courses, to give prompts for the reflective introduction, students electing which one to pursue:

1. Pinpoint the final versions of your included assignments and, using some of the features of good writing I stressed in

conferences and in class workshops, explain why they represent better versions than the originals and what you have learned from the course.

2. Discuss what you now understand, based on the content of this course, by using the terms defined in the course.

3. Explore your strengths in writing; explore also your weaknesses and the steps you've taken to overcome them as you go on to other courses and other worlds that require writing; use the language and the content of the course as an ongoing solution to your writing problems. (Discussing weaknesses is a strength, not a weakness!)

Once writers decide on a prompt, encourage them to freewrite the introduction first, all the while thinking of ways to document their progress, to show evidence of changes in their understanding of the course content and their writing. For instance, they could show before-and-after snippets of their writing, structured as body quotes. They can posit paragraphs that they rewrote and are positioned side by side with the originals in parallel columns. They can narrate rewritten sentences that interpret what they did. They can use disciplinary vocabulary accurately from the course to establish that they can perform an experiment, discuss the Hittite civilization, or analyze an empirical study. Finally, they can employ techniques from the course that they applied—and applied rightly—to their rewritten discourses.

Again, students need some help showing what they have learned in writing so that they do not simply announce what they hope to do. One strategy is to preview such work by excerpting passages and arguments from other pieces of writing—ones they haven't decided to rewrite—and show them how they meet or exceed many of the things you've taught in this course. For example, you can take the sample introduction for a student's literature review and critique it in class after students offer their feedback. Another is the standing offer I have with students after the tenth week: if they e-mail me their draft of the introduction, I will mark it up with comments on the first page, but only if I can show them to the class with their names removed. I then ask for rewritten or revised first pages, based on the class discussion, and distribute those in a handout or web page.

Only one caution do I issue: Students must qualify their arguments so that their reflections do not exceed reasonable expectations. In describing their writing, for example, one student wrote, "I have no mispellings [sic] in this paper" or the frequent *writing* as *writting*! Such are not occasions for ridicule but indications of how arguments can be weakened considerably when students overestimate. I invite students to speculate as to why their colleagues make such comments, which usually comes back to what they perceive the prof wants. This discussion is fruitful because you can now have a propitious moment to tell them what you want: to review their work even after they believe they have finished. Until honed, students cannot accurately perceive when their work is done. That's one reason students need you as a coach and writer, even in the final conference.

The Body in the Final Portfolio

In my courses, I elect to have writers select which final pieces appear in their portfolio. In introductory courses, I give a little more help with selection, such as specifying that they need to include a range of pieces—say, 2–4—an offer that always provokes lively class debate.

"I don't understand why anyone would choose more than two pieces!" states Nicole.

"That's funny," says Austin. "I can't understand why you wouldn't include four!"

If you have just a few minutes for discussion, it's fascinating to hear students speculate on the reasons a writer might choose less rather than more (and the reverse). In my experiences, student writers conclude the fewer number is where students have already shown writing excellence in their previous drafts, been told so by the instructor, and just need polishing work on a few. The greater number is for those who haven't shown that kind of writing quality yet but who are eager to prove it in various kinds of writing situations: hence, the greater number. It's wonderful when students come up with these justifications, ones that mirror the way a writer would reason in making an argument.

I return them to the misspellings example, after which someone asks, "Can we check with you or the writing center when we think we're close to being finished?"

"Sure, but I can tell you now," I say. "We can still say you're doing finishing work on the body of your work until deadline."

Since the final portfolio is a selection of pieces, not a complete collection of all their writing, the body reveals what student writers believe is their best work. Such best work should follow mechanical conventions too, so specify what you expect in a presentation-quality portfolio to avoid endless, draining discussions about mechanics. Get them out of the way quickly so writers can center on their writing, such as these:

- Manuscript format: double-spaced, header with page number, simple Roman font (Courier, Times New Roman, and Optima are common choices)

- Loose manuscript sheets (no paper clips or staples or other binding)

- An attractive and neat paper portfolio to house all your finishing work, with your name on its front cover

- Clean pages (no penned-in corrections)

- Documentation pages (Works Cited or References) at the end of the portfolio

Proofreading and Copyediting

As with most things writing, it's best to define proofreading and copyediting by example. Whenever I assigned a second draft during the semester, I ask that writers copyedit—correct errors that academic or professional audiences would expect in near-finished works: standardized spelling, mechanics, capitalization, punctuation, and grammar. The final portfolio should be without patterned errors (i.e., multiple instances of where the comma should read as a period) that repeatedly interrupt your reading. Encourage students to get help in editing from their writing lab.

Copyediting involves fact-checking and correcting; proofreading involves checking formatting in the final versions.

You can show examples in your own writing, displaying editing symbols or fact-checks where you've changed important parts in a manuscript. These can be scanned and shown on a slide. Students like seeing what their professors do in their own writing. A librarian colleague shows her handwritten note taking for articles and places where she wasn't precise enough when it came time to convert her notes into sentences.

Unless you're fortunate to have expert writers in your class, you should really limit activities of error correction. Most students have done this kind of work throughout their school lives and still are tripped by the same errors or commit new ones in their corrections. A study by Perrault (2011) found three broad categories comprising why students seem to regress into less proficient levels of error. A professor's simple explanation of error and the correct counterparts will not overcome these problems. Building on Perrault's research and the earlier work of Ronald T. Kellogg, we can even conclude that students, when confronted with any taxonomy of error, quickly become overwhelmed and actually increase their error rate. When you appreciate that students have so much competition for working memory among writing processes, you can understand, on an anecdotal level, why error escalates with high-stakes writing. Even when I taught error correction directly, I still had to point out students' errors in their papers despite their having practiced correcting those errors.

The best method I have found is to have students keep an error log in their daybooks that record the errors you point out in conferences or the writing lab identifies. As Perrault notes, the metaphor of a web rather than a building block best illustrates how students become proficient writers. Therefore, mass effort to teach error correction in the context of high-stakes writing produces little results. I haven't found any method better than a well-kept error log with a gentle professor's and tutor's prodding for other errors. It's a slow process, but it's better than wasting huge blocks of time that only produces widespread regression.

Perhaps you've noticed the same things in your own writing. I know that until I started giving my drafts to trusted others I could never spot errors in my own writing. It's the hardest thing to do, the demands on working memory being so great. In my own writing, I know, after a certain point, I become so consumed with the individual trees in my essay that I can't remember they belong to a forest that I cannot neglect. Or I become so consumed with the forest that I cannot see the trees and their faulty branches and wormwood. It is only practice that will help writers automate those processes; the more practice you can accumulate—for both you and your students—the better.

Yet there are limits. Writers will always need good readers to help them see the forest for the trees (or the trees for the forest?). Writers can become so familiar with their rewritten work that they cannot see the errors contained with it. I advise students to print out their near-final drafts with a different font or spacing that helps them see the page anew.

10

Offer But Two Cheers for Grading Writing

The hardest component in using writing to carry course content is grading, and for students it is the hardest to accept. Colleen, a former student from my first-year classes, was suffering from grade fatigue in a course when I received an e-mail from her, asking if she could meet with me soon.

"It's been a long time since we talked," she wrote.

We bantered gingerly back and forth for some time about exactly when we could meet. Her tone approached urgency in her last e-mail, however, when it looked like we might have to postpone:

> Right now, I think I just need a reassuring voice to talk to. Taking [an advanced class with writing] has been a real shock to the system. I thought I was prepared for the criticism, but it's hard to write when you get so much negative feedback.

When we met, I was the outsider, but I could still hear her reflecting on her learning. How much better it would have been for her if the insider—the professor in her class—allowed for such reflection in writing.

True, Colleen and all writers need the professor's critical language, but that language must persevere to help rather than hurt, admittedly a difficult task when all students remember is a series of grades. Trying to honor learning while grading reminds me of the icon of the Last Judgment that hangs in my office, depicting abundant mercy and great justice. Early in my career, I often wondered, as mere mortals, how we as teaching professors could ever honor those two values when it comes time for us to grade writing, seemingly the most difficult task of all.

Bad Things Happen When Grading Is Applied to Course Writing

Of course we want students to reflect thoughtfully about their work in a way that we can factor into our grading just as thoughtfully. Mechanical approaches just don't suffice. That's why it's a bad idea to divide grades between *content* and *writing* as if a student could be described as knowing a subject without being able to write about it. Likewise, rubrics are so lock-tight they intimidate rather than teach. If we are treating students as fellow writers, we know their struggles as our own. That realization is one approach to resolving the writing problem.

I can appreciate colleagues' frustration in grading writing, for I have read and tried many schemes of grading applied to writing and found them all wanting. Just assigning grades A through F is time-consuming and labor-intensive enough; the promise of machine-scored essays seems empty to me, an abdication of our professional responsibilities. But even if we could grade concisely and accurately, formulated in carefully constructed rubrics, scales, percentages, weights, traits, or uneasy combinations of these—and all in ways that students could understand—we would still conclude they don't help us very much in teaching our courses with writing. They certainly don't make better writers. That single grade at semester's end tells us very little (if anything) about students' learning experiences and nothing about their writerly work habits, all of which contribute to good writing.

In academia, administrators, parents, and students just expect you will grade as part of your professional responsibility.

In addition, accrediting agencies have renewed their interest in learner outcomes, placing even more torque on student grades. Faculty are preoccupied with grading writing: the workload, the mechanics, its efficacy. As Toby Fulwiler wryly observes, "[m]any teachers have signed up for the writing workshop in the first place because they hoped we'd have some magical suggestions for grading student papers" (1986, 29).

Of course, there is no magical solution, nor can there be. As we've all seen, the burdens of workload, reliability, and necessity associated with grading writing—that grand but not glorious super-structure of terminal comments, marginalia, editing marks, and the like that everyone expects professors to perform—is overwhelming. We can easily conclude, as Peter Elbow did many years ago, that any reform for the grading of writing is "hopeless," especially if the goal is to make it "reliable" or to possess "clear meaning" (n.d., 187–88).

Grading as Contronym

Grading, quite simply, cannot be reformed for writing. In the end, what Colleen needs—indeed, what all our students need—is meaningful feedback that gives them energy as writers. Student writers need our language to supply them the energy that works toward superior writing. We cannot supply that strengthening language if we are spending—no, wasting—all our feedback energies grading their writing.

However, we still have to be realists. Grading writing is the established norm of evaluation that will not break, and there's no reason to believe it will cease anytime soon. But we can bend it to accomplish our learning goals if we qualify our grading in four ways.

First, we must concede that grading writing is a contronym, a self-refuting proposition. Instead, we must convince students that we all want to become better writers but acknowledge that grading doesn't accomplish that. We know it is our professional responsibility to issue grades, but it is also our responsibility to enhance learning. Some schools complicate that process by requiring even more grading: midterm letter grades for freshmen and students on probation.

Second, since the Forces That Be require grading for writing, we must settle for the next best thing: limiting its frequency. Once we realize our predicament, we can pull students into our side of the battle to accept *the-best-we-can-do* grading. That means grading writing as infrequently as possible and not until the end of the course. Your goal is to inform students all along how they're doing—sans grades—since grades signify the end of your conversation with student writers.

Third, we do far better coursework when we replace grading with assessing. That means the time you would have spent grading—deliberating over them, broadcasting them to students, defending them—can now be spent on low-stakes responding and conferencing. You can also eliminate the apparatus such constant grading requires: for example, profuse commenting to defend a grade and precise recordkeeping in a gradebook. When released from that restraint, you can spend all of your time responding to the writing and no time building that superstructure. The assessments you provide will be much more understandable to your students too. They can also respond to your feedback using the same language. That interchange is a conversation about writing in your discipline, started on the very first day with the syllabus and student responses and carried throughout the semester in your classroom writing. When you must grade, you can perform it as best-we-can-do: a professional responsibility performed once as a concluding act.

Fourth, you are now free to do consistent assessing, formative measuring that prepares students for the one-time summative grade at the end. Assessing gives students practice in understanding your feedback of their work and gives them time to apply that understanding in rewriting their work. As a result, you push students to commit to constant improvement.

The First Day and Grading

I spend a lot of time talking about grading in the first week of class and particularly on the first day. Whatever you decide, I recommend addressing the subject of grades as soon as possible because it is what students have on their mind in any course that uses writing. They feel anxious and apprehensive and want to know specifically how you will grade their writing. Playing into that expectation, explain that your goal for their writing is to solicit their best possible writing, writing that they may have never performed before. You can tell them, too, that you know they come to your class motivated by a grade and, when it comes to their writing, they believe a good grade is unreachable. In these ways, you establish common ground because both you and they are writers and have our own take on the writing problem.

Next, tell them your values as they relate to writing but make them reachable. For example, in my introductory courses, I want students to own their own writing, taking control for it independent of the high-stakes criticisms we believe our professional responsibilities demand. I let them know I want students to care about the language they use, to be mindful of it; in attending to their writing, I say, they must see its value, whether it receives a grade or not. In fifteen years of giving variations of this same speech, I still love seeing that shocked—and relieved—majority in the audience.

I tell my students that when I graded writing frequently I graded it too critically, which we all know is bad teaching. As a writer, I want to be ever mindful of my own failed practices and those of all writers, a notion that can guide my responses to student writing because I'm trying to help my fellows. With a letter grade attached, I found I had a harder time detecting my own hypercriticism because I felt like my response focused on defending my grade. On the other hand, as a student I hated to receive teacher commentary disconnected from the grade. Whatever situation applied, the grade just didn't fit the landscape the teacher's response painted.

It doesn't matter if I have rubrics either. Writers are opening their soul to outsiders; they express their vulnerability, even when they carelessly lob words onto a page. Confronting their writing in a conference, students grow embarrassed when they read it out loud or become angry or frustrated when what they intended to do in language doesn't surface. These are the teachable moments that grading doesn't supply.

Communicating About Writing Anxieties

When professional writers speak of their craft, they frequently share their own anxieties about writing freely with their audiences. I now also do so with writers in my own class. In many ways, the values well represented in Colleen's anxieties are ones I share as a professor and writer. As a professor, I'm anxious when mailing a journal article or reading the criticisms of referees. As a student writer, I still remember an essay I had returned from a professor who had written, "This essay is strong at the center but soft around the edges . . . . You should think of sending it to a journal, after revision." To this day, I have left that essay unrevised. Was it good? Was it bad? What piece cannot be made publishable with enough revision?

As a student, I remember wanting so much better feedback. I wanted to know what the professor meant by *soft* and what sentences connoted *edges*. Could he cite examples? If he could point to soft sections, would he be willing to look at two or three versions of that section to see if I was applying the right force to my rewritten work? I lacked the gumption to visit him during office hours and to ask for that added help. After all, he was a famous scholar with prodigious output, which I interpreted to mean that he wouldn't be able to relate to me anyway since he obviously never experienced any problems in his own writing. (Or so I thought.) I didn't feel compelled to do so when I saw the A– circled at the conclusion of his terminal comments. To me and to most of my fellows, that signaled a finality to this conversation.

As a professor, I recognize that finality in the standard rejection letter. When I receive one, I want to know why my finished piece, as one publishing house described it, has a "topic with merit" but "does not elicit the kind of enthusiasm on the part of the editorial staff that we feel is requisite for publication." Each statement generates its own set of questions. What kind of enthusiasm should I be eliciting? At one point in my manuscript did the elusive enthusiasm dwindle? If my book is, in their words, not right for this house, why are they encouraging me to find other presses interested in my unenthusiastic project? It is so easy to become defensive when the rejection letters arrive because they elicit more questions than answers, questions that cannot be broached by overworked publishers, stockpiled with unread manuscripts. It's disheartening when publishers state, "We regret we cannot be more encouraging," when I know I haven't made the grade. For many of our students who haven't achieved the grade they wanted, our comments look like support for the final rejection.

What about students who receive the grade they sought? What about the chronic overachievers who want to receive the pat on the back that they think a letter grade will provide? From past experiences, I know putting an A on that paper persuades students implicitly that the paper can't be made any better, so they stop trying because it is an end to the conversation. The situation reminds me of my son, who has a terrific throwing arm. He hasn't thrown all winter long, and after tossing a few wild balls around with me this spring he woke up the next morning with sore muscles, so sore he couldn't throw a ball. Training must be year-round, even for the gifted AAA player. Writing progress trails if writers do not develop an inner sense of continuous rewriting, their writing muscles growing sore after a winter of neglect.

Grading Decenters Writing

Not only do colleges and some accrediting agencies expect us to do grading, but our society also expects grading to be the lingua franca in evaluating anything. Just note how many times our society references common conceptions about grading. The voting guides distributed throughout the nation grade candidates based on factors important to an interest group or voting block. News articles grade the infrastructure of state roads, bridges, airports, drinking water, waterways, rail lines, transit and wastewater systems, and dams. In one such article, a particular state earned a D overall, with discrete grades of B for railway conditions to a low of D– for navigable railways and wastewater systems. In such situations, no one defends letter grading as a system of measure—why a twelve-point range over a five?—because our school experiences are so ingrained. That familiarity doesn't make them fair or helpful.

Students participate, too. They can grade professors in anonymous evaluations at the end of the semester or on a website. These grades profoundly affect professors' feelings and unduly influence how professors teach those courses in the future. These grades also close the conversation between students and their professor, making sharing writer identity more difficult.

Empirical studies about grading and writing are even more revealing. Two of Wagner's (1975) studies show that, because grading is a labor-intensive process, professors are less likely to assign frequent writing. Grading moves us away from writing in a discipline to writing under the constraints of an overworked faculty (Meikle, 1982). Grading as a whole, no matter the focus, is fraught with problems. Liesel O'Hagan's (1998) study of 1,500 articles on grading found only a handful willing to argue for conventional grading. Likewise, Robert J. Marzano's (2000) noteworthy study of postsecondary grading practices notes that universal acceptance of conventional grading for a variety of tasks and circumstances proves they "are meaningless" (1). For more than one hundred years, the familiar A–F scale persists despite considerable research that proves its widespread ineffectiveness (Glasser, 1968; O'Hagan, 1998).

In teaching course content through writing, we need the potter's art. We need the instinct of where to apply pressure and where we let up, where to place a correcting hand and where to withdraw.

That's a difficult balance when we face courses filled with writers of differing skills and motivations and weaknesses. Too much pressure at one point and the art suffers. That inevitable collapse occurs when we grade writing throughout the semester.

Therefore, I confront students with my claim: continuous grading has the power to undo all I'm attempting to teach through writing, so I take open steps to limit its influence.

Inductive Teaching and The-Best-We-Can-Come-Up-With Grading

After you present these irreconcilable dilemmas to students, make your offer to grade writing in the class as *the-best-we-can-come-up-with*. Therefore, your solution is to make it as infrequent as the dental visit: the absolute minimum. And that minimum means you will grade only writing that cannot be revised or rewritten any further for credit, work that is *deadlined*—in its final resting spot—sometime during the last two weeks of the semester.

First, a quick overview. As discussed in the introductory chapter, I advocate the inductive teaching approach that starts with the first-day freewriting. Inductive teaching elicits better student writing by starting from the writer's current state and then building to something greater. This approach is as old as creative writing courses, but it took some creative writers like Marie Ponsot to bring it into other classrooms. Students need time to observe and practice their writing before they can discern common features in effective writing pieces. That bottom-up learning enhances the way we use writing to convey content, enabling us to place students on that journey to writing competence in a field that Ronald T. Kellogg (1999) estimates takes as much as twenty years to master.

In such instruction, professors focus their comments on student writing, creating an environment for writing where grades cannot dictate teachers' feedback (Wagner, 1976). That environment keeps letter-grading at the end of the semester where no further commentary or opportunities for learning exist within the course: that last possible moment. At the end of the day, we need a grading system for writing that is nearly invisible for most of the course so we can best support writing as learning. Even prominent aspects of a content course, like examinations, can reinforce your work with writers if you choose the better option: assessing with writing itself.

Assessing Is the Better Option

Since grading conflicts with our instruction, we should do it as infrequently as possible and always after as long a period of assessing that we can provide. By assessing, I mean what conversations the professor starts with her fellow writers, responses that focus both parties on their writing. By giving feedback to fellow writers, such as in postwrite responses or in conferences, I center our attention on teaching. In effect, less grading means more time for assessing, and it is assessing that produces the most valuable resource for writers.

In fact, since I started issuing feedback alone, I find I'm a much faster and clearer writer because I'm doing more writing. I am also assessing infinitely more than grading. I can now glide through the postwrites, the end-of-class exercises that ask students to review what I just taught. I scan them quickly and can comment on them succinctly. When I first introduced postwrites, I was tempted to overwrite, so I timed myself to fifteen minutes for a small section of fifteen, which forced me to read and respond only to what they had written. I found an "OK" and "You got it!" response to be good enough when a student provided a sound answer. But more often than not, I wrote more, becoming a more prolific responder—faster and more proficient in my feedback—while at the same time enjoying the evolving interchanges between students and me. I distinctly remember one late fall afternoon when, immediately after class and in the same classroom, my handwritten comments began to shape me, showing me the primacy of teaching in assessment. I didn't feel that drudgery I associated so particularly with grading either. I felt like I was writing without stopping, much like a focused freewrite.

"Are you grading again?" the religion professor laughed as he entered the classroom, ready for the next class to meet in that room.

I had to think for a moment. Was I grading? "No, I'm just responding to what students wrote at the end of my last class."

"That sure must take a lot of time," he said, shaking his head, looking at the stack of postwrites on the desk.

I looked at that pile too. "Actually, it doesn't," I said. "That is my 'done' pile."

I realized that the nature of the course changed, too. I found students really working to communicate with me in these postwrites rather than doing what was barely acceptable. Of course, it didn't hurt that they were unaware of what was barely acceptable. They escalated their efforts with each succeeding postwrite.

When compared with my previous practice, I also noticed how much time I had wasted grading. For example, I used to compare grades among students, penciling tentative ones until I finished a pack and could go back and differentiate, even for small assignments, before issuing binding grades. This practice is widespread, as is subtracting, when professors mark down from 100 percent when they see grammatical errors or inaccuracies. Not only does it take longer to grade than to assess, but also the process unintentionally paralyzes students so that they need time to mobilize before completing other work. One professor complained that students commit the same errors over and over, unaware that his constant grading never communicated what he wanted his students to learn.

With assessing through writing, you can give formative feedback that anticipates students will use it to produce a better product. This is like what Stephen Adkinson and Stephen Tchudi (1998) call *achievement grading*. Although the professor uses no letter grades, she is observing behaviors and habits crucial to creating a learning environment where good writing has a greater chance to happen. Students should greet their submitted assignments as not yet done until a final deadline when they have at least processed input from you. Formative assessments cooperate with content courses carried by writing because they mirror the very writing process itself. Assessments recognize that writing products come into being as a result of a sometimes long process that cannot always be hurried in developing writers.

Assessing also allows for a more realistic writing process that may turn out well or may go wrong. But those are results, better suited to finishing work when letter grades can emerge as summative evaluations. What we need first in the classroom is an assessment structure that stands apart from what we are trying to instill in the classroom: plenteous writing now, better rewriting later. That means creating time and tasks for students to experiment.

In such a system, I give far more feedback on the quality of various aspects of writing than I would have time and opportunity to do than when I used grading all the time. I can now pass through a short in-class assignment or reflective freewrite at the end of class in twenty minutes for a class of twenty-five. I know in designing those postwrites that there are particular things I want students to know and I can get at that material only if I make my workload manageable. I find the whole postwrite activity invigorating because students focus on my written feedback. There isn't anything to compete—no points, categories, percentages, or abstract symbols. Assessing focuses us exclusively on writing.

The same situation applies during conferencing. As I discussed earlier, conferencing is a tremendous resource in processing students' drafts. In a fifteen-minute conference session, you can read students' written plans or drafts, give specific feedback they want, hear their tentative plans for rewriting or revision, and assess the session. Contrast that with grading a first draft. Even though it's a first draft, you will be tempted to read too deeply, comment too thoroughly, and thus destroy any student experimentation. It's difficult not to probe. When I graded all the time, I always got hung up on some peccadillo, like *that* versus *which*, and ended up writing a comment longer than I should and distant from what they student had written. I fussed about grades and began comparing papers based on grades.

I debated, too, on what the grade told the student if I was expecting a rewrite. I placed proofreading marks, which students may not have understood since we hadn't practiced editing in the class yet. I then would look up at the clock—thirty minutes had elapsed!

In sharp contrast, assessing—whether in conferences or on postwrites—avoids much of this misdirection.

Since I refrain from constant grading, I never take a student paper home. I now have time to do a better prep, such as designing better forms of feedback in my mini-workshops, conferences, postwrites, and handouts. My incentive to design well is that it will save me from laborious grading and give me more time for what I love: teaching. Can you see how liberating such assessment is? As a result, you do not have to abdicate a learning environment when writing takes place. You can now be open to new scenarios for writing, like writing with your students in class and in conferences.

Contract for B Final Grade

With assessment in place, though, how can we find the best role for grades? The best answer I've been able to propose to students is the Contract for B.

In such a system, you talk about grades only on the first day of class, during a conference, and on the last week of class. Confined to such specified times, the question arises in students' minds how you will keep this whole enterprise going and let them know how they're doing. This is where you can adapt what Peter Elbow and Jane Danielewicz (2009) propose in the Contract for B. For instance, I tell students that no matter what course I'm teaching if they complete the assigned tasks—work really, really hard at them—I can assure them of a final grade of B. The contract also allows you to include generic learning behaviors that are important to the writing and learning environment, like attendance. You can even include examinations by moving them into the contract to establish a minimum competence; if students know the subject they should be able to articulate it.

Consequently, the province of the contract is acknowledging learning behaviors you desire and tasks you want mastered. Once you have a basic superstructure for the contract, you can fine-tune it for individual courses. I usually have ten to fifteen stipulations for each course. Some are bipolar conditions, which require yes–no compliance, such as meeting standards of attendance, deadlines, and preparedness. For example, if students miss no more than three classes, that stipulation is met with a *yes, reaching standard.* Another example is making students accountable for their own learning. I require students to keep track of whether they are meeting the contract for B. At a minimum, I have them complete the fifth- and tenth-week self-evaluations that show me they are thinking about assessment at least twice a semester and three times if you use the opening day letter.

Others are by degree, requiring competence in something like being able to use the technical terms of the course accurately in their writing, as evidenced in quizzes and in-class discussions. For example, in a course with three cumulative examinations you could combine that stipulation with a traditional grade. Students would be expected to achieve a minimum of B when the first two examinations are averaged together. If you treat course material within a writing paradigm, you could also weigh individual examinations differently, treating the earliest as a first draft, the second as a second draft, and the last as part of the final portfolio since it is a final draft.

Assessment Recordkeeping

You must be able to record assessments quickly and only when necessary. Here's one way I rapidly record assessments.

First, I record student writers' work in my electronic gradebook, which functions like a private journal. I also reflect on each class, just for a minute or two, in this journal gradebook's class view. In a software program or Web-based grading module, you can record observations (i.e., freewriting) about the class as well as assess in what is sometimes called *standards-based scoring*. You can compose these assessments entirely in low-stakes freewrites.

If you desire more precise tracking, you can formulate standards for the contract components of using one of two scales. The first is for bipolar stipulations (attendance, deadlines) and employs a two-point scale (1—yes, reaching standard; 2—no, not reaching standard). The second is for degree stipulations and uses either a four- or seven-point scale (1—underwritten; 2—developing; 3—reaching expectations for B Contract; 4—exceeding expectations; intermediates include 1.5, 2.5, and 3.5).

Mostly, I use a four-point scale, because I am looking exclusively at effort (1—underwritten effort; 2—insufficient effort; 3—good faith effort for B Contract; 4—superior effort). Some software allow you to feed these score into a Power Law formula, which emphasizes gains in specific skills over time, to chart students' progress and to predict their next performance.

You also have the additional option of using that formula for examinations. Rather than just averaging test scores, you can use the Power Law formula to encourage a developmental dimension to writing performed in tests. If students know the content, they should be able to write about it.

Foremost in our mind here is one thing: bookkeeping must be quick-entry, and it must not demote your attention away from writing responses. Use the software as much as possible to reduce manual entry.

I find there's no need to show students all those numbers. It's not that there's a man behind the curtain directing their fates either. Just as I don't show students my freewriting reflections on the class itself, I don't make available these scores that are shorthand for me alone. Since they figure into making student performance better, they cannot be used against them because they center on effort and tasks. They have meaning for me, reporting what I need to concentrate on in the next class or conference. When it comes time for midterm grade reports my college requires, I can write them quickly based on my contract scoring and daybook notes. In fact, I've found that the midterm writing helps me to practice my structured writing and can also serve as a kind of warm-up before my own writing.

Fine Print in the Contract

It is important to reinforce that you want to help students, as a fellow writer, by providing plenty of practice and assessment. In the syllabus, I repeat what may be obvious but what students may not yet believe:

- The B is accessible to every student—skill, training, bad experiences are irrelevant.

- All decisions about what is required for the B, cited already, are made without judging the overall quality of the drafts.

On first drafts, don't ask that students fuss with discrete issues like grammar and sentence structure since these concerns will arise when the writing is closer to being finished. Have them tackle first things first: thesis or (alternative) hypotheses, unity, development. The Contract for B helps keep you grounded.

Of course, I always hope no student achieves the lower grades. As I state in the syllabus, the quickest way for them to fall to B– and below is to miss classes and conferences, to show up without assignments or with uninvested work. Some items are also nonnegotiable; these will irrevocably break contract and dictate a specific final grade or a range of grades. Typical categories include the percentage of completed low-stakes assignments and activities that must be completed, the number of major draft assignments that must be missed, and the liability student writers incur for underwritten work. For example, you could specify that unless students complete

70 percent of the coursework they cannot even earn a D as a final grade.

Thus, I find that this tiered measurement—formative (Contract for B) and summative (final letter grade)—prizes the practice that can lead to greater performance. The best kind of practice is principled practice with master practitioners; it is we as writers and teaching professors who are more than guides on the side. Our role, nevertheless, is participatory and complementary.

We cannot assure students that their writing will be A's; there are no guarantees. We alone can show them, through example, that we practice what we preach and aim to make writers' practices better.

Responses Appropriate to the Assignment

Assessing is not difficult, and like most everything else, the more you do it, the more effortless it will be as you reach your stride. The important thing when you first start assessing is to begin piecemeal, such as when you assign brief prompts at the beginning or end of class. Whatever form they take—quiz, daybook writing, postwrite—they should require students to generate only one- to five-minutes of low-stakes writing. It's important to keep the questions brief and open-ended, which will keep your feedback focused. Sometimes your feedback can be made while students are composing.

As I explained earlier in discussing postwrites, I still prefer students perform these brief writings by hand, and even though I'm a digital nerd I respond in like mode. In designing these concise assignments, I limit my questions to two that directly address what's occurring in class or which reference some skill or task addressed in the B contract so that I can similarly focus my ensuing response. When you apply this strategy—say you're stressing a particular theory of human behavior—ask the class to write several thesis statements in their daybooks. When you walk around the class after a few minutes of their composing, ask a few students who wrote good thesis statements for their essays to write them on the board.

Working inductively, explain to the class why these work: that is, for their accuracy and their grammatical coordination, for which I underline coordinate pairs. (Okay, I'm a grammar nerd too.) At the end of class, I ask students to demonstrate their own examples in a postwrite:

> Write your own grammatical, coordinate sentence like the ones we practiced in class today.

In that prompt, I assess two stipulations from the contract: #5, Observations/inferences, and #8, Style, using the four-point scale cited earlier. Of course, you can distribute postwrites just during the last five minutes of class, but if you're asking students to write something structured for homework—like a thesis statement or concluding paragraph—why not incorporate the postwrite as a practice into the lesson?

When I get a stack of these, I quickly fan through them, looking for what kinds of insights they garnered from the first activity and what they missed. I can score these quickly in my gradebook journal, recording only those who exceed or fall short of those criteria in the B contract. But I only write responses on the student papers, such as two students who performed exceptionally well:

> *John, this work is really stellar. I can't wait to see how you're going to compose your ending.*
>
> *Alice, what a superb coordinated sentence. I'm glad you're keeping that conjunction separated with a comma.*

With students who are weak or struggling with these skills, I give them some pointers:

> *Tom, the first part of the sentence is strong, but only the verb appears in the second half (after and). What else do you need?*

Angela, the sentence doesn't have a verb. I placed a caret
where you could slot one. Any clearer?

After just a few weeks, the better students, of course, want to know about getting an A, A–, or B+ final grade. Here again I reinforce the formative nature of the Contract for B; that is, the grade of B depends on completing tasks and discrete skills that anyone in the class should be able to complete. Grades of A, A–, and B+, however, depend on outstanding performance in written communication. Students earn a B if they put in good effort and writerly behavior. But to earn the higher grades, they must attend to the quality of their writing (summative) on top of keeping the stipulations for the B contract (formative).

You have many options to share quality writing with the class. You could show previous or current student papers as artifacts of excellent writing in a portfolio context. You can also have class discussions, conferences, and mini-workshops about excellence in writing—as much or as little as needed. By using examples that are on their way to greatness, you can better illustrate where students should be headed in their rewriting.

You can also solicit examples from your current students. After my request in class for samples, one student wished me to look at a first draft of a portfolio introduction. I asked her to e-mail me the first page of the draft, which I distributed to students during the next class. In a subsequent class workshop, we then ranked the page as a class on the same four-point assessment scale, this time with specific criteria. Then we had an open discussion in class or online forum so I see how students and I read the final portfolio. At such end times in a course, I seek to widen our area of agreement on assessment, when students are best equipped to make inferences. You can sponsor this activity, too, refining the criteria on the scale if there is confusion.

I sponsor three activities to teach the same lesson or until 80 percent of the students succeed, whichever comes first. After having assessed students for a whole semester, you have prepared them to understand how one audience, their instructor, reads for superior writing. The goal is not to teach nuances of assessment but rather how to make informed judgments about writing quality. Using inductive teaching, you can show students they can take writing they already have made, assess it within broad categories, and make decisions on possible rewriting. For them, this assessment near the end of the semester brings them one step closer to preparing their final portfolio for the final grade.

The Final Response to Grading

Despite best intentions and a minimalistic grading system, you will still find students responding to you as a grader. Students have learned these behaviors throughout school life and the systems will kick in whenever students question themselves. One sincere and gifted student wrote me a frantic e-mail after class:

> I'm sincerely confused and concerned about my progress in this class. I understand the mistake I made in today's essay, but is that all you took from it? I worked really hard on it trying to make beautiful sentences and have it run smoothly. I had others read it and got extremely positive feedback, so when you had nothing to say but an error in your observation of my essay I became discouraged. Get back to me when you have time.
> – Marcia

In that day's lesson, we wrote observations of one another's essays as they were read, which we all later read in turn. I joined one group and participated in writing observations, not judgments but recordings of what we noticed in the writing as the writer read it to us. I looked over my observations in my daybook and didn't see that I pointed out any mistake:

I wrote back to Marcia, mindful of her concerns:

> Marcia,
>
> I loved your essay. I think it, perhaps, the best of the class, although I won't see them all until later today.
>
> I'm sorry you were under the misapprehension that you made a "mistake" or that was all I noticed. Not true at all, and I apologize for any confusion. (I think I made at least two mistakes today!) I'm positive I wrote much more in my observations. Would you like to see them?
>
> Can you come see me tomorrow morning? Do you have time? I can promise polite conversation and the best Macintosh apple you have ever eaten.

Almost immediately I received this reply:

> I'm so glad you liked my essay and I was just paranoid! Its fine, I'm sure I was just being overly sensitive. I wish I had time to see you tomorrow, but unfortunately I have classes and then work again: Thanks so much for clearing things up.

It only takes a few moments to step from behind even the simplest and kindest grading mechanism to offer a gentle word, a note of praise and apology (where merited), and an openness to meet. No grading system is complete without them.

Ending to Begin Again

Some writers refer to the end of a major stage in a project as *cooling*. It is the time when the subconscious writer's mind takes over and the conscious self lies dormant. It could be for a specific time. I've heard it often: "Take a week off; take two if one is not enough. Try not to think about your writing project at all."

But you cannot carry out that admonition completely. The writing may cool, but it still remains warm within you. Go ahead and plan your own writing, but place it in parallel with how writing can teach your course content. You do that by cultivating a habit of mind that builds a double life into your professional activities. When you assign practice for your students, assign a parallel writing activity for yourself. When one life cools, shift your furnace to the other life, always looking for how one area can feed the other. You'll appreciate the struggles and the joys more closely because you are experiencing them parallel (not perpendicular) to your students. Writing provides an inexhaustible supply for subjects; we just need to be looking. Just see how your daily writing works in your classroom and keeps your skills taut.

As time goes on, reflect on how your relationship with writing has changed. In a more instrumental role, writing should function less as a supplement or a requirement to a course and more as a way of knowing that both reinforces and delivers what you teach. Note the differences in the way students learn how to study for your course, building on written language skills they already possess. That action, in turn, strengthens their writing skills because the writing-to-learn activities are linked together for an academic purpose and a specific audience. Students are now free to work out their own understanding of course content in their writing, work that you can observe and respond to, which also helps them learn. Because you embraced writing as a course norm, you were thoroughly absorbed into the writing process, which benefited students and spilled over into your own writing practice.

Are you now freewriting in the class? Are you using responses on postwrites as a catalyst for your own thinking and learning? Do you use a daybook to get started before conferences and your own scholarly writing? The daily writing, responding, assessing, and conferencing activities reinvigorate that old adage, "If you want to learn something well, teach it to others."

Let your subconscious rise to the foreground now. Let it ruminate in your writing and your teaching that has been informed by writing. Later, after you've cooled a bit, start writing your next scholarly project and your course syllabus, now that you're embracing writing.

References

Adkinson, Stephen, and Stephen Tchudi. "Grading on Merit and Achievement: Where Quality Meets Quantity." *Alternatives to Grading Student Writing.* Ed. Stephen Tchudi. Urbana, IL: NCTE, 1998, 192–208.

Albers, Cheryl. "Using the Syllabus to Document the Scholarship of Teaching." *Teaching Sociology* (2003): 60–72.

Baecker, Diann L. "Uncovering the Rhetoric of the Syllabus: The Case of the Missing I." *College Teaching* 46.2 (1998): 58–62.

Belanger, Joe. "Conflict Between Mentor and Judge: Being Fair and Being Helpful in Composition Evaluation." *English Quarterly* 18.4 (1985): 79–92.

Bloom LLC. DayOne, 2012. Computer software.

Blount, Keith. *Scrivener.* Cornwall, England: Literature and Latte, 2009. Computer software.

Braine, John. *Writing a Novel.* New York: McGraw-Hill, 1975.

CCCC Committee on Assessment. "Writing Assessment: A Position Statement." *College Composition and Communication* 46.3 (1995): 430–37.

Council of Writing Program Administrators, National Council of Teachers of English, National Writing Project. *Framework for Success in Postsecondary Writing.* January 2011.

Deen, Rosemary. "Notes to Stella." *College English* 54.5 (1992): 573–84.

Eberly, Mary B., Sarah E. Newton, and Robert A. Wiggins. "The Syllabus as a Tool for Student-Centered Learning." *Journal of General Education* 50.1 (2001): 56–74.

Elbow, Peter. *A Contract for a Final Grade of B*. n.d.

—. *Vernacular Eloquence: What Speech Can Bring to Writing*. Oxford: Oxford University Press, 2012.

—. *Writing without Teachers*, 2d ed. Oxford: Oxford University Press, 1998.

Elbow, Peter, and Jane Danielewicz. *A Unilateral Grading Contract to Improve Learning and Teaching*. Unpublished ms., 2009.

Elbow, Peter, and Mary Deane Sorcinelli. "High-Stakes and Low-Stakes Writing." *Teaching Tips: Strategies, Research, Theory for College and University Teachers*, 12th ed. Eds. Wilbur McKeachie and Marilla Svinicki. Boston: Houghton Mifflin, 2006, 192–93.

Emig, Janet. *The Composing Processes of Twelfth Graders*. Urbana, IL: NCTE, 1971.

—. "Writing as a Mode of Learning." *College Composition and Communication* 28.5 (1977): 122–28.

Fulwiler, Toby. "The Argument for Writing Across the Curriculum." *Writing Across the Disciplines: Research into Practice*. Ed. Art Young and Toby Fulwiler. Upper Montclair, NJ: Boynton/Cook, 1986, 21–32.

Fink, L. Dee. *Creating Significant Learning Experiences: An Integrated Approach to Designing College Courses*. San Francisco: Jossey-Bass, 2003.

Glasser, William. *Schools Without Failure*. New York: Harper, 1968.

Glater, Jonathan D. "To: Professor@University.Edu Subject: Why It's All About Me." *New York Times*, 22 February 2006, Washington ed., sec. A:1.

Graves, Donald H. *The Energy to Teach*. Portsmouth, NH: Heinemann, 2001.

Habanek, Darlene V. "An Examination of the Integrity of the Syllabus." *College Teaching* 53.2 (2005): 62–64.

Haven, Cynthia. "The New Literacy: Stanford Study Finds Richness and Complexity in Students' Writing." Stanford Report, 9 October 2009. http://news.stanford.edu/news/2009/october12/lunsford-writing-research-101209.html.

Heath, Dan, and Chip Heath. *Made to Stick*. New York: Random House, 2007.

Hoffman-Kipp, Peter, Alfredo J. Artiles, and Laura López-Torres. "Beyond Reflection: Teacher Learning as Praxis." *Theory into Practice* 42.3 (2003): 248–254.

Jabr, Ferris. "The Reading Brain in the Digital Age: The Science of Paper Versus Screens." *Scientific American* 11 Apr. 2013.

Kellogg, Ronald T. *The Psychology of Writing*. Oxford: Oxford University Press, 1999.

—. "Training Writing Skills: A Cognitive Developmental Perspective." *Journal of Writing Research* 1.1 (2008): 1–26.

Kellogg, Ronald T., and Bascom A. Raulerson. "Improving the Writing Skills of College Students." *Psychonomic Bulletin and Review* 14.2 (April 2007): 237–42.

Khanna, Maya M., Amy S. Badura Brack, and Laura L. Finken. "Short- and Long-Term Effects of Cumulative Finals on Student Learning." *Teaching of Psychology* 40.3 (2013): 175–182.

Lauer, Janice M. *Four Worlds of Writing: Inquiry and Action in Context*. 4th ed. Boston: Pearson Custom Publishing, 1991.

Lawrence, Natalie K. "Cumulative Exams in the Introductory Psychology Course." *Teaching of Psychology* 40.1 (2013): 15–19.

Liberatore, Matthew. "Two Minutes of Reflection Improves Teaching." *Chemical Engineering Education* 40.4 (2012): 271.

Lunsford, Andrea. Lycoming College, Williamsport, PA. 20 January 2003. Personal communication.

Marzano, Robert J. *Transforming Classroom Grading*. Alexandria, VA: Association for Supervision and Curriculum Development, 2000.

McKeachie, William J. *Teaching Tips*. Boston: D.C. Heath, 1986.

Meikle, Robert J. "Traditional Grade-Based Writing Evaluation and the Process Approach: Systems in Conflict." *British Columbia* (1982): 1–29.

Murray, Donald M. *A Writer Teaches Writing*. Boston: Houghton Mifflin, 1968.

—. *The Essential Don Murray: Lessons from America's Greatest Writing Teacher*. New York: Heinemann, 2009.

O'Hagan, Liesel K. "It's Broken—Fix It." *Alternatives to Grading Student Writing*. Ed. Stephen Tchudi. Urbana, IL: NCTE, 1998. 1–13.

Paul, Annie Murphy. "Your Brain on Fiction." *New York Times*, 18 Mar. 2012: 6.

Perrault, S. T. "Cognition and Error in Student Writing." *Journal on Excellence in College Teaching* 22.3 (2011): 47–73.

Ponsot, Marie, and Rosemary Deen. *Beat Not the Poor Desk*. Portsmouth: Boynton-Cook, 1982.

Ramirez, Gerardo, and Sian L. Beilock. "Writing About Testing Worries Boosts Exam Performance in the Classroom." *Science*, 14 January 2011, 211–13.

Reynolds, Nedra, and Richard Aaron Rice. *Portfolio Keeping: A Guide for Students*, 2nd ed. Boston: Bedford/St. Martins, 2006.

Roberts, Marilyn. "Creating a Dynamic Syllabus: A Strategy for Course Assessment." *College Teaching* 61.3 (2013): 109.

Schwartz, Barry. *The Paradox of Choice: Why More Is Less*. New York: Ecco, 2004.

See, Carolyn. *Making a Literary Life*. New York: Ballantine, 2003.

Singham, Mano. "Death to the Syllabus!" *Liberal Education* 93.4 (2007): 52–56.

Sommers, Nancy. "Responding to Student Writing." *College Composition And Communication* 33.2 (1982): 148–56.

Straub, Richard. "Students' Reactions to Teacher Comments: An Exploratory Study." *Research in the Teaching of English* (1997): 91–119.

Tanner, Kimberly D. "Reconsidering 'What Works.'" *CBE Life Sciences Education* 10.4 (2011): 329–33.

Wagner, Eileen Nause. *The Impact of Composition Grading on the Attitudes and Writing Performance of Freshman English Students.* Diss., University Microfilms (1975): 1–146.

—. "When the Bookkeeping System Takes Over: The Effects of Grading Compositions on Student Attitudes" (1976): 1–16. Paper presented at the annual meeting of the Conference on College Composition and Communication, Philadelphia, 25–27 March, 1976.

White, Edward M. "The Damage of Innovations Set Adrift." *AAHE Bulletin* 44 (1990): 3–5.

Ziegler, Alan. *The Writing Workshop Note Book: Notes on Creating and Workshopping.* New York: Soft Skull Press, 2007.

Appendix

Chapter 2: Plan with the Syllabus

1. Administer a First-Day Quiz

Record your most correct answers on the answer sheet. Keep this quiz in your new working folder after you hand in your answer sheet.

1. Which of the following features will break the Contract for B?
   A. Missing more than four classes and/or conferences
   B. Failing to keep abreast of whether you're fulfilling the B contract
   C. Handing in homework without coming to class
   D. Missing deadlines
   E. Completing less than 90% of homework assignments
   F. All of the above

2. When are writers ineligible—or, at best, unlikely—to receive even a passing final grade of a D?
   A. Attending fewer than eleven of the first fourteen classroom weeks
   B. Refusing to revise

    C. Absent six times by the end of the course

    D. Completing fewer than 70% of activities, homework, and assignments

    E. Absent five times by midterm

    F. All of the above

3. At the end of the semester, some students, unfortunately, will break contract. Which of the following is true as a result of that broken contract?

    A. They fail the course if they have not attended eleven of the first fourteen classroom weeks.

    B. If they miss three or more genre assignments, the highest grade they can earn is a C–.

    C. They fail the course if they have fewer than 70% of homework completed.

    D. Their final grade will be judged solely on the quality of their final portfolio, up to a B.

    E. They cannot earn higher than a B for the course.

    F. All of the above.

4. The following conditions hold true for all students receiving a final grade *above* a B EXCEPT ...

    A. Writing quality of their final portfolio is above a B.

    B. All the tasks for the B Contract are met.

    C. They received mostly A's on their assignments.

    D. They met or exceeded all goals of the course.

    E. They did not miss more than four classes and/or conferences.

5. Why are there no grades in the course until the end?

    A. So we may concentrate solely on our writing.

    B. Because grading in writing frequently interferes with assessment.

    C. To allow for more practice.

    D. To benefit students who work really, really hard.

    E. Writing is a subjective experience of the reader.

    F. All of the above.

6. What are examples of plagiarism?

    A. Stealing key phrases from another's writing

    B. Stealing sentence structure from another's writing

    C. Constitutes a piece of writing submitted for two courses

    D. "Mosaic" plagiarism

    E. Always reported to the dean

    F. All of the above

7. Which is NOT true of Demolition Day?

    A. It occurs on the Tuesday of the last class week (fifteenth week).

    B. Students may drop only three scores.

    C. Students may drop up to two days of low scores.

    D. Dropping scores does not drop absences.

    E. Students must be present at that class to drop scores.

    F. Students may drop "mi" (missing) scores for days that they were absent.

8. How many missed class *weeks* during the first fourteen weeks of the semester constitute *failure* for the course?

    A. One

    B. Two

    C. Three

    D. Four

    E. Five; or two by midterm

    F. Six; or five by midterm

9. When is late work accepted?

    A. Once per semester

    B. Twice per semester

    C. Never

    D. Depends on the circumstances

    E. Depends on the weather

    F. Depends on what is due

10. For homework to be accepted, which one of the following must be true?

    A. It was submitted in person at the class or conference in which it was due.

    B. The student e-mailed the paper.

    C. It was perfect!

    D. It was late.

    E. A friend dropped it off.

    F. The student successfully removed the spaghetti stains from the paper. (At least he thinks they're spaghetti stains!)

11. For what kind of assignment may the instructor assign a grade for *more* than just hard work?

    A. Homework

    B. Midprocess drafts

    C. First versions

    D. Drafts

    E. Activities

    F. Writing excellence in the final portfolio

12. Which of the following is NOT true?

    A. Intelligence is improvable.

B. Revision is one way to improve.

C. Practice is necessary for improvement.

D. An A is reachable with hard work alone.

E. Writing ability is not fixed.

F. A B is reachable with hard work alone.

13. What weight is given to the portfolio grade category?

    A. 40%

    B. 50%

    C. 60%

    D. 70%

    E. 80%

    F. No weights

14. What is PlanbookConnect?

    A. Syllabus

    B. 50% percent online

    C. Required textbook

    D. Website featuring the calendar of assignments and class agenda

    E. Recommended textbook

    F. None of the above

15. What holds the final portfolio together as *one* piece of work rather than a loose collection of unrelated work?

    A. Theme or metaphor

    B. The body composed of revisions from previous drafts

    C. An introductory essay

    D. A and B

    E. A, B, and C

    F. None of the above

PLEASE PRINT YOUR ANSWERS:

16. Write a grammatically correct sentence using a colon.

17. Write a grammatically correct sentence with a subordinate (dependent) clause and a main (independent) clause.

18. In word count, what is your longest discourse—a sustained piece of writing—you have ever written, figuring 250 words per typed page? What was your purpose for writing that discourse?

Answer Key for First-Day Quiz

No.	Correct Answer
1	F
2	F
3	F
4	C
5	F
6	F
7	B
8	C
9	C
10	C
11	F
12	D
13	F
14	D
15	A
16, 17, 18	Answers vary

2. Sample Syllabus

Dr. Hafer   tel: (321)-4293

The John P. Graham

  Teaching Professor

Department of

  English

Lycoming College

          Academic Center D314

          Office hours: Wednesdays, 10-12 and by

            appointment

          e-mail: <hafer@lycoming.edu>

          Class web page on PlanbookConnect:

            <http://www.planbookconnect.com/teachers/25>

          Conference appointments:

            <http://hafer.youcanbook.me>

          Electronic submissions: <turnitin.com>

            Class ID: 6394749 Password: Go30Sox

ENGL 106

Composition

Fall 2013

Welcome to the course. I hope that, through our opening exercise, you see writing is the most important thing we can do in this class.

To keep writing in that central role, I teach by syllabus, a guide to the standards, responsibilities, policies, and purposes of any course, but especially of a writing course. I also have composed this "syllabus" as an open agreement between us as we pursue the craft of writing together. I reserve the right to modify the provisions outlined in this syllabus if a need arises, but I will strive to be equitable and fair.

The syllabus also keeps us on-task. I will hold you to its terms, and I expect you to hold me to them just as rigorously. As writers — as people who write and count words, as John Braine defines us[1] — we need to be mutually accountable to one another. Therefore, view this syllabus as one approach to sharing our responsibilities as writers.

Along with these responsibilities are specific learning goals I expect you to reach. I also introduce here my philosophy of assessing (vs. grading), class policies, and perspectives on writing. These areas all reflect my experiences as a writer and as a teacher of writers.

In every course I teach, I enlist student writers to engage course subject matter through their writing. This course is no exception. That means, as a writer, you must work to strengthen all aspects of your writing process — inventing, drafting, rewriting, copy-editing — which will help you and your peers to become better writers and rewriters. Since writing is a process — a long and complicated one — I will give you plenty of both practice and guidance.

I work hard to have all students in the class meet these goals:

Foundational Knowledge

1. Recognize the features that distinguish various genres of writing.

2. Identify the terms and components of the writing process.

3. Discern these major dimensions that characterize writing: focus, development, structure (organization), style, conventions.

Application

1. Find your voice in writing: to hear it, perhaps, for the first time.

2. Be able to write competently in various genres.

3. Read your own writing as a "text."

4. Discover more subjects for writing than you have time and opportunity to explore.

5. Rewrite and copy-edit effectively and competently.

Integration

6. Connect writing to your life: to discover, to explore, to make decisions, to deal with problems, to learning in this course and others.

Human Dimension

7. Reflect on your writing process, thereby knowing how to solicit specific help when you need it.

8. Share writing with others, increasing your independence and understanding.

Caring

9. Enjoy writing, to throw yourself headlong into its fury!

Learning How to Learn

10. Be able to write in genres that are new to you.

11. Know how to pursue a writing project independent of instructor involvement.

I recognize that there are many ways to teach writing. The approach I use works best for my students, the college, and me. Please know there is no one or "correct" way to teach and to learn writing. As a writer, I am always learning new ways that benefit my writing and, I hope, my students' writing.

Nature of Writing

It is my purpose to invoke you as a writer in this course and beyond.
One belief common among writers is the conviction that insight and inspiration in writing occur primarily when they are found working at their craft.

Short story writer and essayist Flannery O'Connor was known to work her writing every weekday morning, poised at a typewriter. She stated that, if inspiration chose to hit her during those early hours, she was ready. Similarly, I ask you to attend to your writing craft with that same commitment so that you will be ready when inspiration appears. Thus, every day we will write in class; we'll see if we can coax inspiration to come to us.

Because it is difficult (impossible?) for me to talk precisely about the craft of writing until you make writing for this class, there will be some uncertainty in our daily operation. I want the freedom, when I notice a particular writing problem or question persists, to write a handout and share it during workshop without worrying about keeping pace with the syllabus. Similarly, you may ask for additional help in class regarding any specific writing topic with which we are struggling. Given these realities, you should expect that I will expand upon the calendar of activities and assignments I will distribute.

As you read through this syllabus, I want you to notice that three things dominate. Every class features discussion. Every class showcases a workshop. Every class, we write together.

Here's the Point

Good writing is "accidental." It makes sense that writers — people who write and count words — produce the most good writing. They work hard at it daily and thus bring about the most "accidents."

Required Texts

- Ruszkiewicz, John J. *How to Write Anything: A Guide and Reference*. 2nd ed. New York: Bedford-St. Martin's, 2012. I prefer you purchase the print edition because it's spiral bound and easy to transport. ISBN: 978-1-4576-0243-6

- Reynolds, Nedra and Rich Rice. *Portfolio Keeping: A Guide for Students*. 3rd. ed. New York: Bedford-St. Martin's, 2013. ISBN: 978-1-4576-3285-3

- A "working folder"; it could be a three-ring binder, an accordion file, file jackets, etc. — a working container to collect all the "stuff" of our writing classroom. It should be used to house all your "process" class work — handouts, outlines, notes, homework. All writers in the class need this working folder. Expect that I'll ask you to produce your working folder at some point.

- A final portfolio, due at the end of the course, but we'll develop it throughout the whole semester by way of the "working folder."

- Daybook, a bound notebook, exclusively for prolific, daily, unstructured writing.

Class Web Resources

I post the class agenda, including handouts and assignments, at the end of each class day: <http://www.planbookconnect.com/teachers/25>. I require conference attendance as part of the coursework. To schedule a conference, go to <http://hafer.youcanbook.me> and select an available day and time. Electronic submissions can be uploaded at <http://www.turnitin.com>.

Grading vs. Assessing

No subject in the writing classroom provokes more mistrust, distrust, resentment, hostility, anxiety, bitterness, resignation, envy, and rancor between students and their professors than grading. At best, students perceive traditional grading as a subjective judgment of their learning and their person. At worst, they discern it as a weapon used against them.

My best answer (so far) is to introduce better measures of fairness into the grading process, but those are not enough. I want to ease student writers into thinking constructively about their writing more often and that means grading less often. Together, we must "forget" grading up to the point where learning to be a better writer takes over. You see, I choose far less grading in favor of far more assessing; I choose one grade at one time rather than many grades all the time.

That reduction doesn't mean I won't evaluate, respond, comment, judge, and even like your writing. I will reserve plenty of time for feedback. I use what writing professor Peter Elbow calls a "home studio" approach, and which is commonly called assessment.[2] Imagine you are enrolled in a painting or cooking class; perhaps you could be a scout looking to complete a merit badge or a new driver looking to pass a competency test. These contexts are the ones I covet for my writing classes, ones where assessment — not grading — is the rule.

I first thought along these lines after a student showed me a news article in which some school districts proposed "homework-free weekends," but found that students used these time-outs to catch up on overdue homework. In short, they worked harder than ever. What if I could host grade-free weeks in which we worked "harder than ever," but instead of "catching up" to a grade, we strove for writing excellence, something we should be doing as writers anyway? Peter Elbow and Jane Danielewicz arrive at the same notion: *We would have classes or workshops or lessons, but there would be no official grading. Of course I'd give you evaluative feedback ..., pointing out where you've done well and where I could suggest an improvement. But I wouldn't put grades on your individual paintings or omelets or give you an official grade for the course.*[3]

Imitating those same evaluative conditions, I sponsor workshops, conferences, and handouts in this course. My job is to create a learning environment: as professor, I also am your mentor and fellow writer. I will give you a rich supply of feedback on your writing; I will even write with you in class. In these roles, I will not assign letter grades for fourteen weeks — big assignments and small — but I will provide plenty of feedback for rewriting (or revising, at your discretion).[4] In fact, after the first day until midterm, I refuse to talk about grades entirely and will do so only by request during a conference.

That said, if you complete the tasks assigned to this course — work really, really hard — I can assure you of a final grade of a B. I call this understanding the Contract for B.

The Contract for B

So, just to be clear, here is what I mean by working really, really hard and therefore being assured of a B final grade. Any student who works hard can achieve these tasks:

1. *Attendance*. Don't miss more than three classes/conferences. For any classes you miss, you are still responsible for the learning of that day. Also, be habitually on time. I count lateness as half-absences. Be certain you attend conferences and the trial-run conferences I schedule periodically.

2. *Deadlines*. Meet them. I do not take late work or late tasks/activities.

3. *Communication*. Read your college e-mail account daily so you can keep abreast of class communications. In addition, check the class Planbook site and sign up promptly for conferences online.

4. *Preparedness*. Be ready for our work together. Prepare for the reading, for example, so that you've digested it rather than picked meagerly at it.

When you come to class, have a pen, your daybook, and your textbook ready. Try to come rested. When I write something on the board or repeat it, I expect you to copy it into your daybook. Preparedness encompasses completion too: You must complete at least ninety percent (90%) of the assigned work.

5. *Rhetorical terms*. Know the set of terms we use in class and are defined in your textbooks.

6. *Observations/inferences*. You must be able to write observations of work that is read aloud. During workshop, your peers will be observing what you wrote, which will tell you a lot about what they notice in your writing. I will do the same, but I'll also be inferring what your piece means to an interested reader like me, which may entail giving advice and options. You will then be using these distinctions to structure and develop your own writing.

7. *Daily, prolific (unstructured) writing*. I expect you to be able to produce prolific, unstructured writing daily and at will. We will be writing in class every day, and I expect you to write for ten minutes outside of class every day. Expertise in prolific writing means you always have something to write about.

8. *Structured writing*. I expect you to be able to produce structured, edited writing that grows out of some of your earlier prolific, unstructured writing. For example, the major genre assignments should evidence a good faith effort in structuring your writing for an academic audience and show care in your use of language. These major discourses also need to travel; they need to move your mind (and your readers') through a subject.

9. *Style*. Show adequate progress in learning how to write effective sentences, using these features: coordination, subordination, clarity, economy, emphasis, rhythm, grammaticality.

10. *Concrete and abstract language*. You must be able, self-consciously, to write both concretely and abstractly.

11. *Rewriting*. I require rewriting; endeavor to produce some substantial change in your writing. Here I'm following Ponsot and Deen's distinction.[5] Rewriting is "recasting key sentences" or sections that

require clearer meaning or more graceful expression. Revising, however, re-imagines your manuscript and is outside the scope of this course.

12. *Copy-editing and proofreading*. When the assignment is for a second draft and especially for the final portfolio, copy-edit it — that is, release it from mistakes in spelling, mechanics, capitalization, punctuation, and grammar. The final portfolio should be virtually free of these errors. It's fine to get help in editing, such as from the Writing Center or a good student writer. (Copy-editing involves fact-checking and correcting; proofreading involves checking formatting in the final versions.)

13. *Portfolio keeping*. You must have a portfolio prepared for the final "trial run" review (see #2) during the last class week, the fifteenth week of the semester. That portfolio must meet the "gateway" requirements for our last conference, my first reading of your portfolio (more on this later in the semester). To prepare for that review, maintain your daybook and working (writing) folder — that collection of all the work of the course — throughout the semester. Show me in the conferences your working folder and the work that you're doing in writing.

14. *Awareness*. Keep track of whether you are meeting this Contract for B. At a minimum, complete the 5th- and 10th-week self-evaluations on time. Schedule a conference to get my feedback on your Contract-keeping when you don't know for sure.

I realize that better students always want to know how well they're doing. To chart your progress in the course, I will comment profusely on your work in the various stages of writing — inventing ("getting started"), drafting, revising, and editing. Sometimes, when you're working hard, you will just want to know if I'm seeing any results yet. My feedback will help you determine your standing.

I will help you, as a fellow writer, by providing plenty of practice. Let me stress once again what may not be obvious or yet believed:

- The B is accessible to every student — skill, training, bad experiences are irrelevant.

- All decisions about what is required for the B, cited above, are made without judging the quality of your writing.

On first drafts, I don't ask that they be fussy, well organized, and perfectly unified. I don't expect homework always to be correct. I care more about you using writing to work through writing problems than about your etiquette. It's fine if not everything is perfect (it won't be) if it shows signs of your mind working. Each draft I see should show movement from the rough cut to the polished product. Likewise, homework and in-class activities should show a working mind, evidenced in a complete set of work.

If there's lack of effort in one area, I need to see greater effort in others. I fully expect superior effort.

Getting An A, A-, or B+

As you can see, the grade of B depends on completing tasks. Grades of A, A-, and B+, however, depend on outstanding performance in written communication: writing excellence. Thus, you earn a B if you put in good time and effort and writerly behavior; I will push you to get a B. But to earn the higher grades, you must attend to the quality of your writing while also keeping the stipulations for the B Contract.

Notice (again) that for grades up to B, you don't have to worry about my standards of excellence; you can ignore what I tell you or see my feedback as what would come from any interested reader. That is the way it should be. Becoming a self-conscious writer means you must take control of your own writing — to find your own way, one that resonates for you and your community of readers.

For the higher grades, you must translate that self-conscious behavior into excellent writing. Your final portfolio plays the biggest role in decisions about excellence. Of course, we'll have class discussions, conferences, and workshops about excellence in writing, and I will communicate those throughout the semester in precept and example.

Knowing Where You Stand

This system is better than regular grading for giving you a clear idea of your writing and thus of your final grade. For whenever I give you feedback on any major assignment, I will ask you questions about meanings in your text and the expressions you use. I also will tell you, when we reach the later writing, if I judge your draft to be genuinely excellent and thus to exceed the Contract for B. That does not mean the work of rewriting is over; we still have much to accomplish and to apply to your writing. Expect me to praise effort at the same time encouraging further rewriting.

Of course, you may speak to me about your grade as often as you like; your writing conference in my office is the best place for that conversation. I will post open office hours too on the class websites. Remember that keeping abreast of your work effort is part of fulfilling the Contract for B.

Grades Lower Than B

I hope no one aims for the lower grades. The quickest way to fall to a B– and below is to miss classes and conferences, to show up without assignments or with uninvested work. Being unprepared and unaware are unacceptable behaviors for a writer and especially for a writer in this class.
So here's what's nonnegotiable:

- You are not eligible for a passing grade of D unless you have completed 70% of the coursework: activities and assignments.

- If you miss three or more major writing assignments — the genre assignments — the highest grade you can earn is a C–.

- Failure to turn in a final portfolio in paper form (to me) and/or electronic form (to turnitin.com) means you will fail the class.

- You cannot offer work that's late, e-mailed, or passed from a friend to me. If you are missing classes and fall behind in work, check the assignments on the website; by all means, stay in touch with me about your chances of passing the course.

I grant one absolution for a minor lapse from the Contract. But two minors equal a major and will break Contract, leaving you exposed to the lower grades of B– and below. I then judge the quality of writing in your final portfolio without the safety net of the Contract. While work performed under a broken

Contract can still be improved to a B with a stellar portfolio, such occurrences are rare.[6] Writers who do not "keep Contract" cannot earn higher than a B final grade. Please note this.

If you are uninterested in achieving a B in the course and think a "Gentleman's C" is just fine, better talk with me first. My approach may not be for you.

Workload and the B Contract

It is easy to underestimate or misinterpret what I've just written about the Contract. Since I'm always in favor of alternative explanations, here's one from a student in his final portfolio:

I will be honest. I thought when I chose to take Dr. Hafer's course I only had to show up, complete the assignments, and end up with at least a B for the semester. This was not the case. I ended up falling short of staying on track to get a B grade. ... I was doing below average in most of my assignments. I believe my reasons for myself doing so poorly was that I came in with the wrong attitude.

It was the best writing he did all semester.

> Let's dispense with grades as long as possible and see what benefits real writing practice will bring you. So do what the weak student does not do: finish assignments with distinction; read the textbook with an eye toward improving your writing; and, most importantly of all, write, write, write.

Connections to the College

In addition to meeting departmental competencies for composition (listed later), I have designed this course to meet the liberal arts mission of the college: "The mission of Lycoming College is to provide a distinguished baccalaureate education in the liberal arts and sciences within a coeducational, supportive, residential setting." (<http://www.lycoming.edu/aboutlycoming/mission.aspx.>)

Portfolio

I expect you to collect all the coursework throughout the semester (a working folder), and later, to showcase the best writing you can do in the course (a final portfolio).

In other words, you will compile this working folder from all the work of the course — constantly adding to it as the course progresses — until finishing with a selection of your best work in a final portfolio. That final portfolio is not a loose collection of unrelated materials, but rather

- a selection of work you did in the course and

- a complete whole, represented in a theme or a metaphor.

Assignment Design

I make writing assignments for specific reasons, which I categorize under the headings in Table A.1. I'll be explaining more about these in class as we practice them.

All of these manuscripts must be nonfiction prose; the majority must be researched.

I require "original" compositions, whether in the form of essay, letter, article, report, etc. — no recycled high school papers or writing destined for double-duty in other classes (plagiarism).

Normally, whenever written work is due during the semester, you will make two copies, one for you and one for me. Your copy should be archived in your working folder. I archive the copy you give me in my working folder of your writing.

From the collection you will compose during the semester, you must recast several into polished final versions, rigorously rewritten and edited; one additional, reflective essay should also introduce your final portfolio to me. These artifacts comprise your "best works" final portfolio.

Seldom do we have time in courses to revise extensively: to labor in depth, and in uncompressed time, as real writers do. The portfolio system gives us that opportunity.

Table A.1. Assignment Design

Category of writing	Stakes	Baseball Analogy	Purpose for Writing	Example Assignments	Assessments
Unstructured	Low	Spring training	To think, to practice, to learn	Daily writing In-class writing Planning Postwrites Workshop practice	B CONTRACT: Responses from professor and peers
Transitional	Mid	Regular season	To practice structured writing; to demonstrate learning	Drafts Working folder	B CONTRACT: Responses from professor and peers
Structured	High	World Series	To inform, to persuade, to express, to emphasize language	Final portfolio	FINAL GRADE: Feedback from professor

Plagiarism

Plagiarism kills. It is the deliberate or irresponsible submission of another's intellectual property as your own. It may take the form of mosaic plagiarism, stealing key phrases and sentence structure from another's text without attribution. Likewise, printed matter or Internet research that lacks citations or documentation constitutes theft of intellectual property, just as surely as if you robbed the author of his billfold!

Whatever form plagiarism takes, it is stealing; it compromises every relationship with fellow writers. Any evidence of plagiarism will result in a broken Contract. No exceptions. Since I am compelled to report plagiarism to the Provost and Dean of the College, it is he who will decide your future at our institution.

In my experience, student writers know a good deal about plagiarism but not how to avoid it. So here's some good news: If you have doubts about citations, raise them when we have regular conferences or class. As Peter Elbow and Mary Deane Sorcinelli wryly observe, "admitting ... [you] don't know something is much better than making a mistake that could constitute plagiarism."[7] I use <turnitin.com> with that aim in mind.

Last year, a colleague suspended all paper-writing in favor of hour-long tests while he and the class studied Internet plagiarism and how to detect it. He and I are pals.

Offering Work and Yourself

I never accept late homework because writing does not readily lend itself easily to "makeups."

Therefore, all homework must be offered in person — being sure to make two copies, one for you and one for me — at the start of class or at the beginning of each conference, whichever applies. Conversely, "dropping off" homework, e-mailing it to me, sending it through a friend or classmate, and all associated submissions in absentia are unacceptable. If you're going to be absent, realize I cannot accept work ahead of time since we process together that first work during class or conference. Those combinations only occur during class time.

I argue aggressively in this course that growth in writing is a reasonable expectation when writers and their craft become accountable to all in one time and in one place. No one will defend, advise, promote, or argue effectively anyone's writing when its writer is absent. Please do not ask me to violate my own principles. Instead, work by deadline.

Absences

Of course, I recognize lateness and absences cannot always be avoided, that everyone becomes ill, suffers a family loss, participates in a critical sports meet or game, crashes a hard drive, forgets to buy an inkjet cartridge, or has some other Bad Day Incident at some point in the semester and cannot attend. I know I do. Like you, I face those circumstances every semester; I've had illnesses (my kids and my elderly father too!) that have pulled me out of school for a period. I accept all of these situations (and countless others) as valid.

To compensate for these eventualities, I have designed the course to incorporate as much of the human experience as possible and still have it retain its academic integrity. Therefore, I will drop two days of work — not two assignments, but two days of work — from the first fourteen weeks of classes. These demolished days never erase absences from the totals in the B Contract, only assignments due. If you attend every class and conference, I will drop two days of low performance.

Remember, late work is never accepted, but may qualify as assignments to be dropped.

If you play on a college sports team and you know some games will conflict with class commitments, take the time now to plan for those absences. My advice also applies to trips you're planning that interfere with the daily classwork.

Here's a summary of all things pertaining to attendance and the final grade:

- Miss more than three classes/conferences and you break the Contract for a B. The highest grade you can get now is a B; the lowest, an F.

- Miss five classes/conferences by midterm (or six up to the last day you can drop the course), the highest grade you can attain is a D.

- I don't erase absences.
- During the first fourteen weeks, you get a pass for work missed on any two days. The absences still "count," however.
- I count lateness as half-absences.
- For any classes you miss, you are still responsible for the learning of that day.
- If you complete less than 70% of the work — in-class activities and assignments — the highest grade you can receive is a D.
- If you miss three or more major writing assignments — the genre assignments — the highest grade you can earn is a C–.
- Failure to turn in a final portfolio in paper form (to me) and electronic form (to turnitin.com) means you will fail the course.
- You cannot offer work that's late, e-mailed, or passed from a friend to me and expect it to "count" as class attendance. I never take work without you.

If your absences reach five during the semester or four by midterm — that total includes conferences — I reserve the right to give you a "drop card," which means that you should withdraw from the course. A passing grade of even a D is unlikely.

Therefore, plan your absences wisely.

What If I Miss Class?

1. E-mail me before class or conference to inform me you will not be attending.
2. Keep up with assignments by consulting the calendar on the website (address on p. 1 header).
3. Archive missed work in your working folder for later use; remember that I do not accept late nor "absent" work, but both may be included in the final portfolio.

4. If you want feedback on work that's late, schedule a conference and we'll review it.

Outcomes

Last year, three major college organizations identified a "framework" that they believe "describes the rhetorical and twenty-first–century skills as well as habits of mind and experiences that are critical for college success"[8]:

- Curiosity – the desire to know more about the world.

- Openness – the willingness to consider new ways of being and thinking in the world.

- Engagement – a sense of investment and involvement in learning.

- Creativity – the ability to use novel approaches for generating, investigating, and representing ideas.

- Persistence – the ability to sustain interest in and attention to short- and long-term projects.

- Responsibility – the ability to take ownership of one's actions and understand the consequences of those actions for oneself and others.

- Flexibility – the ability to adapt to situations, expectations, or demands.

- Metacognition – the ability to reflect on one's own thinking as well as on the individual and cultural processes used to structure knowledge.

I forge these habits of mind into the way I teach writing. Specifically, I teach students how to gain these competencies:

- Rhetorical knowledge – the ability to analyze and act on understandings of audiences, purposes, and contexts in creating and comprehending texts;

- Critical thinking – the ability to analyze a situation or text and make thoughtful decisions based on that analysis, through writing, reading, and research;

- Writing processes – multiple strategies to approach and undertake writing and research;

- Knowledge of conventions – the formal and informal guidelines that define what is considered to be correct and appropriate, or incorrect and inappropriate, in a piece of writing; and

- Composing in electronic environments – Ability to compose in multiple environments, from traditional pen and paper to electronic technologies.

A more specific list appears on pp. 1–2.

Courtesies

My policy is not to add students as "friends" on social networking sites.

I have a dry sense of humor. Some students aren't always sure when I'm joking. If necessary, I will raise my hand after telling a joke to signal my intention.

Only students who earn an A and thus have completed the course with distinction are eligible for a written recommendation.

In an in-class writing activity, I will ask for a show of hands to see if anyone needs more time; I also will ask if there's anyone who does not need more time. I make this request because I want to hear from everyone. (I will not raise my hand to avoid confusion with the joke signal listed above.)

If you write me an e-mail, put a title on the subject line. Otherwise, it may end up in my junk mail folder and I'll never see it.

Turn off all cell phones during class. Normally, I will remind you; if I forget, it's my fault. If you forget after my announcement, it's your fault.

If you bring a laptop to class, put it to sleep and collapse the screen when class begins. Reopen it when we're writing.

When you're absent, send me a note before the start of class to let me know you'll be out. It isn't necessary to give me a reason, but I want some communication from you. I do believe in the right to privacy.

Check the website when you're absent or unsure of assignments; I update it at the end of every class day.

If you come to class late, try not to be disruptive. Close the door behind you quietly and find a close, convenient seat. Better yet, don't come late.

Do visit the Writing Center. But if you think the Writing Center will give you extra credit or a proofreader's hard work, you will leave unfulfilled.

Notes

1. Braine, John. *Writing a Novel*. New York: McGraw-Hill, 1975.

2. Peter Elbow, Professor Emeritus of English at University of Massachusetts, Amherst, has greatly influenced my thinking on grading and writing; this section reflects that influence.

3. Elbow, Peter and Jane Danielewicz. *A Unilateral Grading Contract to Improve Learning and Teaching*. Unpublished ms., 2009. 10 December 2009.

4. The college requires a midterm grade report. I make a good faith effort (GFE) to predict one, but never resulting in levels higher than a B since your writing is not yet ready to be graded.

5. Ponsot, Marie and Rosemary Deen. *Beat Not the Poor Desk*. Portsmouth: Boynton Cook, 1982, p. 6.

6. Again, I don't want to give the delinquent false hope. This situation is a lot like baseball's. If a player didn't complete spring training and the regular season, he shouldn't expect to hit a home run during the World Series.

7. Elbow, Peter and Mary Deane Sorcinelli. "High-Stakes and Low-Stakes Writing." Eds. Wilbur McKeachie and Marilla Svinicki. *Teaching Tips: Strategies, Research, Theory for College and University Teachers, 12th Edition*. Boston: Houghton Mifflin, 2006: 192-93.

8. Council of Writing Program Administrators, National Council of Teachers of English, National Writing Project. *Framework for Success in Postsecondary Writing*. January 2011. Print.

Chapter 3: Open That First Class with Writing

3. Have a Discussion After First-Day Writing

After the first-day writing and pair-and-share, ask the class why you introduced the first class in this way. See what their responses are. I am often surprised by their inventive answers, some of which eventually become my reasons for starting this exercise. This exercise reinvents itself every time you begin with it.

I normally teach my course during two-hour, twice-per-week blocks. That's a great chunk of time, so after a few powerful answers I give students a ten-minute break. At that point, they know only one thing about the course: we write together and always at the beginning.

After break, I pass out a syllabus and give them a ten-minute quiz on it. (See a sample in Chapter 1 Appendix.) I ask for questions after I give them another ten minutes to look over the syllabus. Then I ask them to write for another ten minutes on some double-sided paper packets I distribute; I write with them.

Subsequent classes all need to start with writing and end with writing. I know, too, there will be forces and obstacles exerting pressure to forgo the writing just one time, which will turn into two times and three until writing that bookends the course is abandoned altogether. So I really work to keep this schedule, even if I can only spare a minute or two at either end of the class period.

4. Use Paper Packets/Double-Entry Paper

Another way to elicit participation early in the class is to use paper packets that form the pages for a loose-leaf daybook notebook. The packet, which I call *double-entry paper*, is composed of a white sheet on top and a yellow sheet below; both are bonded along the top edge and three-hole punched. They are also known as carbonless packets, but that description doesn't register with modern students. (It costs about $100 per year for me to use packets, and since I know in advance what they will cost I can often get the department budget to include it.) The underneath of the top white sheet has a special coating that records as a copy on the yellow underneath, like carbon paper used to work for typists but much more neatly because the image on yellow develops like an old Polaroid camera. (Some comb-bound student laboratory workbooks use the same principle with a writing surface overlay.) I furnish a lined notebook page for the printer to reproduce on the white sheet so student writers have a guide for their handwritten drafting. Students write on the white sheet; a second copy develops on the yellow sheet.

If you're comfortable with this method after a semester, see if your campus printing services can make daybook notebooks with these packets bound together. You can ask them to include card stock that can be moved easily between packets so the writing doesn't bleed onto subsequent papers. The white sheets should be perforated too for easy removal from the notebook after the classroom writing. The notebook has the obvious advantage of keeping the daily classroom writing intact: no paper shuffling during class. I like these prepackaged books because I'm not hauling paper to classrooms and students seem to take the notebook seriously since they have to purchase one in the campus store.

Chapter 4. Write Daily: Practice Before Polish

5. Show Different Daybook Designs

Show different media—sizes, shapes, styles, textures—of daily notebooks that students can use as daybooks. Even if you use a daybook of double sheets that you sell in the campus bookstore, consider requiring students to carry small notepads everywhere as collection devices because they will forget any ideas if they don't have writing tools at the ready. Tell them that if you see them out of class you will stop them and ask if they have their daybooks. Beware—they should be able to ask you too.

6. Have Students Use Their Daybooks

After students finish their daily writing at the beginning of class, I ask them to discuss with their neighbors what they wrote about to start the discussion again. If you're using double-entry packets, you can collect the top, white form while they are looking at their yellow copy. Then craft the discussion to whatever you're currently emphasizing about writing.

7. Make the Unstuck Flyleaf

Tell students to list ideas they've collected for writing in the flyleaf of their daybooks. They can use the list to get unstuck.

Table of Contents

Date	Title	Page #

9. Ask Students to Cross-Index

Some notebooks have index pages at their opening section, or you can design a daybook for that purpose. Student writers could use these notebooks in a chronological arrangement as usual but then "key" any ideas that crop up in their daily writing to these front index pages. Pretty soon, they should begin to notice themes or stock ideas that are approached from several angles.

10. Discuss a Writer's Responsibility to Collect Ideas

Tell student writers they are responsible to collect ideas to write about. If you lecture regularly, you can sprinkle budding topics or prompts. Carry a compact daybook around or an electronic one like DayOne where you collect ideas for papers or for the course. You can also turn student questions into opportunities to write in their daybooks (the notebook that collects daily writing), even just five or ten minutes with peer-to-peer sharing immediately afterward. You can do the same. As you write with them at such junctures, your engaging in the same process valorizes the task. If you fail, tell your class and report why such is part of the writing process.

Collecting ideas means looking at, inspecting, and examining subjects that surround writers. That action is alien to beginning writers who cannot find anything to write about while billions of subjects pass over them undiscovered. Show them they are discoverable by not assigning subjects if possible. Instead, encourage them in their daily notebooks to list subjects as they encounter them—in lectures, between class, in discussions with classmates. The daybook will alert them to be on the lookout for subjects, especially ones that intrigue or puzzle them. Even in list form, the daybook daily writings become the genesis of discourse.

11. Begin Discourse Using Collection

In class, have students retrieve their daybooks. Ask them to list subjects about which they are obsessed: subjects in your discipline that they've always been too afraid to write about; subjects they think everyone writes about but to which they have a unique contribution; subjects that they can never use in school-sponsored writing. After ten minutes, have them pick one and begin with a ten-minute freewrite: just a production of prose without stopping, their brains now tied to the pen point. Then discuss the exercise and ask for volunteers to discuss theirs.

12. Reflect on Collecting

For one week, keep a log of when and how you complete your daily writing outside of class time. Record your own version of your writing process: what was the most difficult, the most time-consuming, the most productive time to work? Share with students a few select entries. Ask them to record their process, and have them share when you have a few moments at the end of class. It is a good idea to solicit student responses often about planning to write and talking about what they write. You can learn from your students in this way too. Make it easier for them to create writerly habits. It will also improve your own.

13. Use Double-Entry Daybooks to Keep the Two-Copy Rule

This exercise requires some preparation and expense at the beginning of each semester, but it is well worth the effort.

Visit your local stationery store and see if its services include making double-entry packets: two sheets, white and yellow, held together with binding glue at the top. The white paper underside is treated with a carbonless material that allows every entry on top to be copied instantly onto the bottom yellow copy. Stationers prepare these for tax and office professionals, but they can just as easily be assembled as unprinted packets for daily writing in class. Some campus print shops offer the same services.

As students file in, distribute these double-entry packets, starting on the first day and continuing throughout the semester. Get students warmed up for writing and the class: that is, before writing, write. Encourage a brief in-class write as the first activity, even when you feel rushed or overwhelmed and especially when you feel rushed or overwhelmed. Write with them, too. If students are collecting subjects throughout the semester, they can write on one of them or on a question you pose on the board related to the previous class. If I assign a research or similar expository paper, I invite students to write first—all their questions, anxieties, and even ideas come forth. After a two-minute write with them, ask them to turn to a neighbor (or a groupmate if you use teams) and ask them to share what they just wrote. Meanwhile, you walk among them, collecting the white sheets and scanning them for problems, questions, insights. Then share that feedback as a class discussion when the crosstalk dies down, using the chalkboard or other visual to record common themes. Ask students to add notes on their yellow copies, all taken from the class discussion, so that they leave the class with a complete set of notes on that activity.

14. Have Writers Write Their Own Prompts

Have students practice answering writing prompts by sending them to you via e-mail before the next class meets. The first one can focus on the reading assignment due that day. But be strict with requirements: they need subject lines and a formal, proofread question. Then select one at random by asking one student in the class to pick from a pool of appropriate prompts you've received. After a quick freewrite, have them structure their answer in rewriting.

After ten minutes, review the other responses with students, explaining, without revealing names, why you would deem some better than others (and less so—not bad—since improvement is always possible with rewriting and revising). Repeat a second time for the next reading assignment.

15. Compose an Apology Letter

To decrease writing apprehension, have students write an apology letter in one of their daily writings. In it, they ask the class to forgive them for any writing they will do the rest of the semester. They can even name the kinds of things they typically do in their writing. Acknowledging persistent problems can be liberating and can motivate students to work on them afresh. You can do the same assignment and list your expectations. Make copies for students so they can see we all have different manifestations of the writing problem.

16. Monitor Your Own Process and Then Broadcast It

Take notice of your own writing practices as they occur, and let students know your findings. Then you must immediately encourage them to be on the lookout for daily writing sensibilities. Have them report their daily writing processes and environment as a daybook entry or a short, focused freewrite that you collect. Ask students to write a letter to you about how they prepare to write for your class and other classes. It isn't uncommon for professors to ask for self-reflection in the course, and this letter about daily writing can document their efforts. This letter, too, can be the impetus to getting the practice of daily writing started.

Sometimes students need focused prewriting when they are reluctant to come up with their own topics; this selection may be intimidating for many since school-sponsored writing is seldom self-selection. For example:

- Where do you perform your best practice writing?

- What's your mood like when you write?

- What tools work best, or do you like to vary among laptop, desktop, pen, 3 x 5 cards, eye-ease notebook?

- Do you ever stand while writing, like Ben Franklin did, or assume a different pose or place for writing?

- Notice what you do and have done in writing during the last week—together with what you haven't done and haven't made work—and narrate those in your daybook or schedule pad. Your process may not be the grind mine is, but at least it's fine. (Ouch, forgive me for those two bad puns!)

17. Design a Writing Program for Another

Have students compose a writing profile for someone very different from themselves. As part of the plan, have them design a major and a career goal for that someone: a personality, hobbies, vocational interests, and possible writing obstacles. After an interval, ask them to design a writing plan for one week. Discuss with the class or have students pair-and-share. You can even ask, in a class discussion after pair-and-share, if anyone in the class fits the description set by the students who discuss their profile; there may be some who find the plan helpful, but also, this activity gives the writer a sense of audience. If you think this activity might be helpful for some students, have them keyboard their plan and you can post it to the course website or blog.

18. Solve Your Own Problems

As an undergraduate, I remember hearing scurrilous talk about why students choose certain majors, much of it malicious. One spiteful comment that I heard repeated often was that many psychology majors chose their field so that they could solve their own problems. Later I heard the same diagnosis for writers. Now a professor, I still hear students make the same rationalizations.

So here's a project that perhaps hooks into that human behavior. Solicit students to work on a Dear Abby/Dear Annie column in which they give feedback to a writer who is blocked. You can also write to a hypothetical student and show the results to the class after they've submitted theirs.

Chapter 5. Make Long Assignments Manageable for Everyone

19. Have Students Author a Checksheet

Ask students to compose a checksheet for an assignment. Then excuse yourself and leave the room; they will need to work quickly and without your interposing when there's a problem. Return twenty minutes later and have a spokesperson from each group read his or her version. Then develop a set of criteria that emerge from the checksheet and the ensuing class discussion. Critique each, awarding bonus points for the better ones. Then post that one, with your critique, on the class website.

Chapter 6. Prepare for Rewriting

20. Rewrite After Freewriting

In daily freewriting, ask students to take one sentence and rewrite it three ways. Build on that concept by gradually increasing the requirement to a paragraph. You can even identify needs in this way. For instance, if you're having trouble with students writing good opening sentences or paragraphs, have them compose three different versions. Then have them choose the best. You can even entertain arguments as to which qualify as such, generating criteria that you can elaborate on or even challenge. Some of the liveliest class discussions I've had work from such situations. Alternately, you can have them pair-and-share: have a classroom neighbor identify the better among the three. These sessions do not require a lot of time but expose students to rewriting all semester long.

21. Collect First Drafts for Rewriting

On the day a major assignment is due, have students make two copies that they must bring to class at the beginning of the class period. Write on the board or on a slide that you would like your copy before class begins and that they should keep their other copy at the ready for workshop. As the papers crawl in, scan them quickly for bright, vibrant sentences. No matter how dull you think the writing is overall, you should be able to find, at an absolute minimum, a grammatical sentence with a clear subject and verb. Highlight it and move on to another paper; set the goal to identify five to ten grammatical sentences from as set of papers. (The more you practice this quick review, the more you can select in the available time.) Copy the better one to a slide or blackboard and ask the class to copy it in their notebooks:

> Now, compose three alternative sentences that keep the same basic meaning.

While they compose, you do the same. After a few minutes, walk around the classroom and nudge those who need help, providing encouragement for those phrases and words choices—even sentences—they are doing well. Ask a few to copy particular sentences that you identify to the blackboard.

After students finish, review the sentences on the board and narrate their effectiveness. You might even ask a few to explain to the class how they reinvented their sentences. Have the rest of the class copy these down.

At the end of class, pick another of the ten you identified earlier and transfer it to the blackboard. Ask students to compose three versions, preferably writing on double-sided paper so they have a copy when they hand in the other when leaving the class. You can read these quickly, placing an asterisk around the best of the three. If that one needs some grammatical or punctuation editing, do so gently in a light-colored pen or pencil. Then return them by next class period. Repeat throughout the semester.

22. Eliminate a Paper for Rewriting

Consider eliminating a required paper from your usual assignment regimen to encourage a thorough rewriting of a present assignment, perhaps one that students have difficulty grasping in just one rough draft. You can record your expectations in a checksheet, basing the rewritten draft on what you would expect to see on a second or final draft. As a variant, you can encourage students to rewrite sections that are particularly troublesome for students, such as three versions of a transitional or beginning or ending paragraph; you can then choose the better, giving the student credit for the process. To encourage wide-scale rewriting, you could require a change of 25–75 percent when they compare it with the first version, showing that you demand a serious accounting for rewriting, much like the effort (but better performance) that would be required in another paper.

To prepare them, show examples of effective rewriting from your own prose in the same genre in which students are writing; in other words, if they are composing a report, show one of your reports that you've struggled with or are currently struggling with. Rewrite the opening paragraph three different ways—or a closing one or a transitional one—to spotlight three sections that are traditional sites students have difficulty. Have students pick which the ones you show them of your own prose, perhaps in a secret vote that you count you tabulate and show in the same class.

23. Rewrite for Quality

To show that quality derives from rewriting, take fifteen minutes in class to have students rewrite five or six sentences from their daybooks or in-class freewriting, the emphasis laying on producing beautiful sentences. Nudge a few while you walk around the room to help them along, asking a few that you've spied to have produced some good work to read their paragraph at class end.

Chapter 7. Offer Feedback for Classwork

DR. HAFER · ENGLISH 106

POSTWRITE.W6C1

Last name												
First name												

Tuesday, February 12, 2013

1. REVIEW.
   A few weeks ago, I gave you a handout on subjects/verbs which reviews what I taught on that subject thus far in the course. You "know" subjects and verbs intuitively or else you wouldn't be able to speak English sentences at all! Making that knowledge readily accessible, however, is the key to writing clearer English sentences.

2. To see if you're prepared, <u>underline</u> the complete subject and ~~strikethrough~~ the verb in the following first version, student sentences:

   a. The night that started it all was when my friend Krista said, "Nicole, I am not sitting here again all night with the same people watching the Yankee game; let's do something."

   b. The first reason, low salary jobs, is the most important reason why poverty does not stop.

3. ASSIGNMENT. Look up the answers for this postwrite on the class PlanbookConnect site; consult today's agenda and you will find the answers at the bottom of the web page.

Exhibit A.7.1 24. Development of Postwrites

DR. HAFER · ENGLISH 106

POSTWRITE.REWRITING

Last name	R	u	m	m	e	l							
First name	J	o	n										

Tuesday, September 3, 2013

1. In ONE phrase, give me one compelling title from the group you submitted for homework OR invent a new title that might work for your narrative. Then rewrite that title to form at least two significant others.

STILL THE BEST ONE

The Monotonous Work of Landscaping

Acheiving perfection and beauty

Landscaping and losing track of time

What ONE THING from TODAY is the hardest for you to understand or is the most confusing? You could also respond to our last POSTWRITE to form an ongoing conversation between us. (Please respond on the REVERSE side.)

Exhibit A.7.2 25. Simple Responses to Postwrites

DR. HAFER · ENGLISH 106

POSTWRITE.REWRITING

Last name	W	h	i	t	m	a	n						
First name	T	a	y	l	e	r							

Tuesday, September 3, 2013

1. In ONE phrase, give me one compelling title from the group you submitted for homework OR invent a new title that might work for your narrative. Then rewrite that title to form at least two significant others.

Living as a Doormat   SUPER!

Everyone's "Welcome" mat.

Soles on my Soul.

Life as a People-Pleaser

What ONE THING from TODAY is the hardest for you to understand or is the most confusing? You could also respond to our last POSTWRITE to form an ongoing conversation between us. (Please respond on the REVERSE side.)

It hard for me to picture how all
this free writing is going to fit into
a final writing piece. Guess I will
see very soon though.

IT "FITS" AS YOU MAKE IT FIT.'FREEWRITING
GETS YOU THINKING ABOUT MAKING
LANGUAGE, FREEING YOU FROM
HOLDING BACK/EDITING TASKS, SO THAT
YOU CAN CONCENTRATE SOLELY ON MEANING.

What exactly is a Memoir?
   Can you explain a little more.

SURE, IT'S A PERSONAL REFLECTION
ON AN ASPECT OF ONE'S LIFE,
(YOU PRACTICE REFLECTION IN A
   SMALL WAY IN THESE POSTWRITES.

From today, the hardest thing for me to understand is how to form the purpose and meaning for our drafts after already writing the middle portion, which is where the core purpose should be apparent.

GREAT POINT. SOMETIMES THE PURPOSE IS ELUSIVE, ISN'T IT? SOMETIMES WE JUST CAN'T FIND THE WORDS TO ARTICULATE WHAT WE'RE PROCESSING IN OUR HEAD. IT'S A LOT LIKE WHAT ANNE LAMOTT WAS TALKING ABOUT— IN WRITING, WE FREQUENTLY HAVE TO "TRY OUT" LANGUAGE SO WE CAN FIND OUT WHAT WE MEAN.

HAVE YOU EVER HAD AN ARGUMENT WITH SOMEONE WHERE THE WORDS CAME OUT WRONG? IF ONLY YOU COULD GO BACK TO THAT TIME, YOU WOULD CHANGE WHAT YOU SAID, RIGHT? WRITING/FREEWRITING/DRAFTING HELPS US MAKE THAT "RIGHT WORD" POSSIBLE.

From todays class the hardest thing....
for me is going to make my narrative
personal enough so its not just another
dog story.

I HAVE CONFIDENCE THAT YOU CAN.
TRY BURSTS OF FREEWRITING WHEN YOU
FEEL THE TOPIC IS STALE OR TRITE OR
SOMETHING YOU'VE HEARD MANY TIMES
BEFORE. IT TAKES PRACTICE — BUT
THAT'S WHAT THIS CLASS IS FOR!

Chapter 8. Give Feedback During Short Conferences

26. Conduct Self-Assessments During a Conference

Give students a lowercase letter scale for them to use in judging the state of completeness of the draft they're submitting; they'll be less prone to numerical numbing. For example, to the dumbfounded who exclaim, "You mean I need a sixth draft?!" you reply, "No, you need an 'e' draft."

They can indicate their ranking on their cover sheet. Absent descriptions mark a draft caught between map points.

Draft Process

Zero—I got it down on paper. I don't know where I'm going or what I'm doing. Help, but don't hurt, me!

a—The paper's much better than nothing.

b—I have an intention in my writing but is it discernible to my readers?

c

d

e—I'm midprocess. I'm open to feedback at all levels.

f

g—I'm getting close.

h

i—Am I there yet?

j—I'm editing; don't give me any advice on focus or development, even if you're right!

27. Consider a Workshop

You no doubt pack your classes full of information, so why not create some breathing space for reflection and practice for learning' sake? Ask students to bring in the first typed page of any assignment that's due later in the semester. Assign them to read their opening in small groups, with their groupmates performing a two-minute freewrite on what they just heard without taking notes beforehand. When all have read and written, groupmates can take turns reading what they freewrote, as ordered by the author. In other words, John hears all the records composed by his groupmates before moving on to another writer in the group. As an alternative, you can build rewriting into the workshop by requiring writers to produce three different versions of an opening paragraph.

28. Present Two Versions

Bring a piece of your own writing into workshop—say, two versions of an introduction that you're exploring for a new article. Make copies for the class and let them workshop the two versions with you staying silent, just as in a workshop environment. You can list terms and figures that may be unfamiliar to them on a separate cover sheet that lists your purpose and struggles. Let writers see that you are willing to use the process that you've set up for them.

29. Hold Workshop Self-Evaluations

Consider employing a self-evaluation checklist that you can distribute to the class immediately after the peer workshop. These should be tiered, moving from low-stakes to high as students become familiar with what you want. But they should always focus on the frequency and kinds of responses. In the last few workshops, assign points or issue encouraging comments for specific answers. If there's a dramatic change in the point structure, hand out the response sheet before the workshop begins so students know what to expect. For instance, if a few writers are dominating the workshops, designate negative points for any more than five responses in a workshop. I want to hear from everyone in the class.

30. Distribute Progress Reports for a Contract Conference

Consider sponsoring a conference that invites students to compare their task achievements compared with the Contract for B. This conference could coincide with the fifth-week self-assessment that you have collected in a previous class or at this conference. When they arrive, provide students a printout of their progress as you have charted it thus far in the semester. The printed matter focuses discussion on their individual progress.

Using an electronic gradebook that has standards-based grading keeps the bookkeeping light.

Chapter 9. Finish What You Started: Portfolio and Conference

31. Have Students Record a Motion Picture

When a motion picture is shot, the director frequently calls for multiple takes on a single scene, some radically different than one another. Sometimes the dramatic effect and overall outcome are difficult to predict at the planning stages, so the director makes several cuts to compensate. Similarly, conferences can be unpredictable since there are actors there too, fulfilling their roles in ways that are hard to predict.

Have your students direct a scene from a movie, using a scriptwriting format, with two likely outcomes: one where a writing conference is working and one where it is not. Give the two roles—writer/professor and writer/student—and provide key motivations for those roles. For instance, the student may be looking solely for specific advice on getting an A and to be done with the paper while the professor is looking for the student to work toward becoming a reflective writer. This assignment could be used when you've reached a point where students have attended several conferences or when you feel like you're repeating the same advice to every student writer who conferences with you.

Chapter 10. Offer But Two Cheers for Grading Writing

Exhibit A.10.1 Self-Assessments

5th-Week Self-Assessment

1. Are you meeting the Contract for a B? (Check out the Contract again.)
2. How many absences — conference and classroom — have you had?
3. Are you producing ten minutes of nonstop prolific freewriting in your Daybook every day?
4. If you are meeting the Contract, is there any draft that you have prepared so far that opens the door to a higher grade — that is, work I mentioned that is "excellent" or "strong" or better than what's stipulated in the Contract? If so, which ones?

If you are NOT meeting the Contract, what do you need to do to restore your standing?

I list in the syllabus — and have included below — the kinds of skills I want you to develop, those common to all successful writers. Please give yourself a "+," a "−," or a "√" (ok) for each of these items. Let your answer reflect your sense of self **now** — five weeks through the semester.

5. Are you able to produce concrete prolific writing at will?
6. Are you able to write for others in whole discourses, composing the complete structure?
7. Can you write observations rather than inferences?
8. Can you "textualize" your writing — write both concretely and abstractly in the appropriate sections of your "structured" writing?
9. Can you rewrite to craft effective sentences so that you know your options and can choose the "better" among them?
10. Can you consciously produce grammatical coordinated and subordinated sentences?

Now make the same judgments — "+," a "–," or a "√" — for each of the following descriptions in the same way.

11. "Getting Started":

    Are you able to find lots of ideas and words and subjects for your writing?

12. Discovery:

    Are you able to dig for real insight in your subjects, to get to what really matters — to puzzle through something, to push you understand — and thus create an energy of thinking?

    Do you use writing to solve your writing "problems"? Other problems? For instance, if you "can't write," do you use prolific writing to lead you into (later) structured writing?

    Are you risking something, exploring a subject rather than sitting on the sidelines?

13. Style:

    Can you make your writing sound comfortably like you? In structured writing too?

    Can you energize your sentences?

14. Feedback:

    Can you give good feedback to others in class? Can you get classmates to give you the feedback you need?

15. Can you "show" when needed and "not tell": find concrete words that make readers see what you see, feel what you feel? If so, attach an example (no longer than one page) that proves your point.

16. Can you do "real rewriting" rather than just proofreading or editing?

17. Can you write coordinated and subordinated sentences with correct punctuation: comma, semicolon, colon?

18. Which later drafts of "structured" writing have you proofread successfully to rid your work of errors in conventions?

19. Have your proofread any e-mails that you sent to me? Did you address me (correctly) by name and use the subject line in your e-mail?

20. Tell me briefly ONE compelling example of how much you have improved so far.

10th-Week Self-Assessment

1. Were you meeting the Contract during the 5th week?

2. Are you meeting the Contract for a B now? (Check out the Contract again in the syllabus.)

3. How many absences — conference and classroom — have you had?

4. Are you producing ten minutes of nonstop prolific freewriting in your Daybook every day?

5. **If you are meeting the Contract,** is there any draft that you have prepared so far that opens the door to a higher grade — that is, work I mentioned in conference that is "excellent" or "strong" or better than what's stipulated in the Contract? If so, which ones?

I list in the syllabus — and have included below — the kinds of skills I want you to develop, those common to all successful writers. Please give yourself a "+," a "−," or a "$\sqrt{}$" (ok) for each of these items. Let your answer reflect your sense of self **now** — six weeks through the semester.

6. Are you able to produce concrete prolific writing at will?

7. Are you able to write for others in whole discourses, composing the complete structure?

8. Can you write observations rather than inferences when the occasion demands?

9. Can you "textualize" your writing — write both concretely and abstractly in the appropriate sections of your "structured" writing?

10. Do you know how to make sentences "clearer"?

11. Can you rewrite to craft effective sentences so that you know your options and can choose the "better" among them?

12. Can you produce "clearer" sentences through agent subjects and action verbs?

13. Can you consciously produce grammatically coordinated and subordinated sentences?

Now make the same judgments — "+," a "–," or a "√" — for each of the following descriptions.

14. "Getting Started":

Are you able to find lots of ideas and words and subjects for your writing?

15. Thinking, investing:

Are you able to dig for real insight in your subjects, to get to what really matters — to puzzle through something, to push so to figure something out — and thus create an energy of thinking?

Do you use writing to solve writing "problems"? For instance, if you "can't write," do you use prolific writing to lead you into (later) structured writing?

Are you risking something, exploring a subject rather than sitting on the sidelines?

Are you rewriting on your own to prepare a final portfolio?

16. Voice:

Can you make your writing sound comfortably like you? Can you build life and energy into your sentences?

17. Feedback:

Can you give good feedback to others? Can you get classmates to give you the feedback you need?

18. Can you do "real rewriting" rather than just proofreading or editing?

19. Can you write coordinated and subordinated sentences with correct punctuation — comma, semicolon, colon — and use conjunctions successfully?

20. Which later drafts of "structured" writing have you proofread successfully to rid your work of all errors in conventions?

21. Have your proofread any e-mails that you sent to me? Did you address me (correctly) by name and use the subject line in your e-mail?

22. What is your level of effort thus far?

23. Tell me briefly ONE compelling example of how much you have improved so far.

10th Week Self-Assessment

1. Were you meeting the Contract during the 5th week?

2. Are you meeting the Contract for a B now? (Check out the Contract again in the syllabus.) Prove it.

32. Freewrite on Grading

Ask students to focus freewrite for ten minutes—writing continuously, without stopping for editing or correcting—on their experiences with school-sponsored writing and grades. Invite them to share specific stories. Then ask for volunteers to narrate what they just wrote about, letting the writing prompting class discussion. Let them speak as long as discussion continues, offering brief commentary and interpretation, preferably to connect the class's stories. In this way, you can initiate students for assessment, such as at portfolio-keeping time in the course or as preparation for a major, upcoming writing assignment.

33. Teach Students to Grade

This assignment shows the difficulty of the task and the levels of judgment required of a competent grader and how assessment, as defined in the syllabus, works as a fairer measure.

Working in groups of three, have students grade some project on campus: the cafeteria, parking availability for students, the campus newspaper, a new building construction on campus. Instruct them that they must first invent criteria that would be accessible and pertinent to all audiences affected: administration, students, even local government officials and citizens. If they have difficulty envisioning this task, ask them to imagine the best features of the subject: the best student newspaper has a vigorous writing style with some humor interspersed.

Then, using five basic levels (A–F), have students compare the subject (the project) to their criteria.

When finished, each student in the group should compose a letter detailing the results of the study, with each member assigned a different constituency, or audience. Ask them to comment as to whether the five levels were too many or not enough to judge their subjects.

Before accepting final drafts, hold a class discussion, focusing on the grade variations. Why did members assign different letter grades, even if they are using the same criteria? Is audience a deciding factor in grading? How difficult were the criteria to come up with? How did you distinguish among the various levels? Is there any overlap or fuzzy boundaries? How is this exercise different from traditional grading of writing where specific criteria are usually invisible to the student or are vague? How would this same exercise using assessment be different from grading?

Allow students to review their drafts among themselves in class in light of the class discussion. Do not accept any drafts until at least one class period has passed.

34. Draw Up an Assessment Table for Planning How to Review Writing

Construct a simple assessment table with topics along the vertical axis. Have students read a sample student paragraph and rate it (1.0–4.0) based on the topics you want them to measure. By taking on the role of critical audience, they judge the paragraph while you poll their answers as you walk around the classroom. Then ask them to pair-and-share before holding a class discussion. When you reach consensus, try the same exercise again with another sample paragraph. During discussion this time, ask students how the weaker and the stronger paragraph could be made stronger. Real examples are especially powerful reinforcement for fairness and accountability. The samples should just be excerpts, however.

TOPIC	Sample #1	Sample #2
STYLE: Clarity		
DEVELOPMENT: Accuracy		
DEVELOPMENT: Documentation		

Index